Advances in Applied General Equilibrium Modeling

CH00786702

Series editors

James Giesecke, Victoria University, Melbourne, Australia
Peter B. Dixon, Victoria University, Melbourne, Australia
Robert Koopman, World Trade Organization, Geneva, Switzerland

This series has a companion series in *SpringerBriefs in Applied General Equilibrium Modeling*.

The series publishes advances in the theory, application, parameterisation and computation of applied general equilibrium (AGE) models. AGE analysis is now an essential input in many countries to the discussion of a wide range of economic topics relevant to public policy. This reflects the capacity of AGE models to carry extensive economic detail, their flexibility in accommodating new policy-relevant theory and data, and their capacity to project economic outcomes for a large number of macroeconomic and microeconomic variables.

Topics in AGE modeling addressed by the series include: macroeconomic forecasting and adjustment; public finance; economic growth; monetary policy and financial markets; environmental policy; energy policy; income distribution and inequality; global modeling; country-specific modeling; regional modeling; economic effects of natural disasters and other catastrophic events; productivity; demography; foreign direct investment; economic development; model solution algorithms and software; and topics in estimation, calibration and validation.

AGE applications are increasingly multi-disciplinary, spanning inputs from such diverse fields as engineering, behavioral psychology, energy modeling, land use modeling, demography, and climate modeling. The series allows for the comprehensive documentation and careful exposition of not only the AGE models themselves, but also the inter-disciplinary inputs to the modeling, and the interactions between each.

For AGE modelers, the series provides a format supporting: clear exposition of data work, attention to the theoretical modeling of relevant policy detail, and thorough discussion of simulation results. This aids both academic and policy readerships.

Academic readers will appreciate: the capacity to see details of the full complexity of relevant components of model equation systems; comprehensive documentation of data manipulation algorithms; supporting analysis and discussion of model input and closure assumptions; and careful discussion of results grounded in AGE theory, data and closure assumptions.

Policy readers will appreciate: a format that supports the reporting of the comprehensive set of model outputs of interest to policy makers; discussion of elements of the theory and data that exert a heavy influence on research findings; and nuanced and qualified discussion of the policy implications of AGE research.

More information about this series at http://www.springer.com/series/13860

Peter B. Dixon · Michael Jerie
Maureen T. Rimmer

Trade Theory in Computable General Equilibrium Models

Armington, Krugman and Melitz

 Springer

Peter B. Dixon
Centre of Policy Studies
Victoria University
Melbourne, VIC
Australia

Maureen T. Rimmer
Centre of Policy Studies
Victoria University
Melbourne, VIC
Australia

Michael Jerie
Centre of Policy Studies
Victoria University
Melbourne, VIC
Australia

ISSN 2520-8268 ISSN 2520-8276 (electronic)
Advances in Applied General Equilibrium Modeling
ISBN 978-981-10-8323-5 ISBN 978-981-10-8325-9 (eBook)
https://doi.org/10.1007/978-981-10-8325-9

Library of Congress Control Number: 2018931508

Printed on acid-free paper

This Springer imprint is published by Springer Nature
The registered company is Springer Nature Singapore Pte Ltd.
The registered company address is: 152 Beach Road, #21-01/04 Gateway East, Singapore 189721,
Singapore

Preface

We are applied economists working in the Centre of Policy Studies (CoPS) at Victoria University, Melbourne. CoPS is largely self-funding, relying on contracts with governments and businesses around the world on a variety of topics including trade, taxation, environment, labor markets, immigration, major projects, microeconomic reform, and macrostabilization. We find contract research exciting and feel that it gives our work real-world relevance. But it means that the elapsed time for preparing this book has been elongated and unpredictable. We thank Springer for patience and faith that we would eventually get it done.

During the years of preparation, we accumulated many debts of gratitude. The greatest of these is to Bob Koopman who gave us the motivation, confidence, and opportunity to undertake this work. Motivation: As Director of the Office of Economics in the US International Trade Commission (USITC), Bob invited us to present a paper to an audience of top trade economists at the NAFTA@20 conference held in 2014. This was an invitation requiring us to be across modern trade theory and its implications for policy analysis. Confidence: On our many visits to the USITC, Bob took a keen supportive interest in what we were doing. Opportunity: Bob organized finance that made it possible for us to allocate time to the project. We also thank the US Department of Commerce and the Discovery Scheme of the Australian Research Council for financial support.

Earlier versions of material in this book were presented at: the 2013 Open Economy Lectures of the Institute for Applied International Trade, Beijing, organized by Shunli Yao; the annual GTAP conferences of 2012, 2014, 2015, and 2016; a Productivity Commission seminar in 2013; and the National CGE workshop at Victoria University in 2014. Participants at these events provided lively feedback, improving our understanding of the field and our ability to communicate it to others.

We are grateful to our CoPS colleagues, particularly the Director, James Giesecke, for providing a wonderfully encouraging environment for our research. We also thank Victoria University for giving CoPS institutional arrangements under which we can flourish.

In writing this book, we have drawn on material from our article in the Journal of Global Economic Analysis (JGEA, vol 1, 2016). We thank Tom Hertel, Ed Balistreri, and Tom Rutherford for detailed pre-publication comments on our JGEA submission. All of the JGEA material has been revised for this book. In many places, it has been expanded and clarified. Chapter 7 is entirely new. In that chapter, we present a simple method for converting an existing Armington model into a Melitz model and apply it to GTAP.

The book is dedicated to the memory of Ken Pearson who died of cancer in 2015. Ken was the original creator of the GEMPACK software. This software has facilitated the development and application of CGE modeling throughout the world. Its profound influence on our own work will be apparent to any reader of this book. Ken was our great friend and colleague. We miss him.

Melbourne, Australia   Peter B. Dixon
March 2018   Michael Jerie
                                                                                   Maureen T. Rimmer

Contents

In the Melitz model, both types of fixed costs are non-zero. As for Krugman, firms are monopolistically competitive, correctly perceiving the elasticity of demand for their product. In a major departure from Armington and Krugman, Melitz allows for productivity variation across firms in country s. As in Krugman, the number of firms in country s adjusts endogenously to achieve industry-wide zero pure profits. Whereas in Armington and Krugman, all firms in country s sell on all trade links, in Melitz only high productivity firms can sell on trade links for which there are high fixed costs (large values for F_{sd}).

Chapter 3 investigates the optimality properties of an equilibrium in the Melitz model. Given the departures in Melitz from perfect competition, we wondered whether a Melitz market equilibrium is distorted, and if so, whether that provides a justification for policy intervention. However, despite monopolistic competition and economies of scale, we find that in the absence of tariffs, the market equilibrium described by Melitz is cost minimizing. That is, a Melitz world widget industry minimizes the costs of satisfying given widget demands in each country. Although Melitz does not introduce new *within*-industry distortions, a model in which some sectors are Melitz while others are Armington exhibits *between*-industry distortions.

Chapter 4 shows how parameters for Melitz-style models are being estimated. We review a leading example, Balistreri et al. (2011). For their estimation procedure, they use data on the values of trade flows in manufactured goods. These data include domestic flows (s to s flows) as well as international flows (s to d flows, s ≠ d). The parameter set in a Melitz model provides excess degrees of freedom. There are many choices of parameter values compatible with reproducing the observed data on trade flows. We derive $R^2 - R$ conditions on the parameter space for data compatibility where R is the number of countries. Balistreri et al. impose strong priors on the values of many parameters and on relationships between their values. These priors are not consistent with the $R^2 - R$ conditions implied by the data. This gives Balistreri et al. an econometric estimating method. They choose the values of their free parameters to be as compatible as possible with the data. Nevertheless, we are left wondering whether they would have been better off to simply calibrate. That is, choose parameter values that are completely compatible in a Melitz model with observed trade flows.

Chapter 5 starts our work on Melitz in CGE modeling. We review Balistreri and Rutherford's (2013) method for solving a Melitz CGE model. Balistreri and Rutherford use GAMS software.[6] They describe difficulties in solving Melitz models which they attribute to high dimensionalities and non-convexities. To overcome their computational difficulties, they adopt a decomposition or "divide and conquer" iterative procedure. They guess values for economy-wide variables such as wage rates and demands for each product in each country. Given these guesses, they solve a single-sector Melitz model for each product. These single sector solutions reveal values for industry productivity variables and love-for-variety preference variables. These values are fed into a global Armington

---

[6]See Bisschop and Meeraus (1982), Brooke et al. (1992), Horridge et al. (2013).

model which generates revised estimates for wage rates and demands for each product in each country. These revised estimates are then fed back into the single-sector Melitz models. The procedure continues until the economy-wide variables that go into the Melitz single sector models are the same as those that come out of the next run of the global Armington model. We establish why this method works. However, computation is not our main interest in Balistreri and Rutherford's algorithm. To us, what the algorithm reveals is that a Melitz model can be viewed as an Armington model with extra shocks to productivity and preference variables. This finding is valuable in interpreting Melitz results.

Chapter 6 sets out an illustrative numerical general equilibrium model with Melitz sectors. We show how Melitz results can be computed directly (without decomposition) by an off-the-shelf application of GEMPACK software.[7] Coding errors can easily occur in CGE modeling. Test simulations, that is simulations for which the results are known a priori, are an important checking device. We present a series of test simulations for a Melitz CGE model. Then we compare results for the effects of a tariff change in the illustrative Melitz model with those obtained in the corresponding Armington model. The corresponding Armington model uses the same input-output and trade database as the Melitz model, and its inter-country substitution elasticities are set so that the Armington and Melitz models imply similar trade responses to tariff changes. In interpreting the tariff results, we use the insight from Chap. 5 that Melitz equals Armington with extra productivity and preference shocks. This insight allows us to decompose the welfare effects of tariff changes in a Melitz model into terms-of-trade and efficiency effects, derivable from an Armington model, plus extra Melitz effects associated with productivity and love of variety. In our illustrative Melitz tariff simulation, these extra effects have opposite sign and tend to cancel out. Consequently, the welfare results in the Melitz simulation are close to those in the corresponding Armington simulation. We relate this outcome to the optimality result of Chap. 3.

Chapter 7 demonstrates how an existing Armington-based CGE model can be converted into a Melitz-based CGE model. The conversion method involves minimal changes to the code for the Armington model. It is achieved by adding equations to the bottom of the code. With these equations in place, Armington and Melitz solutions can be computed through closure swaps, that is, changes in the choice of exogenous and endogenous variables. Given the enormous effort that has been put into the creation of Armington models and the unavoidable complexity generated by the inclusion of policy-relevant detail, being able to make the conversion with minimal changes to the Armington model is a major advantage. It is an advantage that distinguishes our conversion method from that of Akgul et al. (2016). It means that conversion to Melitz of different Armington models around the world can be achieved without requiring rethinks and recoding of these models.

To explain our conversion method we first apply it to what we call the BasicArmington model. This is the Armington version of the illustrative model

---

[7]See Pearson (1988), Harrison et al. (2014), Horridge et al. (2013).

used in Chap. 6. With the conversion equations added, we obtain the A2M (Armington to Melitz) system for BasicArmington. To check the validity of the conversion, we compare Melitz results from this BasicArmington-A2M system with the Melitz results from Chap. 6.

Then, we apply the conversion method to a 10-region, 57-commodity, Armington-based GTAP model. GTAP is the world's most widely applied global CGE model.[8] Using our GTAP-A2M system, we compare Melitz and corresponding Armington results for the effects of a tariff imposed by North America on all imports of Wearing apparel (Wap). As in Chap. 6, we use a welfare decomposition equation to explain and interpret the results. The Wap tariff simulations with the GTAP-A2M system give significantly different welfare results for Melitz and Armington. This contrasts with results from the BasicArmington-A2M system where the differences are negligible. In the BasicArmington-A2M system, all sectors in the converted model are treated as Melitz whereas in the Melitz simulation with the GTAP-A2M system, only the Wap sector is treated as Melitz. With only Wap treated as Melitz, the movement of resources into and out of the Wap sector in each country causes important welfare effects that are not present in Armington. Our computations with the GTAP-A2M system confirm that GEMPACK software easily handles a full-scale, policy-detailed CGE model with Melitz sectors.

Chapter 8 provides concluding remarks and lists the main findings from the earlier chapters.

1.2 How to Read This Book

Modern trade theory is difficult for applied economists to absorb in a limited amount of time. While we would like to describe this book as "Melitz made easy", that would set up false expectations. Rather, we can describe the book as Melitz made accessible.

Readers of a technical book like this should decide on a reading strategy. Here we try to give some hints to help with this process.

Chapters 2 and 3 are for people who want to master Melitz theory. In these chapters we try to explain the theory intuitively. At the same time, we don't shy away from the underlying mathematics.

Chapter 4 is for people who want to understand about estimation and calibration issues in implementing Melitz in a CGE model.

Chapters 5–7 are for people who want to know how to do Melitz-based CGE modeling.

Chapter 8 is for people who need a quick summary of what we found out.

---

[8]The GTAP website is at https://www.gtap.agecon.purdue.edu/. The key reference on GTAP is Hertel (1997).

We use appendices to set out a lot of the underlying mathematics. This is elementary but comprehensive and unavoidably detailed. Our own understanding of the properties of Melitz theory and its implications for CGE modeling was forged in preparing these appendices. We hope that readers will benefit from working through at least some of them.

Appendices are also used to set out the GEMPACK code for the simple models that are discussed in Chaps. 6 and 7. Download instructions for the code and the reported simulations are given in Appendices 6.1 and 7.1. The code for the GTAP-A2M system is too voluminous for display in the book. However, instructions for downloading it with our reported simulations are in Chap. 7 (Sect. 7.5).

References

Akgul, Z., Villoria, N. B., & Hertel, T. W. (2016). GTAP-HET: Introducing firm heterogeneity into the GTAP model. *Journal of Global Economic Analysis, 1*(1), 111–180.

Armington, P. (1969). A theory of demand for products distinguished by place of production. *Staff Papers-International Monetary Fund, 16*(1), 159–178.

Balistreri, E. J., Hillberry, R. H., & Rutherford, T. F. (2011). Structural estimation and solution of international trade models with heterogeneous firms. *Journal of International Economics, 83,* 95–108.

Balistreri, E., & Rutherford, T. (2013). Computing general equilibrium theories of monopolistic competition and heterogeneous firms (Chapter 23). In P. B. Dixon & D. W. Jorgenson (Eds.), *Handbook of computable general equilibrium modeling* (pp. 1513–1570). Amsterdam: Elsevier.

Bisschop, J., & Meeraus, A. (1982). On the development of a general algebraic modeling system in a strategic planning environment. *Mathematical Programming Study, 20,* 1–19.

Brooke, A., Meeraus, A., & Kendrick, D. (1992). *Release 2.25: GAMS a user's guide.* San Francisco: The Scientific Press.

Deardorff, A. V., Stern, R. M., & Baum, C. F. (1977). A multi-country simulation of the employment and exchange-rate effects of post-Kennedy round tariff reductions (Chapter 3). In N. Akrasanee, S. Naya, & V. Vichit-Vadakan (Eds.), *Trade and employment in Asia and the Pacific* (pp. 36–72). Honolulu: The University Press of Hawaii.

Dixon, P. B., Parmenter, B. R., Ryland, G. J., & Sutton, J. (1977). *ORANI, a general equilibrium model of the Australian economy: Current specification and illustrations of use for policy analysis* (pp. xii + 297). First Progress Report of the IMPACT Project, Vol. 2. Canberra: Australian Government Publishing Service.

Dixon, P. B., Parmenter, B. R., Sutton, J., & Vincent, D. P. (1982). *ORANI: A multisectoral model of the Australian economy* (pp. xviii + 372). Contributions to Economic Analysis, Vol. 142. Amsterdam: North-Holland Publishing Company.

Evans, H. D. (1972). *A general equilibrium analysis of protection: The effects of protection in Australia.* Contributions to Economic Analysis, Vol. 76. Amsterdam: North-Holland Publishing Company.

Harrison, J., Horridge, J. M., Jerie, M., & Pearson, K. R. (2014). *GEMPACK manual,* GEMPACK Software. ISBN 978-1-921654-34-3. Available at http://www.copsmodels.com/gpmanual.htm.

Hertel, T. W. (Ed.). (1997). *Global trade analysis: Modeling and applications.* Cambridge, UK: Cambridge University Press.

Horridge, M., Meeraus, A., Pearson, K., & Rutherford, T. (2013). Software platforms: GAMS and GEMPACK (Chapter 20). In P. B. Dixon & D. W. Jorgenson (Eds.), *Handbook of computable general equilibrium modeling* (pp. 1331–1382). Amsterdam: Elsevier.

Johansen, L. (1960). *A multisectoral study of economic growth*. Contributions to Economic Analysis, Vol. 21. Amsterdam: North-Holland.

Krugman, P. (1980). Scale economies, product differentiation, and the pattern of trade. *The American Economic Review, 70*(5), 950–959.

Melitz, M. J. (2003). The impact of trade on intra-industry reallocations and aggregate industry productivity. *Econometrica, 71*(6), 1695–1725.

Pearson, K. R. (1988). Automating the computation of solutions of large economic models. *Economic Modelling, 5*(4), 385–395.

Zhai, F. (2008). Armington meets Melitz: Introducing firm heterogeneity in a global CGE model of trade. *Journal of Economic Integration, 23*(3), 575–604.

Chapter 2
Armington, Krugman and Melitz as Special Cases of an Encompassing Model

Abstract This chapter is built around a general, theoretical, multi-country model of production, pricing and trade by firms in the widget industry. We refer to this as the Armington, Krugman, Melitz Encompassing (AKME) model. We explain the Armington, Krugman and Melitz models and the relationships between them by showing that they are successively less restrictive special cases of AKME. All CGE modelers are familiar with the Armington model in which country of origin distinguishes one widget from another and firms play no role. For Krugman and Melitz, widgets are distinguished by firm rather than country. However, before these models can be taken into the CGE framework, the firm dimension must be eliminated. "Typical" firms must replace individual firms. Defining a typical firm in each country for Krugman is straight forward. While different firms produce distinct varieties of widgets, all widget firms in a given country have the same productivity and face the same demand conditions. Consequently, any widget firm in a country will do as typical. For Melitz, there is a richer specification of inter-firm heterogeneity. While firms in a given country face the same demand conditions, they can have different productivity levels. This makes identification of the typical firm challenging. We show how Melitz defines multiple typical firms, one for each trading link. Throughout the chapter we explain the modeling strategy in non-technical terms but we do not shirk the mathematics, particularly for Melitz. Understanding the mathematics is essential for accurate translation of Melitz into the CGE framework and for interpreting results.

Keywords Trade models · Armington · Krugman · Melitz · Encompassing model

In this chapter we present an encompassing 10-equation system that describes production, pricing and trade for a particular commodity, say widgets. We refer to this as the AKME model: Armington, Krugman, Melitz Encompassing model.

In AKME, each country's widget industry is composed of monopolistically competitive firms. Each firm has the potential to produce its own variety of widget,

© Springer Nature Singapore Pte Ltd. 2018
P. B. Dixon et al., *Trade Theory in Computable General Equilibrium Models*,
Advances in Applied General Equilibrium Modeling,
https://doi.org/10.1007/978-981-10-8325-9_2

distinct from widgets produced by other firms. To give itself this potential, a firm incurs a fixed setup cost. The firm then faces an additional fixed setup cost for every market in which it chooses to operate. The potential markets are the domestic market and the market in each other country.

After explaining the 10-equation system in Sect. 2.1, we show in Sect. 2.2 that the Armington, Krugman and Melitz models are progressively less restrictive special cases. In Sect. 2.3 we demonstrate the completeness of our specifications of the Armington, Krugman and Melitz models. We do this by showing that with these specifications we could generate multi-country solutions for the widget sector for given values of economy-wide variables such as aggregate demand for widgets and wage rates in each country.

2.1 An Encompassing Model of Trade: The 10-Equation AKME Model

We start by simply laying out the 10 equations of the ACME model and defining the notation. Then we explain and discuss each equation in turn. The 10 equations are:

$$P_{ksd} = \left(\frac{W_s T_{sd}}{\Phi_k}\right)\left(\frac{\eta}{1+\eta}\right) \qquad k \in S(s,d) \tag{2.1}$$

$$P_d = \left(\sum_s \sum_{k \in S(s,d)} N_s g_s(\Phi_k)(\delta_{sd}\gamma_{ksd})^\sigma P_{ksd}^{1-\sigma}\right)^{1/(1-\sigma)} \tag{2.2}$$

$$Q_{ksd} = Q_d(\delta_{sd}\gamma_{ksd})^\sigma \left(\frac{P_d}{P_{ksd}}\right)^\sigma \qquad k \in S(s,d) \tag{2.3}$$

$$Q_{sd} = \left(\sum_{k \in S(s,d)} N_s g_s(\Phi_k)\gamma_{ksd}Q_{ksd}^{(\sigma-1)/\sigma}\right)^{\sigma/(\sigma-1)} \tag{2.4}$$

$$\Pi_{ksd} = \frac{P_{ksd}}{T_{sd}}Q_{ksd} - \left(\frac{W_s}{\Phi_k}\right)Q_{ksd} - F_{sd}W_s \quad k \in S(s,d) \tag{2.5}$$

$$\Pi_s = \sum_d \sum_{k \in S(s,d)} N_s g_s(\Phi_k)\Pi_{ksd} - N_s H_s W_s \tag{2.6}$$

$$L_s = \sum_d \sum_{k \in S(s,d)} N_s g_s(\Phi_k)\frac{Q_{ksd}}{\Phi_k} + \sum_d \sum_{k \in S(s,d)} N_s g_s(\Phi_k)F_{sd} + N_s H_s \tag{2.7}$$

$$S(s,d) = \left\{ k : \Phi_k \geq \Phi_{\min(s,d)} \right\} \qquad (2.8)$$

$$\Pi tot_s = 0 \qquad (2.9)$$

$$\Pi_{\min(s,d)} = 0 \qquad (2.10)$$

In these equations,

N_s is the number of widget firms in country s and $g_s(\Phi_k)$ is the proportion of these firms that have productivity at level Φ_k. A firm's productivity level, assumed to be a given constant for each firm, is the number of additional units of output generated per additional unit of labor (for simplicity we assume that labor is the only input). When we refer to firms in class k in country s we mean the set of firms in s that have productivity Φ_k. The number of firms in this class is $N_s g_s(\Phi_k)$. By $\Phi_{\min(s,d)}$ we mean the minimum value of productivity Φ_k over all firms operating on the sd-link. Technically we do most of the mathematics in this book as if the possible productivity levels are discrete. This is for ease of exposition.

P_{ksd} is the price in country d of widgets produced in country s by firms in productivity class k. We assume that each class-k firm operating on the sd-link charges the same price for its variety as each other such firm. This assumption is justified because, as we will see, all class-k firms in country s are assumed to be identical: they have the same costs and face the same demand conditions.

W_s is the cost of a unit of labor to widget makers in country s.

T_{sd} is the power[1] of the tariff or possibly transport costs associated with the sale of widgets from s to d. We assume that tariffs are charged on the cif price which in the model being explained here is the same as the factory door price which is the same as the fob price.[2]

η is the elasticity of demand (restricted to be <-1) perceived by producers in all countries on all their sales.

F_{sd} is the fixed cost (measured in units of labor) incurred by a firm in s to enable it to set up the export of its variety to d.

H_s is the fixed cost (measured in units of labor) for every firm in country s, even those that don't produce anything.

$S(s,d)$ is the set of all firms k in s that send widgets from s to d. With all firms in country s facing the same fixed costs, we can assume that if any class-k firm in country s operates on the sd-link then all firms in country s with productivity greater than or equal to Φ_k operate on the sd-link.

P_d is the average price paid by consumers in d for their widgets from all sources.

---

[1]Power is one plus the rate.

[2]We do not follow Melitz (2003) who assumed (rather strangely) that tariffs are charged on the value of the production-labor used in creating imports (excludes fixed costs).

γ_{ksd} is a positive parameter reflecting d's preference for varieties produced by firms in class k in country s relative to other varieties from s.

δ_{sd} is a positive parameter reflecting d's preference for varieties in general from s relative to those from other countries.

σ (restricted to be >1) is the elasticity of substitution between varieties, assumed to be the same for all consumers in every country and for any pair of varieties wherever sourced.

Q_{ksd} is the quantity of widgets sent from country s to country d by each firm in class k (this includes the s-to-s flows).

Q_{sd} is the effective (or welfare-relevant) quantity of widgets of all varieties sent from s to d (a CES aggregate of the Q_{ksd}s).

Q_d is the total requirement for widgets in d. As we will explain later, this is a CES aggregate of the Q_{sd}s.

Π_{ksd} is the contribution to the profits of a class-k producer in country s from its sales to d. In particular, $\Pi_{\min(s,d)}$ is the contribution of sd-sales to the profits of firms with the lowest productivity [$\Phi_{\min(s,d)}$] of those on the sd-link.

Πtot_s is total profits for widget firms in country s.

L_s is the employment in the widget industry in country s.

Equation (2.1) is an example of the Lerner mark-up rule. If a class-k firm in country s perceives that its sales to country d are proportional to P_{ksd}^{η} and that its revenue and variable cost per unit of sales in country d are P_{ksd}/T_{sd} and W_s/Φ_k, then to maximize its profits it will set its price to country d according to (2.1).[3] With η being less than -1, the mark-up factor on marginal costs [$\eta/(1+\eta)$] is greater than 1. If firms perceive that they are in highly competitive markets [η approaches $-\infty$], then the mark-up factor is close to 1, that is prices are close to marginal costs. On the other hand, if firms perceive that they have significant market power [η close to -1], then the mark-up factor is large and prices will be considerably greater than marginal costs.

Equation (2.2) defines the average price (P_d) of widgets in country d as a CES average of the prices of the individual varieties sold in country d (P_{ksd}). Equation (2.3) determines the demand in country d for the product of each class-k firm in country s. This is proportional to the total demand for widgets in country d (Q_d) and to a price term which compares the price in d of class-k widgets from s with the average price of widgets in country d. The sensitivity of demand for widgets from a particular class and country to changes in relative prices is controlled by the substitution parameter, σ. Equation (2.4) defines the total effective quantity of widgets sent from s to d as a CES aggregate of the quantities of each

---

[3]Equation (2.1) applies to varieties that are actually sold from s to d, those in the set S(s,d). As to be discussed later, these are the varieties for which non-negative profits can be generated on the sd-link.

variety sent from s to d. Underlying Eqs. (2.2)–(2.4) is a nested CES optimization problem. People in country d are viewed as choosing Q_{sd} and Q_{ksd} to minimize

$$\sum_s \sum_{k \in S(s,d)} Q_{ksd} P_{ksd} \tag{2.11}$$

subject to

$$Q_{sd} = \left(\sum_{k \in S(s,d)} N_s g(\Phi_k) \gamma_{ksd} Q_{ksd}^{(\sigma-1)/\sigma} \right)^{\sigma/(\sigma-1)} \tag{2.12}$$

and

$$Q_d = \left(\sum_s \delta_{sd} Q_{sd}^{(\sigma-1)/\sigma} \right)^{\sigma/(\sigma-1)} \tag{2.13}$$

Equation (2.5) defines profits for a class-k firm in country s from its sales to country d as: revenue *less* variable costs *less* the fixed costs required to set up sales of a variety on the sd-link. Equation (2.6) defines total profits in the widget industry in country s as the sum of profits over all flows *less* fixed costs in developing the potential for producing varieties. Equation (2.7) defines total employment in the widget industry in country s as the sum of labor used as variable inputs and fixed inputs.

Equation (2.8) defines the set of firms on the sd-link. This is all the firms with productivity levels greater than or equal to $\Phi_{min(s,d)}$.

Equation (2.9) imposes zero profits in the widget industry in country s. Via Eq. (2.10) it is assumed that firms with the minimum productivity level on the sd-link [$\Phi_{min(s,d)}$] have zero profits on that link.

In considering the 10-equation system, (2.1)–(2.10), it is reasonable to think of W_s, Q_d and T_{sd} as exogenous. In a general equilibrium model, W_s and Q_d would be endogenous but determined largely independently of the widget industry, and T_{sd} can be thought of as a naturally exogenous policy variable. We assume that the technology and demand parameters and the distribution of productivities [$g_s(\Phi_k)$] are given. If, initially, we also take as given the number of firms in each country (N_s) and the minimum productivities on each link [$\Phi_{min(s,d)}$] so that (2.8) can be used to generate S(s,d), then (2.1)–(2.7) can be solved recursively: (2.1) generates P_{ksd}; (2.2) generates P_d; and so on through to (2.7) which generates L_s. The role of (2.9) and (2.10) is to determine N_s and $\Phi_{min(s,d)}$. It is assumed that the number of firms in country s adjusts so that the industry earns zero profits and that the number of firms on the sd-link adjusts so that the link contributes zero to the profits of the link's lowest productivity firm.

2.2 The Special Assumptions Adopted by Armington, Krugman and Melitz

Equations (2.1)–(2.10) involve variables for individual firms. However, practical modeling is done at the industry level, with industries represented by aggregate variables (e.g. industry employment) and by variables for a representative firm (e.g. the price charged by the representative firm in the widget industry in country s). Table 2.1 shows assumptions adopted by Armington (1969), Krugman (1980) and Melitz (2003) that assist in translating (2.1)–(2.10) into systems of equations connecting industry variables. These assumptions are largely implicit for Armington who did not start at the firm level but explicit for Krugman and Melitz who did start at the firm level.

As shown in Table 2.1, there are no fixed costs in the Armington model. Krugman recognises a fixed cost for each firm but not an additional fixed cost for each trade link. Melitz recognises both types of fixed cost.

For Armington, firms operate as if they have no market power: they price at marginal cost. Both Krugman and Melitz assume that firms are aware of the elasticity of demand for their variety implied by (2.3). Consequently they set prices by marking up marginal costs by the factor $\sigma/(\sigma - 1)$. This factor is greater than 1: recall that $\sigma > 1$. Also note that in using (2.3) to calculate country d's demand elasticity for a variety produced by a class-k firm in country s, we ignore the effect of changes in P_{ksd} on P_d.

In all three models, d's preferences for varieties from s are symmetric, implying that γ_{ksd} has the same value for all k. Without loss in generality, the γ's can be set at 1.

For Armington and Krugman all firms in country s have the same productivity. For Melitz, productivity varies across firms within a country. As set out in

Table 2.1 Assumptions in the Armington, Krugman and Melitz models

	Armington	Krugman	Melitz
Fixed costs for a firm to exist, H_s	0	+	+
Fixed costs for entering a trade link, F_{sd}	0	0	+
Perceived demand elasticity, η	$-\infty$	$-\sigma$	$-\sigma$
d's preference between varieties from s, γ_{ksd}	1 for all k, s, d	1 for all k, s, d	1 for all k, s, d
Productivity for firms in s	$\Phi_{\bullet s}$ ∀ firms	$\Phi_{\bullet s}$ ∀ firms	Pareto distribution
No. of firms (or potential varieties) in s, N_s	1	Endogenous	Endogenous
Fraction of s firms on the sd-link, $\sum_{k \in S(s,d)} g_s(\Phi_k)$	1	1	Endogenous

$$W_s \sum_d \sum_{k \in S(s,d)} g_s(\Phi_k) * \left(\frac{Q_{ksd}}{\Phi_k} + F_{sd} \right) + W_s H_s - \sum_d \Lambda_d \sum_{k \in S(s,d)} g_s(\Phi_k) \delta_{sd} Q_{ksd}^{(\sigma-1)/\sigma} = 0 \quad \forall s$$

$$(3.28)$$

$$W_s \left[N_s g_s(\Phi_k) \left(\frac{1}{\Phi_k} \right) \right] - \Lambda_d N_s g_s(\Phi_k) \delta_{sd} \left(\frac{\sigma - 1}{\sigma} \right) Q_{ksd}^{-1/\sigma} = 0 \quad \forall s, d \quad \& \quad \forall k \in S(s,d)$$

$$(3.29)$$

Equations (3.25)–(3.29) are necessary conditions for a solution of the planners cost minimizing problem. To demonstrate proposition (3.22), we need to show that any set of variable values satisfying (3.25)–(3.29) is consistent with an AKME market equilibrium with zero tariffs. To demonstrate proposition (3.23), we need to show that an AKME equilibrium with zero tariffs satisfies (3.25)–(3.29).

Proving proposition **(3.22)**
Let $\Phi_{\min(s,d)}$, N_s, Q_{ksd} and Λ_d satisfy (3.25)–(3.29) for given values of the exogenous variables W_s and Q_d. Let P_d and P_{ksd} be defined by

$$\Lambda_d = P_d Q_d^{1/\sigma} \tag{3.30}$$

$$P_{ksd} = \frac{W_s}{\Phi_k} \left(\frac{\sigma}{\sigma - 1} \right). \tag{3.31}$$

We also define Q_{sd}, Π_{ksd}, Πtot_s and L_s as in (T2.4)–(T2.7) of the AKME model with zero tariffs. With these definitions, we show in Appendix 3.1 that $\Phi_{\min(s,d)}$, N_s, Q_{ksd}, P_d, P_{ksd}, Q_{sd}, Π_{ksd}, Πtot_s and L_s satisfies (T2.1)–(T2.10) and is therefore an AKME solution.

Proving proposition **(3.23)**
Let $\Phi_{\min(s,d)}$, N_s, Q_{ksd}, P_d, P_{ksd}, Q_{sd}, Π_{ksd}, Πtot_s and L_s satisfy (T2.1)–(T2.10) for given values of the exogenous variables W_s and Q_d and with T_{sd} equal to one for all s,d. Define Λ_d by (3.30). We show in Appendix 3.1 that $\Phi_{\min(s,d)}$, N_s, Q_{ksd} and Λ_d satisfies (3.25)–(3.29).

3.3   Interpretation and Significance

Classical presentations of the optimality of market economies generally rely on models in which there are constant or diminishing returns to scale in production and a predetermined or exogenous list of commodities that can be produced (see for example Debreu 1959, Chap. 6; Negishi 1960). The propositions outlined in

Sect. 3.2, which can be thought of as a generalization of Dixit and Stiglitz (1977), show that market optimality can also apply in a model in which production processes exhibit increasing returns to scale and the range of commodities (varieties) produced is endogenous. Thus we have found that the phenomena introduced by Melitz do not necessarily provide a case for policy intervention in a market economy.

Apart from its theoretical and policy implications, we find the equivalence between the AKME model with zero tariffs and cost minimization to be of interest for three reasons.

First, it implies that the envelope theorem is applicable. This is helpful in result interpretation. It means that if we start from a specification in the AKME family with zero tariffs, then small movements in exogenous variables will display the usual "envelope" effects. For example, small movements in tariffs will have zero welfare effects; and small movements in production parameters (such as H_s) will have welfare effects reflecting relevant cost shares (the share of $N_s W_s H_s$ in world widget costs). We illustrate this computationally in Chap. 6.

Our second reason for being interested in the AKME cost-minimization equivalence is also related to result interpretation. In explaining the effects of changes in exogenous variables such as tariffs (T_{sd}) or fixed costs (H_s, F_{sd}), it is convenient to argue from the point of view of an all-encompassing agent. For example, if H_s goes up we would expect an all-encompassing agent to satisfy given widget demands (Q_d for all d) by reducing output in country s (in response to the cost increase) but substituting longer production runs for varieties in s (an increase in output per firm and a decrease in the number of firms). This would create a need to produce more in other countries particularly via greater variety. Thus, in other countries we would expect to see an increase in output with the percentage increase in the number of firms exceeding the percentage increase in output. The cost minimizing problem (3.24)–(3.26) legitimizes such explanations, based on the behaviour of an all-encompassing optimizing agent, as a way of understanding results from AKME multi-agent market models.

Third, understanding the equivalence between the AKME model and cost minimization may be valuable in computations. Balistreri and Rutherford (2013) report that solving general equilibrium models with imperfect competition and increasing returns to scale can be challenging. [We review their computational approach in Chap. 5.] A potential role for problem (3.24)–(3.26) is as a computational framework or at least as a tool for diagnosing computational difficulties. If direct solution of AKME equations proves difficult, then examination of the optimization problem (3.24)–(3.26) may reveal the reason.

Appendix 3.1: Equivalence Between Worldwide Cost Minimizing and the AKME Model

***Proof of proposition* (3.22): Cost minimizing $\Rightarrow$ AKME with zero tariffs**

Let $\Phi_{\min(s,d)}$, N_s, Q_{ksd} and Λ_d be a solution to (3.25)–(3.29) for given values of the exogenous variables W_s, and Q_d. Let P_d and P_{ksd} be defined by (3.30) and (3.31) and define Q_{sd}, Π_{ksd}, Πtot_s and L_s as in (T2.4)–(T2.7) of the AKME model. We show that $\Phi_{\min(s,d)}$, N_s, Q_{ksd}, P_d, P_{ksd}, Q_{sd}, Π_{ksd}, Πtot_s and L_s then satisfy the remaining AKME equations, (T2.1)–(T2.3) and (T2.8)–(T2.10), and is therefore an AKME solution.

Equations (T2.8) is satisfied: (T2.8) is the same as (3.26).

Under (3.21) and with zero tariffs ($T_{sd} = 1$), (T2.1) is the same as (3.31).

From (3.29)–(3.31) we have

$$P_{ksd} = P_d Q_d^{1/\sigma} \delta_{sd} Q_{ksd}^{-1/\sigma}, k \in S(s,d). \tag{3.32}$$

Hence

$$Q_{ksd} = \delta_{sd}^\sigma Q_d \left(\frac{P_d}{P_{ksd}}\right)^\sigma \quad k \in S(s,d). \tag{3.33}$$

Under (3.21) this establishes (T2.3).

From (3.27)

$$-W_s \left(\frac{Q_{\min(s,d)}}{\Phi_{\min(s,d)}} + F_{sd}\right) + \Lambda_d \delta_{sd} Q_{\min(s,d)}^{(\sigma-1)/\sigma} = 0. \tag{3.34}$$

Combining (3.30) and (3.33) gives

$$P_{ksd} = \Lambda_d \delta_{sd} Q_{ksd}^{-1/\sigma}. \tag{3.35}$$

In particular

$$P_{\min(s,d)} = \Lambda_d \delta_{sd} Q_{\min(s,d)}^{-1/\sigma}. \tag{3.36}$$

Putting (3.36) into (3.34) gives

$$-W_s \left(\frac{Q_{\min(s,d)}}{\Phi_{\min(s,d)}} + F_{sd}\right) + P_{\min(s,d)} Q_{\min(s,d)} = 0, \tag{3.37}$$

establishing (T2.10) via (T2.5) with T_{sd} equals one.

From (3.28) and (3.35) we obtain

$$\left[W_s \sum_d \sum_{k \in S(s,d)} g_s(\Phi_k) * \left(\frac{Q_{ksd}}{\Phi_k} + F_{sd} \right) \right] + W_s H_s$$
$$- \sum_d \sum_{k \in S(s,d)} \frac{P_{ksd} Q_{ksd}^{1/\sigma}}{\delta_{sd}} g_s(\Phi_k) \delta_{sd} Q_{ksd}^{(\sigma-1)/\sigma}$$
$$= 0. \tag{3.38}$$

Simplifying, rearranging and multiplying through by N_s gives

$$\left[W_s \sum_d \sum_{k \in S(s,d)} N_s g_s(\Phi_k) * \left(\frac{Q_{ksd}}{\Phi_k} + F_{sd} \right) \right] + N_s W_s H_s$$
$$= \sum_d \sum_{k \in S(s,d)} N_s g_s(\Phi_k) P_{ksd} Q_{ksd}. \tag{3.39}$$

Via (T2.5) with T_{sd} equals one and (T2.6), (3.39) leads to (T2.9).

Now all that remains is to establish (T2.2). We start by rearranging (3.33) as

$$\delta_{sd}^\sigma P_{ksd}^{1-\sigma} = Q_{ksd}^{(\sigma-1)/\sigma} \delta_{sd} Q_d^{(1-\sigma)/\sigma} P_d^{1-\sigma}. \tag{3.40}$$

Then multiplying through by $N_s g_s(\Phi_k)$, aggregating over s and k, and using (3.25) we obtain (T2.2) under assumption (3.21).

Proof of proposition (3.23):

AKME with zero tariffs ⇒ first−order optimality conditions for cost minimizing

Let $\Phi_{min(s,d)}$, N_s, Q_{ksd}, P_d, P_{ksd}, Q_{sd}, Π_{ksd}, Πtot_s and L_s satisfy (T2.1) to (T2.10) for given values of the exogenous variables W_s and Q_d and with T_{sd} equals one for all s,d. Define Λ_d by (3.30). We show that $\Phi_{min(s,d)}$, N_s, Q_{ksd} and Λ_d is a solution to (3.25)–(3.29).

Condition (3.26) is the same as (T2.8).

Under (3.21), (T2.3) gives

$$\delta_{sd} Q_{ksd}^{(\sigma-1)/\sigma} = Q_d^{(\sigma-1)/\sigma} \delta_{sd}^\sigma P_d^{\sigma-1} P_{ksd}^{1-\sigma}. \tag{3.41}$$

Multiplying through by $N_s g_s(\Phi_k)$, summing over all s and all $k \in S(s,d)$ and using (T2.2) and (3.21) gives (3.25).

Equation (T2.5) with $T_{sd} = 1$ and (T2.10) give

$$P_{\min(s,d)}Q_{\min(s,d)} - \left(\frac{W_s}{\Phi_{\min(s,d)}}\right)Q_{\min(s,d)} - F_{sd}W_s = 0. \tag{3.42}$$

To establish (3.27) we need to eliminate $P_{\min(s,d)}$ and introduce Λ_d. We do this via (T2.3), (3.21) and (3.30) which give

$$P_{ksd} = \delta_{sd}\Lambda_d Q_{ksd}^{-1/\sigma} \tag{3.43}$$

and, in particular

$$P_{\min(s,d)} = \delta_{sd}\Lambda_d Q_{\min(s,d)}^{-1/\sigma}. \tag{3.44}$$

Multiplying (3.42) through by $N_s g_s(\Phi_{\min(s,d)})$ and using (3.44) quickly leads to (3.27).

From (T2.5) with $T_{sd} = 1$, (T2.6) and (T2.9) we obtain

$$\sum_d \sum_{k \in S(s,d)} g_s(\Phi_k)\left[P_{ksd}Q_{ksd} - \left(\frac{W_s}{\Phi_k}\right)Q_{ksd} - F_{sd}W_s\right] - H_s W_s = 0. \tag{3.45}$$

Then, substituting from (3.43) gives (3.28).

To obtain (3.29), we start from (3.43), multiply through by $N_s g_s(\Phi_k)$ and use (T2.1) with $T_{sd} = 1$ and (3.21).

References

Balistreri, E., & Rutherford T. (2013). Computing general equilibrium theories of monopolistic competition and heterogeneous firms (Chap. 23). In P. B. Dixon & D. W. Jorgenson (Eds.), *Handbook of Computable General Equilibrium Modeling* (pp. 1513–1570). Amsterdam: Elsevier.

Debreu, G. (1959). *Theory of value: an axiomatic analysis of economic equilibrium* (pp. xi + 114). New Haven: Cowles Foundation, Yale University Press.

Dhingra, S. & Morrow, J. (2012). The impact of integration on productivity and welfare distortions under monopolistic competition (pp. 50), *Centre for Economic Performance Discussion Paper No. 1130*, London School of Economics, February.

Dixit, A. K., & Stiglitz, J. E. (1977). Monopolistic Competition and optimum product diversity. *American Economic Review*, 297–308.

Lanclos, D. K., & Hertel, T. W. (1995). Endogenous product differentiation and trade policy: implications for the U.S. food industry. *American Journal of Agricultural Economics, 77*(3), 591–601.

Negishi, T. (1960). Welfare economics and the existence of an equilibrium for a competitive economy. *Metroeconomica, 12*(2–3), 92–97.

Chapter 4
Calibration and Parameter Estimation for a Melitz Sector in a CGE Model

Abstract This chapter is about giving numbers to parameters and unobservable variables in a Melitz CGE model. We start by describing how a Melitz model can be calibrated. This is the process by which unobservable variables (preference and fixed cost variables, δ's, F's and H's) are evaluated so that for given parameter values (inter-variety substitution elasticities and productivity distribution parameters, σ and α) the model reproduces base-year data. We find that for a Melitz model there are multiple legitimate calibration possibilities but that the choice between these does not affect simulation results. Then, we review the method that Balistreri et al. (2011) have pioneered for estimating parameters in a Melitz model. This method combines calibration and estimation. Rather than setting initial values for unobservable variables to reproduce base-year data, Balistreri et al. impose theoretically preferred structures on the unobservable variables. These structures are incompatible with precise calibration, but pave the way for estimation. Parameters can be estimated by choosing the values that allow calibration to base-year data that is as close as possible subject to meeting the preferred structural constraints on the unobservable variables. Balistreri et al.'s approach is likely to be a starting point for many potentially fruitful calibration/estimation efforts.

Keywords Calibration · Estimation · Melitz · Armington · Balistreri

Trade models with heterogeneous firms such as the Melitz model are attractive because they gel with findings from microeconomic studies. As explained by Balistreri and Rutherford (2013), micro studies show that there is considerable diversity within industries in firm size and productivity. Consistent with Melitz theory, these studies typically show that only high-productivity, large firms have significant exports, and unlike models in which all firms in the country-s widget industry have equal productivity, models with heterogeneous firms offer the possibility of explaining trade-related changes in industry productivity via reallocation of resources between firms.

But how can we put worthwhile numbers to a heterogeneous-firm specification within a CGE model? In Sect. 4.1 we explain a calibration method for a Melitz

© Springer Nature Singapore Pte Ltd. 2018
P. B. Dixon et al., *Trade Theory in Computable General Equilibrium Models*,
Advances in Applied General Equilibrium Modeling,
https://doi.org/10.1007/978-981-10-8325-9_4

sector in a CGE model presented in levels equations. We find that there is a range of calibration possibilities, that is a range of possibilities for setting the initial values of preference variables and fixed cost variables (δ's, F's and H's) that are compatible with the base-year data. In Sect. 4.2 we study the question of whether the choice among legitimate calibrations affects simulation results. In Sect. 4.3 we move from calibration to estimation. We review the econometric estimation method for Melitz parameters devised by Balistreri et al. (2011). Concluding remarks are in Sect. 4.4. A considerable quantity of routine algebra is required to support the arguments in the chapter. This is presented in four appendices.

The key to calibration and parameter estimation for a heterogeneous-firm CGE model is not to take the theory too literally. Consider the Melitz model. It relies on stark assumptions: the widget industry in each country is monopolistically competitive; each firm produces a single unique variety of widget; each widget firm throughout the world faces the same elasticity of demand, σ, in every market; σ is unresponsive to the number of available widget varieties—it is treated as a parameter implying potentially strong "love-of-variety" effects; in every country, the marginal productivities, Φ_k, of widget producers form a simple one-parameter distribution (a Pareto distribution); and every widget firm in country s faces the same fixed cost, W_sH_s to enter the widget industry and the same fixed cost, W_sF_{sd}, to set up trade with country d. If we try to implement such a theory in a literal fashion with data on numbers of firms and firm-specific costs split into variable costs and different types of fixed costs, then we are likely to become lost in a maze of unsatisfactory data compromises. For example, how would we handle multi-product firms? How would we identify fixed costs specific to different trade links?

By treating the Melitz model as an underlying parable, we can devise calibration and estimation methods whereby Melitz sectors can be included in a CGE model in a way that is consistent with robust data and does not depend on impossible definitional conundrums like deciding how many varieties of chemical products are shipped from the U.S. to Japan. Thus, it is possible to build CGE models that can be used to explore the implications of heterogeneous firm theory in the context of observed magnitudes at the industry and country levels for trade, output, demands and employment.

4.1 Calibrating a Melitz Sector in a CGE Model Presented in Levels Form

Calibration means setting parameter values and initial values for unobservable variables so that the actual values of observed variables together with the initial values of the unobservables are a solution of the model. Models are usually calibrated for a particular year, often called the base year. This means that values of observable and unobservable variables for that year when substituted into each of the model's equations generate left hand sides and right hand sides that are equal. Calibration ensures that a model passes at least a minimal criterion for realism: given the values of exogenous variables for the base year, the model generates values for observable endogenous variables that are equal to their observed values for the base year together with values of unobservable endogenous variables that are equal to their assumed initial values.

We illustrate the calibration process for a Melitz sector in a CGE model by reference to the Melitz equations in Table 4.1. These are the Melitz equations from Table 2.2 with four changes that are convenient but do not change the economic interpretation. First, in (T4.3) we have rewritten (T2.3) using the *value* of demand, D_d, for widgets in country d rather than the *quantity*, Q_d. D_d is Q_d multiplied by P_d. Second, in (T4.6) we have rewritten (T2.7) after multiplying through by W_s on both sides. Third, we have used (T2.1), (T2.5), (T2.6) and (T2.9) to create (T4.5) and to eliminate $\Pi_{\bullet sd}$ and Πtot_s. Fourth, we have added equation (T4.11):

$$V(s,d) = N_{sd}P_{\bullet sd}Q_{\bullet sd} \qquad (4.1)$$

where
V(s, d) is the landed-duty-paid value of the flow of widgets on the sd-link.
Equation (4.1) is intuitively appealing. It says that the landed-duty-paid value of the (s, d) flow is the quantity of widgets ($Q_{\bullet sd}$) sent by the typical firm on the link times the number of firms operating on the link (N_{sd}) times the landed-duty-paid price charged by the typical firm ($P_{\bullet sd}$). However, the equation needs to be justified under Melitz assumptions. This is done in Appendix 4.1.

Referring to Table 4.1, we treat the powers of the tariffs (T_{sd}), the trade flows [V(s, d)] and the wage rates (W_s) as the only independently observable variables. For T_{sd} and V(s, d) we can envisage having a data set, such as that provided by GTAP.[1] For W_s we can simply assign values and adopt a complementary definition of units for labor. For example, if the base-year value of the labor input to the widget industry in country s is $1,000, then without loss of generality we can assume that the wage rate is $1 and the quantity of labor input is 1,000 units where a unit is the number of labor hours for which the base-year wage rate is $1.

The wagebill in the widget industry in country s and the value of demand for widgets in country d are also observable, but not independently observable. In the Melitz sector in Table 4.1, these variables are defined by W_sL_s and P_dQ_d. We assume that our observations for demands (D_d) and costs (C_s) satisfy

$$D_d \equiv P_dQ_d = \sum_s V(s,d). \qquad (4.2)$$

---

[1]See Narayanan et al. (2012).

Table 4.1 Equations, variables and parameters for a Melitz sector

	Equation	Corresponding endogenous variable
(T4.1)	$P_{\bullet sd} = \left(\frac{W_s T_{sd}}{\Phi_{\bullet sd}}\right)\left(\frac{\sigma}{\sigma-1}\right)$	$P_{\bullet sd}$
(T4.2)	$P_d = \left(\sum_s N_{sd}\delta_{sd}^\sigma P_{\bullet sd}^{1-\sigma}\right)^{\frac{1}{(1-\sigma)}}$	P_d
(T4.3)	$P_{\bullet sd}Q_{\bullet sd} = D_d\delta_{sd}^\sigma\left(\frac{P_d}{P_{\bullet sd}}\right)^{\sigma-1}$	$Q_{\bullet sd}$
(T4.4)	$Q_{sd} = N_{sd}^{\sigma/(\sigma-1)}Q_{\bullet sd}$	Q_{sd}
(T4.5)	$0 = \frac{1}{\sigma}*\sum_d N_{sd}\frac{P_{\bullet sd}}{T_{sd}}*Q_{\bullet sd} - \sum_d N_{sd}F_{sd}W_s - N_sH_sW_s$	N_s
(T4.6)	$W_sL_s = \sum_d\frac{W_sN_{sd}Q_{\bullet sd}}{\Phi_{\bullet sd}} + \sum_d W_sN_{sd}F_{sd} + W_sN_sH_s$	L_s
(T4.7)	$N_{sd} = N_s*\left(\Phi_{\min(s,d)}\right)^{-\alpha}$	N_{sd}
(T4.8)	$\frac{1}{(\sigma-1)}\left(\frac{W_s}{\Phi_{\min(s,d)}}\right)Q_{\min(s,d)} - F_{sd}W_s = 0$	$\Phi_{\min(s,d)}$
(T4.9)	$\Phi_{\bullet sd} = \beta\Phi_{\min(s,d)}$	$\Phi_{\bullet sd}$
(T4.10)	$Q_{\min(s,d)} = Q_{\bullet sd}/\beta^\sigma$	$Q_{\min(s,d)}$
(T4.11)	$V(s,d) = N_{sd}P_{\bullet sd}Q_{\bullet sd}$	$V(s,d)$

Parameters: σ and α. We don't list β as a separate parameter. It is a function of σ and α, see (2.27).
Exogenous variables: W_s, T_{sd}, D_d, F_{sd}, H_s and δ_{sd}.
Independently observable variables: W_s, T_{sd} and $V(s,d)$.
Notation: See Sects. 2.1 and 2.2 and the text describing Eq. (4.1)

and

$$C_s \equiv W_sL_s = \sum_d\frac{V(s,d)}{T_{sd}}. \tag{4.3}$$

As shown in Appendix 4.1, Eqs. (4.2) and (4.3) are satisfied by the Melitz model. Consequently, if we calibrate to reproduce observed values for $V(s,d)$ then our calibrated model will also reproduce observed values for demands and costs. For this reason we will not count observed values for demands and costs as additional observations that must be reproduced in the calibration process.

For the model in Table 4.1, the calibration task can now be stated as: find values for variables and parameters that satisfy all of the equations with the independently observable variables [T_{sd}, $V(s,d)$ and W_s] set at their base-year values.

With the standard closure indicated at the foot of Table 4.1, we assume that all endogenous variables can be determined as functions of exogenous variables and parameters. In particular, we assume that the trade flows $V(s,d)$ are functions [$V_{sd}(\dots)$] of exogenous variables and parameters:

$$V(s, d) = V_{sd}(\sigma, \alpha, \delta_{jr}, W_j, T_{jr}, D_r, F_{jr}, H_j \quad \text{for all } j, r). \qquad (4.4)$$

For calibration we want (4.4) to generate the base-year values of $V(s, d)$ when W_j and T_{jr} are set on their base-year values. To ensure this we adjust (that is calibrate) parameters or unobservable exogenous variables.

Which parameters or exogenous variables should we calibrate? Not σ or α. These have the wrong dimension. In any case, CGE modelers are normally willing to make judgements about substitution elasticities (σ) and the shape parameter (α) for the distribution of firm productivities. As explained in Sect. 4.3, these judgements might be informed by econometric analysis. Alternatively, they might be based on literature search or they might be set simply on the basis of generating plausible simulation results. Whatever the basis for setting σ and α, these two parameters are not normally candidates for calibration.

What about D_r? When the values of the trade flows are observed, the values of demands are determined via (4.2), in effect the D_r's are observed. Consequently, the D_r's are not candidates for adjustment to help in the process of making (4.4) consistent with the base-year data. That is, they can't be adjusted in the calibration process.

As already explained, W_j and T_{jr} must be set at their base-year values, and are not adjustable for calibration.

This leaves δ_{jr}, F_{jr} and H_j as candidates for calibration.

Rather than make a definite selection from among these candidates, we will think of calibration [the necessity to fit (4.4)] as the imposition of R^2-R relationships between the values of the δ's, F's and H's, where R is the number of regions.

Why R^2-R? At first glance, specifying the base-year values for the $V(s, d)$'s and imposing these on the left hand side of (4.4) seems to give R^2 conditions that must be met through adjustment of the δ's, F's and H's. But being told the values of the $V(s, d)$'s gives us the values of the R regional demands, D_r for all r. These were treated as exogenous and known on the right hand side of (4.4). Being told their values via the base-year $V(s, d)$ matrix either tells us something that we already know or replaces some previous knowledge. In either case the net outcome is that being given the values of the $V(s, d)$s supplies only R^2-R new pieces of information.

To absorb R^2-R new pieces of information we can determine R^2-R new values for a selection of the δ's, F's and H's. Alternatively, we can determine R^2-R relationships between these parameters or exogenous variables that must be satisfied in order for (4.4) to be consistent with the base-year data.

As shown in Appendix 4.2, using base-year values for the trade flows on the left hand side of Eq. (4.4) leads to the R^2-R relationships between the δ's, F's and H's given by:

$$F_{sd} = F_{dd} * \left(\frac{J(s,d)}{\overline{J}(d,d)}\right)^{\frac{(1-\sigma)}{(\alpha+1-\sigma)}} * \left(\frac{\overline{W}_s\overline{T}_{sd}}{\overline{W}_d\overline{T}_{dd}}\right)^{\frac{-\sigma*\alpha}{(\alpha+1-\sigma)}} *$$

$$\left(\frac{\delta_{sd}}{\delta_{dd}}\right)^{\frac{\sigma*\alpha}{(\alpha+1-\sigma)}} * \left(\frac{H_s}{H_d}\right)^{\frac{(1-\sigma)}{(\alpha+1-\sigma)}} \quad \text{for all s, d, } s \neq d \tag{4.5}$$

where $J(s, d)$ is the share of region s's output that is sold to region d and the bars denote base-year values. $J(s, d)$ is defined by

$$J(s, d) = \frac{V(s, d)/T_{sd}}{\sum_j V(s, j)/T_{sj}}. \tag{4.6}$$

Any combination of δ's, F's and H's that satisfies (4.5) calibrates the model in Table 4.1 to fit base-year data for sales shares $[\overline{J}(s, d)]$, wage rates $(\overline{W}_s)$ and tariff powers $(\overline{T}_{sd})$. For example, if we set all δ's, H's and diagonal F's equal to one, then the model would reproduce base-year observations (the bared items) provided that the off-diagonal F's are set according to:

$$F_{sd} = \left(\frac{\overline{J}(s,d)}{\overline{J}(d,d)}\right)^{\frac{(1-\sigma)}{(\alpha+1-\sigma)}} * \left(\frac{\overline{W}_s\overline{T}_{sd}}{\overline{W}_d\overline{T}_{dd}}\right)^{\frac{-\sigma*\alpha}{(\alpha+1-\sigma)}} \quad \text{for all s, d, } s \neq d \tag{4.7}$$

If the base-year share of s's output sold to d is small relative to the share of d's sales to itself, then (4.7) indicates that this feature of the base-year data can be reproduced by the model with F_{sd} set at a high value.[2] We can interpret this as meaning that the model reproduces the low sales from s to d by assuming that trade on the sd-link is inhibited by high set-up costs.

Clearly (4.7) is not the only calibration possibility allowed by (4.5). Rather than setting all the δ's at one, we could set all the F's at one together with all the H's. Then we could calibrate with the diagonal δ's set at one and the off-diagonal δ's set to satisfy the equation

$$1 = \left(\frac{\overline{J}(s,d)}{\overline{J}(d,d)}\right)^{\frac{(1-\sigma)}{(\alpha+1-\sigma)}} * \left(\frac{\overline{W}_s\overline{T}_{sd}}{\overline{W}_d\overline{T}_{dd}}\right)^{\frac{-\sigma*\alpha}{(\alpha+1-\sigma)}} * \delta_{sd}^{\frac{\sigma*\alpha}{(\alpha+1-\sigma)}} \quad \text{for all s, d, } s \neq d \tag{4.8}$$

That is

$$\delta_{sd} = \left(\frac{\overline{J}(s,d)}{\overline{J}(d,d)}\right)^{\frac{(\sigma-1)}{\sigma*\alpha}} \left(\frac{\overline{W}_s\overline{T}_{sd}}{\overline{W}_d\overline{T}_{dd}}\right) \quad \text{for all s, d, } s \neq d. \tag{4.9}$$

---

[2]Recall from Sect. 2.1 that $\sigma > 1$ and from (2.25) that $\alpha - (\sigma - 1) > 0$. Thus, the exponent $\frac{(1-\sigma)}{(\alpha+1-\sigma)}$ is negative.

If the base-year share of s's output sold to d is small relative to the share of d's sales to itself, then (4.9) indicates that this feature of the base-year data can be reproduced by the model with δ_{sd} set at a low value.[3] We can interpret this as meaning that the model reproduces the low sales from s to d by assuming that country d has a low preference for widgets sent from country s.

What about the wage-tariff terms in (4.7) and (4.9)? If $\overline{W}_s\overline{T}_{sd}$ is high relative to $\overline{W}_d\overline{T}_{dd}$ then, on this account, we know that widgets from country s were expensive in country d in the base year relative to own-sourced widgets in country d. This would allow us to explain the observed ratio of s's sales in market d to d's sales in market d with either a relatively low setup-cost ratio [low F_{sd}, (4.7)] or a relatively high preference ratio [high δ_{sd}, (4.9)].

An Armington model relies on preference parameters (δ_{sd}'s) for calibration to base-year trade-flow data. What is apparent here is that a Melitz model can be calibrated in a variety of ways, the most obvious of which rely on either link setup costs or preference parameters. Different calibration choices give different base-year values for unobservable variables such as the number of widget firms in each country (N_s) and the number of firms on each link (N_{sd}). But this is of no concern. Calibration means making sure that parameters and base-year values of exogenous variables are set so that the model reproduces the base-year values for *observed* variables, in this case trade flows, tariffs and wage rates.

However, a major question remains. Will two legitimate calibration choices, that is two choices of the δ's, F's and H's that satisfy (4.5), lead to same simulation results for all variables of interest? For example, if we calibrate assuming all the H's and δ's are 1 and then simulate the effects of 50% tariff on widget imports into country d, will we get the same results for welfare in each country that we would have obtained if we had calibrated assuming that all the H's and F's are 1? As shown in the next section, the answer to this question is yes.

4.2   Showing that Simulation Results in a Melitz Model Don't Depend on the Choice Among Legitimate Calibrations

We assume that the values for the parameters σ and α (and therefore β) are given and that we have chosen values for δ, F and H to calibrate to base-year data for V's, T's and W's. We show for the Melitz model in Table 4.1 that the elasticity of each endogenous variable with respect to each exogenous variable, evaluated at the base-year solution, is independent of the particular choice among the legitimate possibilities that we made for δ, F and H. Thus, we demonstrate that this choice does not affect simulated percentage results for endogenous variables caused by

---

[3]The exponent $\frac{(\sigma - 1)}{\sigma * \alpha}$ is positive.

small percentage changes in exogenous variables away from their base-year values. Having reached this conclusion for small percentage changes in exogenous variables we generalize it to large percentage changes.

We start by representing the model in Table 4.1 as

$$M(Z) = 0 \qquad (4.10)$$

where

Z is the vector of variables including both endogenous and exogenous variables; and
M is the vector of functions formed by the left-hand sides minus the right-hand sides of the equations in Table 4.1.

Let $\overline{Z}$ be the vector of base-year values of the variables. $\overline{Z}$ satisfies (4.10). We can obtain new solutions to (4.10) close to $\overline{Z}$ by finding vectors of small changes in the variables, dZ, that satisfy

$$M_Z(\overline{Z}) * dZ = 0 \qquad (4.11)$$

where $M_Z(\overline{Z})$ is the matrix of first-order derivatives of M evaluated at $\overline{Z}$. More conveniently we can work with percentage changes in the variables by transforming (4.11) into

$$A(\overline{Z}) * z = 0 \qquad (4.12)$$

where

$$A(\overline{Z}) = M_Z(\overline{Z}) * \text{Diag}(\overline{Z}) \qquad (4.13)$$

$$z = 100 * \left(\text{Diag}(\overline{Z})\right)^{-1} * dZ \qquad (4.14)$$

and $\text{Diag}(\overline{Z})$ is the diagonal matrix formed by the components of $\overline{Z}$.[4]

We denote the percentage changes in the endogenous and exogenous variables away from their base-year values by z_1 and z_2. Then we rewrite (4.12) as

$$A_1(\overline{Z}) * z_1 + A_2(\overline{Z}) * z_2 = 0 \qquad (4.15)$$

where $A_1(\overline{Z})$ and $A_2(\overline{Z})$ are the columns of $A(\overline{Z})$ corresponding to the endogenous and exogenous variables. Using (4.15) we can express percentage changes in endogenous variables as functions of percentage changes in exogenous variables:

---

[4]For convenience, we assume that none of the components of $\overline{Z}$ is zero. If this is not true, then we need to work with a version of (4.12) in which some of the variables are changes, rather than percentage changes.

$$z_1 = B(\overline{Z}) * z_2 \qquad (4.16)$$

where $B(\overline{Z})$ is the matrix of elasticities of endogenous variables with respect to exogenous variables calculated according to

$$B(\overline{Z}) = -A_1^{-1}(\overline{Z}) * A_2(\overline{Z}). \qquad (4.17)$$

$A_1(\overline{Z})$ is square because we must have the number of equations (rows) equal to the number of endogenous variables (columns). We assume it is non-singular. Using the implicit function theorem, Dixon et al. (1982, Chap. 5) showed that this is a necessary and sufficient condition for the existence of a function relating endogenous variables to exogenous variables in the neighbourhood of $\overline{Z}$. Put more simply, $A_1^{-1}(\overline{Z})$ exists if and only if we have an economically sensible closure.

Starting from Table 4.1 we have derived a percentage-change version of the Melitz model. This is set out in Table 4.2 and the derivation is explained in Appendix 4.3.

The equations in Table 4.2 could be arranged in the matrix format of (4.12). In this format, the components of the $A(\overline{Z})$ matrix would be made up of combinations of σ, α and β together with 1's, 0's and base-year values of trade flows [V(s, d)] and powers of tariffs [T_{sd}]. Notice that the base-year values of δ, F and H do not appear as coefficients in the equations in Table 4.2. Thus, they are not an ingredient in the formation of $A(\overline{Z})$, which demonstrates that the elasticities of endogenous variables with respect to exogenous variables in the neighbourhood of $\overline{Z}$ computed according to (4.17) are independent of the calibration choices for δ, F and H. Simulation results for the percentage effects on endogenous variables of small percentage changes in exogenous variables will be unaffected by our choice of δ, F and H provided only that this choice is constrained by (4.5).[5]

What happens if the percentage changes in the exogenous variables are not small? Then, as shown in Dixon et al. (1982, Chap. 5) we can derive the true percentage changes in the endogenous variables by applying the percentage changes in the exogenous variables in a series of small steps. At the end of each step, the A matrix is re-evaluated to reflect the V's and T's arrived at in the step and the B matrix is re-computed ready for use in the next step. Algebraically an n-step procedure can be described by:

$$z_1(k, n) = B(V(k-1, n), T(k-1, n), \alpha, \sigma, \beta) * z_2(k, n) \quad \text{for } k = 1, 2, \ldots, n \qquad (4.18)$$

---

[5]The choice is constrained by (4.5) because only under this condition are the equations in Table 4.1 satisfied. As can be seen from Appendix 4.3, we use these equations to derive Table 4.2.

Table 4.2 Percentage change version of Table 4.1

	Equation	Corresponding endogenous variable
(T4.1P)	$p_{\bullet sd} = w_s + t_{sd} - \phi_{\bullet sd}$	$p_{\bullet sd}$
(T4.2P)	$(1-\sigma)*p_d = \sum_s \left(\dfrac{V(s,d)}{\sum_j V(j,d)}\right)*(n_{sd} + \sigma*\hat{\delta}_{sd} + (1-\sigma)*p_{\bullet sd})$	p_d
(T4.3P)	$p_{\bullet sd} + q_{\bullet sd} = d_d + \sigma*\hat{\delta}_{sd} + (\sigma-1)*(p_d - p_{\bullet sd})$	$q_{\bullet sd}$
(T4.4P)	$q_{sd} = \left(\dfrac{\sigma}{\sigma-1}\right)*n_{sd} + q_{\bullet sd}$	q_{sd}
(T4.5P)	$0 = \dfrac{1}{\sigma}*\sum_d \dfrac{V(s,d)}{T_{sd}}*(n_{sd} + p_{\bullet sd} + q_{\bullet sd} - t_{sd})$ $- \dfrac{\beta^{1-\sigma}}{\sigma}*\sum_d \dfrac{V(s,d)}{T_{sd}}*(n_{sd} + f_{sd} + w_s)$ $- \left(\dfrac{1-\beta^{1-\sigma}}{\sigma}\right)*\sum_d \dfrac{V(s,d)}{T_{sd}}*(n_s + h_s + w_s)$	n_s
(T4.6P)	$\left(\sum_d \dfrac{V(s,d)}{T_{sd}}\right)*(w_s + \ell_s) = \left(\dfrac{\sigma-1}{\sigma}\right)*\sum_d \dfrac{V(s,d)}{T_{sd}}*(w_s + n_{sd} + q_{\bullet sd} - \phi_{\bullet sd})$ $+ \dfrac{\beta^{1-\sigma}}{\sigma}*\sum_d \dfrac{V(s,d)}{T_{sd}}*(n_{sd} + f_{sd} + w_s)$ $+ \left(\dfrac{1-\beta^{1-\sigma}}{\sigma}\right)*\sum_d \dfrac{V(s,d)}{T_{sd}}*(n_s + h_s + w_s)$	ℓ_s
(T4.7P)	$n_{sd} = n_s - \alpha*\phi_{\min(s,d)}$	n_{sd}
(T4.8P)	$w_s + q_{\min(s,d)} - \phi_{\min(s,d)} = f_{sd} + w_s$	$\phi_{\min(s,d)}$

(continued)

Table 4.2 (continued)

	Equation	Corresponding endogenous variable
(T4.9P)	$\phi_{\bullet sd} = \phi_{\min(s,d)}$	$\phi_{\bullet sd}$
(T4.10P)	$q_{\min(s,d)} = q_{\bullet sd}$	$q_{\min(s,d)}$
(T4.11P)	$v(s,d) = n_{sd} + p_{\bullet sd} + q_{\bullet sd}$	$v(s,d)$

Notation We use lowercase symbols for percentage changes in the variables denoted by the corresponding uppercase symbols. For example, $P_{\bullet sd} = 100 * \Delta P_{\bullet sd}/P_{\bullet sd}$. The only exception is $\hat{\delta}_{sd}$ which denotes the percentage change in δ_{sd}, that is $\hat{\delta}_{sd} = 100 * \Delta\delta_{sd}/\delta_{sd}$

$$V(k, n) = V(k - 1, n) * \left(1 + \frac{v(k, n)}{100}\right) \quad \text{for } k = 1, 2, \ldots, n \qquad (4.19)$$

and

$$T(k, n) = T(k - 1, n) * \left(1 + \frac{t(k, n)}{100}\right) \quad \text{for } k = 1, 2, \ldots, n \qquad (4.20)$$

where

$z_1(k, n)$ and $z_2(k, n)$ are the vectors of percentage changes in the endogenous and exogenous variables in the kth step of an n-step procedure;

$V(0, n)$ and $T(0, n)$ are the matrices of trade flows and powers of tariffs in the base-year data;

$V(k, n)$ and $T(k, n)$ are the matrices of trade flows and powers of tariffs at the end of the kth step of an n-step procedure; and

$v(k, n)$ which is part of $z_1(k, n)$ and $t(k, n)$ which is part of $z_2(k, n)$ are the percentage changes in trade flows and powers of tariffs in the kth step of an n-step procedure.

The final answer for the percentage effect on the endogenous variables of the large percentage changes in the exogenous variables is obtained by combining the effects at each step.

We assume that the vectors of percentage changes in the exogenous variables applied at each step, $z_2(k, n)$ for $k = 1, \ldots, n$ are set independently of the calibrated values of δ, F and H. Via (4.20) this implies that $T(k, n)$ is independent of the calibrated values of δ, F and H. Consequently, if we can show that $V(k - 1, n)$ for $k = 1, \ldots, n$ is independent of the calibrated values of δ, F and H, then via (4.18) we will have established that $z_1(k, n)$ is independent of these values. This will establish the independence from the calibrated values of δ, F and H of the total percentage effects on the endogenous variables of the large percentage changes in the exogenous variables.

The initial B matrix depends only on the parameters and the data for V and T, and, as already mentioned, we assume that $z_2(k, n)$ is independent of δ, F and H. Looking at (4.18) we see that $z_1(1, n)$ is independent of the calibrated values of δ, F and H. Now we consider $z_1(2, n)$. $T(1, n)$, α, σ, β and $z_2(1, n)$ that appear on the right-hand side of (4.18) in the determination of $z_1(2, n)$ are independent of the calibrated values of δ, F and H. But what about $V(1, n)$? Via (4.19), $V(1, n)$ depends on $V(0, n)$ and $v(1, n)$ which is part of $z_1(1, n)$. Consequently, $V(1, n)$ is independent of the calibrated values of δ, F and H, completing the demonstration that $z_1(2, n)$ is independent of these values. Now we can proceed to $z_1(3, n)$. In this way we quickly establish that $z_1(k, n)$ for all k is independent of the calibrated values of δ, F and H. This completes the demonstration that the solution to the Melitz model in Table 4.1 is independent of the choice of calibration values for δ, F and H among those satisfying (4.5).

4.3 Econometric Estimation of Parameters for a Melitz Sector: The Balistreri et al. (2011) Method

Sections 4.1 and 4.2 show for any legitimate[6] values of σ and α that a Melitz sector in a CGE model can be calibrated to base-year values of trade flows. This can be done by choosing any values of F, δ and H that together satisfy (4.5). But how do we set σ and α?

Balistreri et al. (2011) provide a method based on (4.4). Rather than using (4.4) simply for calibration, they also use it for estimation. In intuitive (but not quite accurate) terms, Balistreri et al.'s strategy is to set W_j, T_{jr} and D_r at their base-year values and assign values to σ, δ_{jr}, and H_j. If they had also assigned a value to α, then they could have used (4.5) to solve for the F_{jr}s so that (4.4) precisely reproduces the base-year values of the V(s, d)s. However, instead of doing this, Balistreri et al. specify a preferred structure for the F_{jr}s. With this structure, (4.4) cannot precisely reproduce the base-year V(s, d)s. This opens the possibility for parameter estimation by choosing parameter values that allow base-year trade flows to be reproduced as closely as possible subject to the F_{jr}s having the preferred structure.

To illustrate this estimation possibility, Balistreri et al. present a 7 industry, 12 region model. Six industries are purely competitive with Armington structures. One industry, Manufacturing, is modelled with a Melitz structure. For this industry, Balistreri et al. estimated α, the F_{jr}s and an additional parameter θ, together with V^e(s, d), T_{sd}, Out_s and In_d, by choosing their values to minimize

$$\sum_{s,d} \left(\overline{V}(s,d) - V^e(s,d) \right)^2 \qquad (4.21)$$

subject to:

$$V^e(s,d) = V_{sd}(\overline{\sigma}, \alpha, \overline{\delta}_{jr}, \overline{W}_j, T_{jr}, \overline{D}_r, F_{jr}, \overline{H}_j) \quad \text{for all } j,r), \qquad (4.22)$$

$$T_{sd} = (1 + \tau_{sd}) Dist_{sd}^{\theta} \quad \text{for all s and d} \qquad (4.23)$$

and

$$F_{sd} = \begin{cases} Out_s + In_d & \text{for } s \neq d \\ Out_s & \text{for } s = d. \end{cases} \qquad (4.24)$$

where

the bars indicate base-year or assigned value;
τ_{sd} is the tariff rate applying to manufactured goods flowing from s to d;

---

[6] $\sigma > 1$ and $\alpha > \sigma - 1$.

Dist$_{sd}$ is a measure of distance between countries s and d, used to represent transport costs for manufactured goods in international and intra-national trade;
θ is a parameter representing the elasticity of transport margins with respect to distance; and
Out$_s$ and In$_d$ are parameters imposing Balistreri et al.'s preferred structure for the F$_{sd}$s.

In the context of (T4.1), Eq. (4.23) implies that transport costs per unit of trade flow are proportional to the fob price of manufactured goods, $(W_s/\Phi_{\bullet sd}) * (\sigma/(\sigma - 1))$, rather than the price of transport services. However, this is only a minor quibble. With data on τ_{sd} and Dist$_{sd}$ Balistreri et al. use (4.23) to reduce the problem of estimating the R^2 components of T to a problem of estimating a single parameter, θ.[7,8]

Equation (4.24) disaggregates setup costs on the sd-link into two parts. First, there are costs (Out$_s$) required for firms in country s to setup in any market. Then there are additional setup costs (In$_d$) required only by foreign firms before they can make sales to country d. In part, these latter costs can be visualized as expenditures to overcome non-tariff trade barriers. While the theoretical validity of (4.24) may be questionable, the econometric payoff is clear. It reduces the dimensions of the F parameter space from R^2 to 2R.

In implementing (4.21)–(4.24), Balistreri et al. implicitly assign the value one to each of the $\bar{\delta}_{jr}$s. In fact the δ's do not appear explicitly in their version of Melitz. Thus they rule out inter-country preference biases. By contrast, inter-country preference biases play a dominant role in the Armington model in determining the pattern of trade flows. For Balistreri et al. (and Melitz), it is differences in link-specific fixed trade costs (the structure of the F matrix) that are used to fill in the explanation of trade patterns beyond what can be attributed to production costs, tariffs and transport costs, and total demands. However, there is empirical support for home bias in inter-country preferences (see for example, Blonigen and Wilson 1999). To recognize this, Balistreri et al.'s estimating procedure could be re-worked with a preferred structure imposed for the δ's as well as the F's.

For $\bar{H}$, Balistreri et al. adopt an arbitrary vector of equal values, $\bar{H}_s$ equals 2 for all s. The value 2 seems a little odd, but the absolute value of the $\bar{H}_s$s is not important. As shown in Appendix 4.4, for given values of σ and α, we can impose a uniform percentage change in all the H's with no effect on the *relative* values of the F's or the observable variables, V, W, T and D. Consequently the absolute values chosen for the $\bar{H}_s$s do not affect Balistreri et al.'s estimates of α and θ, although they could affect the estimates of Out$_s$ and In$_d$. Rather than assuming all of the $\bar{H}_s$s are

---

[7]Normalization of Dist is required so that simulated total worldwide transport costs for trade in manufactured goods is compatible with data on these costs.

[8]As an alternative to using distance, Balistreri et al. could have used more directly relevant data on transport costs derived from differences between fob and cif prices, see for example Gehlhar (1998).

the same, it would be possible to impose a more flexible structure. However, unlike using the idea of home-bias to inform the estimation of the δ_{jr}s, no equivalent idea is available for the H_ss.

For Melitz models the value chosen for each commodity for the *inter-variety* substitution elasticity (σ) is critically important for the simulated effects of trade liberalizations. Similarly, in Armington models, the value chosen for each commodity for the *inter-country* substitution elasticity is critically important. Since the pioneering work of Alaouze and colleagues in the 1970s, substitution elasticities for Armington models have been the subject of intense econometric study.[9] As yet, there is no matching depth of research on inter-variety substitution elasticities. Unfortunately, as shown in the next chapter, inter-country substitution elasticities estimated for an Armington model are unlikely to be a good guide for determining inter-variety elasticities suitable for a Melitz model. In (4.22) Balistreri et al. set $\overline{\sigma}$ at 3.8. In choosing this value they relied on Bernard et al. (2003) who estimated a substitution elasticity of 3.8 from the point of view of consumers of products from different manufacturing plants in the U.S. Whether this is an appropriate value for an inter-variety substitution elasticity in a Melitz manufacturing sector in a global model is an open question.

Using (4.21)–(4.24) with manufacturing data for 2001 for 12 regions, Balistreri et al. obtained interpretable and impressively precise estimates for θ and α. Their estimates of Out_s and In_d seem problematic. But these estimates are unimportant. Having imposed (4.24) to facilitate estimation, Balistreri et al. abandoned it for simulation. For their simulation model they reset the initial values of the F_{jr}s by calibration. That is, given their estimated values of θ and α, their assumed values for δ, σ and H, the base-year data for W_s and D_r, and T's computed according to (4.23), Balistreri et al. created their simulation model by setting the initial values of the F_{jr}s to reproduce the base-year trade flows.

4.4 Concluding Remarks

Calibration in an Armington model normally starts with specified values for inter-country substitution elasticities. Then values of preference variables (δ) can be found so that the model is compatible with base-year data. For a Melitz model, calibration normally starts with specified values for inter-variety substitution elasticities (σ) and shape parameters (α) for the distribution of firm productivities. Then, as described in Sect. 4.1, we can find calibrating values for preference and fixed cost variables (δ's, F's and H's). By contrast, with Armington calibration

---

[9]See Alaouze (1976, 1977) and Alaouze et al. (1977) which produced estimates of Armington elasticities (σ) for about 50 commodities. These papers are summarized in Dixon et al. (1982, Sect. 29.1). Subsequent studies and surveys include Dimaranan and McDougall (2002), Head and Ries (2001), Hertel et al. (2007), McDaniel and Balistreri (2003), Shomos (2005), Zhang and Verikios (2003).

where the calibrating values of the δ's are unique up to a factor of proportionality, for a Melitz model there are multiple calibrating possibilities. Fortunately, as shown in Sect. 4.2, the choice among these possibilities does not affect simulation results.

The work by Balistreri et al. (2011) described in Sect. 4.3 combines calibration and estimation. It is a leading example of what Costinot and Rodriguez-Clare (2013) have in mind when they say:

> … today's researchers try to use their own model to estimate the key structural parameters necessary for counterfactual analysis. Estimation and computation go hand in hand.

Instead of choosing a combination of δ's, F's and H's that are precisely calibrating, Balistreri et al. impose preferred structures on these variables and then estimate parameters so that calibration to base-year data is achieved as closely as possible subject to these preferred structures.

The calibration/estimation method of Balistreri et al. is likely to be the foundation for future efforts to put numbers to the Melitz theory and other emerging theories of international trade. Many improvements can be expected as econometricians develop the method. Focusing narrowly on the work reviewed in Sect. 4.3, obvious directions for improvement are: the use of data for a wider range of variables (e.g. prices and quantities for trade flows, not just values); refinement of the commodity dimension (e.g. 2- or 3-digit industries rather than a 1-digit sector such as manufacturing); refinement of the regional dimension (avoiding the use of aggregates such as Rest-of-Asia, Korea and Taiwan, etc.); and the use of more compelling theoretical restrictions (e.g. relaxation of the assumption of no home bias in preferences). Perhaps the most important improvement will be the introduction of time-series data to supplement cross-section data. Time-series data will facilitate the estimation of inter-variety substitution elasticities. As we will see in Chaps. 6 and 7, these elasticities are of major importance in determining simulation results for the effects of trade policies.

Appendix 4.1: Relating Observables to Melitz Concepts, and Demonstrating the Fixity of the Shares of Production, Link and Establishment Costs in an Industry's Total Costs

In this appendix we derive Eqs. (4.1)–(4.3). Then we show that the Melitz model with a Pareto specification of firm productivities implies a constant split of industry costs between variable, link and establishment costs.

Derivation of (4.1)

In (4.1) we assume that the landed-duty-paid value of trade on the sd-link, $V(s, d)$, is the value for the typical firm, $P_{\bullet sd} Q_{\bullet sd}$, times the number of trading firms, N_{sd}. To derive (4.1) we start from

$$V(s,d) = \sum_{k \in S(s,d)} N_s g(\Phi_k) P_{ksd} Q_{ksd}, \tag{4.25}$$

that is, the landed-duty-paid value of widgets sent from s to d is the value, $P_{ksd}Q_{ksd}$, sent by a k-class firm times the number of such firms, $N_s g(\Phi_k)$, aggregated over all k in S(s, d). Using the AKME versions of (T2.1) and (T2.3) and assuming that $\gamma_{ksd} = 1$ for all k, we find that

$$\frac{P_{ksd}}{P_{\bullet sd}} = \frac{\Phi_{\bullet sd}}{\Phi_{ksd}}. \tag{4.26}$$

and

$$\frac{Q_{ksd}}{Q_{\bullet sd}} = \left(\frac{P_{\bullet sd}}{P_{ksd}}\right)^{\sigma}. \tag{4.27}$$

Combining (4.26) and (4.27) gives

$$Q_{ksd}P_{ksd} = \left(\frac{\Phi_{ksd}}{\Phi_{\bullet sd}}\right)^{\sigma-1} *Q_{\bullet sd}P_{\bullet sd}. \tag{4.28}$$

Substituting into (4.25) we obtain

$$V(s,d) = \frac{P_{\bullet sd}Q_{\bullet sd}}{\Phi_{\bullet sd}^{\sigma-1}} \sum_{k \in S(s,d)} N_s g(\Phi_k) \Phi_{ksd}^{\sigma-1}. \tag{4.29}$$

Then applying (2.19) we arrive at (4.1):

$$V(s,d) = N_{sd} P_{\bullet sd} Q_{\bullet sd}. \tag{4.30}$$

Derivation of (4.2)

Starting from the Melitz version of (T2.3) we have

$$P_{\bullet sd}Q_{\bullet sd}N_{sd} = Q_d \delta_{sd}^{\sigma} P_{\bullet sd}^{1-\sigma} P_d^{\sigma} N_{sd}. \tag{4.31}$$

Adding over s and using (4.30) gives

$$\sum_s V(s,d) = Q_d P_d^{\sigma} \sum_s \delta_{sd}^{\sigma} P_{\bullet sd}^{1-\sigma} N_{sd}. \tag{4.32}$$

Now using (T2.2) we obtain

$$\sum_s V(s,d) = Q_d P_d^{\sigma} P_d^{1-\sigma} \tag{4.33}$$

which leads to (4.2).

Derivation of (4.3)

We start by multiplying the Melitz version of (T2.7) through by W_s:

$$W_s L_s = \sum_d \frac{W_s N_{sd} Q_{\bullet sd}}{\Phi_{\bullet sd}} + \sum_d N_{sd} F_{sd} W_s + N_s H_s W_s. \tag{4.34}$$

The left hand side is total costs in the widget industry of country s. The first term on the right hand side is the industry's total variable costs. The second term is trade-link set-up costs incurred by the industry. The third term is establishment costs incurred by firms in the industry. We work separately on each of these three terms.

Substituting from (T2.1) into the variable-cost term gives

$$\sum_d \frac{W_s N_{sd} Q_{\bullet sd}}{\Phi_{\bullet sd}} = \frac{\sigma - 1}{\sigma} * \sum_d \frac{P_{\bullet sd} N_{sd} Q_{\bullet sd}}{T_{sd}}. \tag{4.35}$$

Working with (T2.10) we find that link set-up costs are given by:

$$\sum_d N_{sd} F_{sd} W_s = \frac{1}{\sigma - 1} * \sum_d \frac{W_s Q_{min(s,d)} N_{sd}}{\Phi_{min(s,d)}}. \tag{4.36}$$

Using (T2.11) and (T2.12) we have $Q_{min(s,d)}/\Phi_{min(s,d)} = \beta^{1-\sigma} * [Q_{\bullet sd}/\Phi_{\bullet sd}]$. Substituting this into (4.36) gives

$$\sum_d N_{sd} F_{sd} W_s = \frac{\beta^{1-\sigma}}{\sigma - 1} * \sum_d \frac{W_s Q_{\bullet sd} N_{sd}}{\Phi_{\bullet sd}}. \tag{4.37}$$

Then using (T2.1) we obtain

$$\sum_d N_{sd} F_{sd} W_s = \frac{\beta^{1-\sigma}}{\sigma} * \sum_d \frac{P_{\bullet sd} Q_{\bullet sd} N_{sd}}{T_{sd}}. \tag{4.38}$$

From (T2.6) and (T2.9) we find that establishment costs are given by

$$N_s H_s W_s = \sum_d N_{sd} \Pi_{\bullet sd}. \tag{4.39}$$

Then using (T2.5) and (T2.1) we obtain

$$N_s H_s W_s = \frac{1}{\sigma} * \sum_d \frac{N_{sd} P_{\bullet sd} Q_{\bullet sd}}{T_{sd}} - \sum_d N_{sd} F_{sd} W_s, \qquad (4.40)$$

which via (4.38) becomes

$$N_s H_s W_s = \frac{1 - \beta^{1-\sigma}}{\sigma} * \sum_d \frac{N_{sd} P_{\bullet sd} Q_{\bullet sd}}{T_{sd}}. \qquad (4.41)$$

Finally we add over (4.35), (4.38) and (4.41) and use (4.30) and (4.34). This gives

$$W_s L_s = \left[\frac{\sigma - 1}{\sigma} + \frac{\beta^{1-\sigma}}{\sigma} + \frac{1 - \beta^{1-\sigma}}{\sigma} \right] * \sum_d \frac{V(s, d)}{T_{sd}}. \qquad (4.42)$$

Simplifying on the right hand side of (4.42) quickly gives (4.3).

The fixity of the shares of variable, link and establishment costs in an industry's total costs

Our derivation of (4.3) brings out an important feature of the Melitz model with a Pareto distribution of firm productivities: the split of an industry's total costs between variable, link and establishment costs is fixed by the variety substitution parameter σ and the Pareto parameter α [recall that β is a function of α and σ, see (2.27)]. The split does not depend on tariff rates (T_{sd}), preferences (δ_{sd}), the number of firms (N_s), the number of firms on links (N_{sd}), and rather remarkably it doesn't depend on establishment costs per firm ($H_s W_s$) or link set-up costs per firm ($F_{sd} W_s$). Variable costs always account for the share $(\sigma - 1)/\sigma$ in total costs; link costs always account for the share $\beta^{1-\sigma}/\sigma$; and establishment costs always account for the share $(1 - \beta^{1-\sigma})/\sigma$. As we will see in Chap. 7, the determination of the cost split via just α and σ sharply simplifies calibration in a model specified in percentage changes.

Appendix 4.2: Calibration: Establishing Relationships Between Unobservables (δ, F and H) and Base-Year Data (V, T and W)

In this appendix we derive (4.5) from the Melitz sectoral model set out in Table 4.1. The algebra is tedious but not hard. Our strategy is to derive expressions for N_{sd}, N_s and $\Phi_{\bullet sd}$ in terms of V(s, d), W_s, T_{sd}, F_{sd}, H_s. σ, α (and β). These expressions lead eventually to (4.5).

Derivation of expression for N_{sd}

Equation (T4.8) in Table 4.1 gives

$$\frac{Q_{\min(s,d)}}{\Phi_{\min(s,d)}} = F_{sd} * (\sigma - 1). \tag{4.43}$$

Then via (T4.9) and (T4.10) we obtain

$$\frac{Q_{\bullet sd}}{\Phi_{\bullet sd}} = F_{sd} * (\sigma - 1) * \beta^{\sigma-1} \tag{4.44}$$

Equations (T4.1) and (T4.11) give

$$V(s, d) = N_{sd} W_s T_{sd} * \frac{Q_{\bullet sd}}{\Phi_{\bullet sd}} * \frac{\sigma}{\sigma - 1} \tag{4.45}$$

Now using (4.44) we find that

$$N_{sd} = \frac{V(s, d)}{W_s T_{sd}} * \frac{\beta^{1-\sigma}}{\sigma F_{sd}} \tag{4.46}$$

Derivation of expression for N_s

Substituting from (4.46) and (T4.11) into (T4.5) gives

$$0 = \frac{1}{\sigma} \sum_d \frac{V(s, d)}{T_{sd}} - \frac{\beta^{1-\sigma}}{\sigma} \sum_d \frac{V(s, d)}{T_{sd}} - N_s H_s W_s, \tag{4.47}$$

leading to

$$N_s = \left(\frac{1 - \beta^{1-\sigma}}{\sigma H_s W_s}\right) * \sum_d \frac{V(s, d)}{T_{sd}} \tag{4.48}$$

Derivation of expression for $\Phi_{\bullet sd}$

Rearranging (T4.7) gives

$$\Phi_{\min(s,d)} = \left(\frac{N_{sd}}{N_s}\right)^{-1/\alpha} \tag{4.49}$$

Now substitute in from (4.46) and (4.48) to obtain

$$\Phi_{\min(s,d)} = \left(\frac{\dfrac{V(s,d)}{T_{sd}} * \dfrac{1}{F_{sd}}}{\dfrac{(\beta^{\sigma-1} - 1)}{H_s} * \sum_j \dfrac{V(s,j)}{T_{sj}}} \right)^{-1/\alpha}. \tag{4.50}$$

Then (T4.9) gives

$$\Phi_{\bullet sd} = \beta * \left(\frac{\dfrac{V(s,d)}{T_{sd}} * \dfrac{1}{F_{sd}}}{\dfrac{(\beta^{\sigma-1} - 1)}{H_s} * \sum_j \dfrac{V(s,j)}{T_{sj}}} \right)^{-1/\alpha}. \tag{4.51}$$

Using the expressions for N_{sd} and $\Phi_{\bullet sd}$ to derive (4.5)

Equation (T4.3) implies that

$$P_{\bullet sd} Q_{\bullet sd} N_{sd} = \delta_{sd}^{\sigma} D_d \left(\frac{P_d}{P_{\bullet sd}} \right)^{\sigma-1} * N_{sd}. \tag{4.52}$$

Then using (T4.11) and (T4.2) we obtain

$$V(s,d) = (D_d) * \frac{\delta_{sd}^{\sigma} P_{\bullet sd}^{1-\sigma} * N_{sd}}{\sum_j \delta_{jd}^{\sigma} P_{\bullet jd}^{1-\sigma} * N_{jd}}. \tag{4.53}$$

Dividing through by $V(d, d)$ leads to

$$\frac{V(s,d)}{V(d,d)} = \frac{\delta_{sd}^{\sigma} P_{\bullet sd}^{1-\sigma} * N_{sd}}{\delta_{dd}^{\sigma} P_{\bullet dd}^{1-\sigma} * N_{dd}} \tag{4.54}$$

which, via (T4.1), can be written as

$$\frac{V(s,d)}{V(d,d)} = \frac{\delta_{sd}^{\sigma} \Phi_{\bullet sd}^{\sigma-1} * N_{sd} * (W_s T_{sd})^{1-\sigma}}{\delta_{dd}^{\sigma} \Phi_{\bullet dd}^{\sigma-1} * N_{dd} * (W_d T_{dd})^{1-\sigma}}. \tag{4.55}$$

Now we use (4.46) and (4.51) to eliminate N_{sd}, N_{dd}, $\Phi_{\bullet sd}$ and $\Phi_{\bullet dd}$ for all s and d:

$$\frac{V(s,d)}{V(d,d)} = \frac{\delta_{sd}^{\sigma}\beta^{\sigma-1} * \left(\frac{\frac{V(s,d)}{T_{sd}} * \frac{1}{F_{sd}}}{\frac{(\beta^{\sigma-1}-1)}{H_s} * \sum_j \frac{V(s,j)}{T_{sj}}}\right)^{\frac{(1-\sigma)}{\alpha}} * \left(\frac{V(s,d)}{W_s T_{sd}} * \frac{\beta^{1-\sigma}}{\sigma F_{sd}}\right) * (W_s T_{sd})^{1-\sigma}}{\delta_{dd}^{\sigma}\beta^{\sigma-1} * \left(\frac{\frac{V(d,d)}{T_{dd}} * \frac{1}{F_{dd}}}{\frac{(\beta^{\sigma-1}-1)}{H_d} * \sum_j \frac{V(d,j)}{T_{dj}}}\right)^{\frac{(1-\sigma)}{\alpha}} * \left(\frac{V(d,d)}{W_d T_{dd}} * \frac{\beta^{1-\sigma}}{\sigma F_{dd}}\right) * (W_d T_{dd})^{1-\sigma}}$$

$$(4.56)$$

By simplifying (4.56) we arrive at:

$$F_{sd} = F_{dd} * \left(\frac{J(s,d)}{J(d,d)}\right)^{\frac{(1-\sigma)}{(1+\alpha-\sigma)}} * \left(\frac{W_s T_{sd}}{W_d T_{dd}}\right)^{\frac{-\sigma*\alpha}{(1+\alpha-\sigma)}} * \left(\frac{\delta_{sd}}{\delta_{dd}}\right)^{\frac{\sigma*\alpha}{(1+\alpha-\sigma)}} * \left(\frac{H_s}{H_d}\right)^{\frac{(1-\sigma)}{(1+\alpha-\sigma)}}$$

$$(4.57)$$

where $J(s, d)$ is, as defined in (4.6), the share of region s's sales accounted for d. Finally, we substitute base-year values (marked with bars) for J's, W's and T's into (4.57) to obtain (4.5).

Appendix 4.3: A Percentage Change Version of the Melitz Model: Derivation of Table 4.2 from Table 4.1

As explained in Dixon et al. (1992) there are three useful rules for converting from a levels presentation of equations to a percentage-change presentation.

Multiplicative rule

$$Z = X * Y \text{ becomes } z = x + y \qquad (4.58)$$

where the lowercase symbols represent percentage changes in the uppercase symbols. (4.58) can be derived by total differentiation:

$$\Delta Z = X * \Delta Y + \Delta X * Y. \qquad (4.59)$$

Dividing on the left-hand side by Z and on the right-hand side by $X * Y$ and multiplying both sides by 100 gives (4.58).

Power rule

$$Z = X^\alpha \text{ becomes } z = \alpha * x. \tag{4.60}$$

To derive (4.60) we start from

$$\Delta Z = \frac{\partial X^\alpha}{\partial X} * \Delta X = \alpha * X^{\alpha-1} * \Delta X. \tag{4.61}$$

Dividing on the left-hand side by Z and on the right-hand side by X^α and multiplying both sides by 100 gives (4.60).

Addition rule

$$Z = X + Y \text{ becomes either } Z * z = X * x + Y * y \text{ or } z = S_x * x + S_y * y \tag{4.62}$$

where S_x and S_y are the shares of X and Y in Z.
To derive (4.62) we start from

$$\Delta Z = \Delta X + \Delta Y \tag{4.63}$$

which can be written as

$$Z \frac{\Delta Z}{Z} = X \frac{\Delta X}{X} + Y \frac{\Delta Y}{Y} \tag{4.64}$$

quickly leading to (4.62).

The conversions from (T4.1), (T4.3), (T4.4), (T4.7), (T4.8), (T4.9), (T4.10) and (T4.11) in Table 4.1 to the percentage change versions in Table 4.2 are achieved by straight-forward applications of the multiplicative and power rules.

Derivation of (T4.2P)

Applying all three rules to (T4.2) we obtain

$$(1 - \sigma) * p_d = \sum_s \frac{N_{sd} * \delta_{sd}^\sigma * P_{\bullet sd}^{1-\sigma}}{\sum_j N_{jd} * \delta_{jd}^\sigma * P_{\bullet jd}^{1-\sigma}} * \left(n_{sd} + \sigma \widehat{\delta}_{sd} + (1 - \sigma) * p_{\bullet sd} \right). \tag{4.65}$$

Then working with (T4.3) and (T4.11) we find that

$$\frac{N_{sd} * \delta_{sd}^\sigma * P_{\bullet sd}^{1-\sigma}}{\sum_j N_{jd} * \delta_{jd}^\sigma * P_{\bullet jd}^{1-\sigma}} = \frac{V(s, d)}{\sum_j V(j, d)}. \tag{4.66}$$

Substituting from (4.66) into (4.65) gives (T4.2P).

Derivation of (T4.5P)

Applying the addition and multiplication rules to (T4.5) we obtain

$$
\begin{aligned}
0 = \frac{1}{\sigma} * \sum_d N_{sd} \frac{P_{\bullet sd}}{T_{sd}} * Q_{\bullet sd} * (n_{sd} + p_{\bullet sd} + q_{\bullet sd} - t_{sd}) \\
- \sum_d N_{sd} F_{sd} W_s * (n_{sd} + f_{sd} + w_s) - N_s H_s W_s * (n_s + h_s + w_s).
\end{aligned}
\tag{4.67}
$$

(T4.11) gives us

$$
\frac{N_{sd} P_{\bullet sd} Q_{\bullet sd}}{T_{sd}} = \frac{V(s, d)}{T_{sd}}.
\tag{4.68}
$$

From (T4.8), (T4.9), (T4.10), (T4.1) and (T4.11) we have

$$
N_{sd} F_{sd} W_s = \frac{\beta^{1-\sigma}}{\sigma} * \frac{P_{\bullet sd} Q_{\bullet sd} N_{sd}}{T_{sd}} = \frac{\beta^{1-\sigma}}{\sigma} * \frac{V(s, d)}{T_{sd}}.
\tag{4.69}
$$

(T4.5) implies that

$$
\begin{aligned}
N_s H_s W_s &= \frac{1}{\sigma} * \sum_d N_{sd} \frac{P_{\bullet sd}}{T_{sd}} * Q_{\bullet sd} - \sum_d N_{sd} F_{sd} W_s \\
&= \frac{1}{\sigma} * \sum_d \frac{V(s, d)}{T_{sd}} - \frac{\beta^{1-\sigma}}{\sigma} * \sum_d \frac{V(s, d)}{T_{sd}}.
\end{aligned}
\tag{4.70}
$$

Substituting from (4.68), (4.69) and (4.70) into (4.67) leads to (T4.5P).

Derivation of (T4.6P)

Applying the addition and multiplication rules to (T4.6) we obtain

$$
\begin{aligned}
W_s L_s * (w_s + \ell_s) = \sum_d \frac{W_s N_{sd} Q_{\bullet sd}}{\Phi_{\bullet sd}} * (w_s + n_{sd} + q_{\bullet sd} - \phi_{\bullet sd}) \\
+ \sum_d W_s N_{sd} F_{sd} * (w_s + n_{sd} + f_{sd}) + W_s N_s H_s * (w_s + n_s + h_s).
\end{aligned}
\tag{4.71}
$$

By using (4.3), (T4.1), (4.69), (4.70) and (T4.11) we arrive at (T4.6P).

Appendix 4.4: The Irrelevance of the Absolute Values of the Initial H_ss for Calibration and Estimation

For given values of the parameters σ and α, denote an initial set of variable values that satisfy the model in Table 4.1 by a superscript I. Then increase all of the H values by 1% while holding constant the observable variables V, W, T and D. A new set of variable values, denoted by the superscript N, that satisfy the equations in Table 4.1 is given by (4.72)–(4.88):

$$H_s^N = H_s^I * (1.01) \quad \text{for all s} \tag{4.72}$$

$$\delta_{sd}^N = \delta_{sd}^I \quad \text{for all s and d} \tag{4.73}$$

$$F_{sd}^N = F_{sd}^I * (1.01)^{(\sigma-1)/(\sigma-1-\alpha)} \quad \text{for all s and d} \tag{4.74}$$

$$V^N(s, d) = V^I(s, d) \quad \text{for all s and d} \tag{4.75}$$

$$L_s^N = L_s^I \quad \text{for all s} \tag{4.76}$$

$$W_s^N = W_s^I \quad \text{for all s} \tag{4.77}$$

$$D_d^N = D_d^I \quad \text{for all d} \tag{4.78}$$

$$T_{sd}^N = T_{sd}^I \quad \text{for all s and d} \tag{4.79}$$

$$N_s^N = N_s^I * (1.01)^{-1} \quad \text{for all s} \tag{4.80}$$

$$\Phi_{\min(s,d)}^N = \Phi_{\min(s,d)}^I * (1.01)^{1/(\sigma-1-\alpha)} \quad \text{for all s and d} \tag{4.81}$$

$$\Phi_{\bullet sd}^N = \Phi_{\bullet sd}^I * (1.01)^{1/(\sigma-1-\alpha)} \quad \text{for all s and d} \tag{4.82}$$

$$Q_{\bullet sd}^N = Q_{\bullet sd}^I * (1.01)^{\sigma/(\sigma-1-\alpha)} \quad \text{for all s and d} \tag{4.83}$$

$$Q_{\min(s,d)}^N = Q_{\min(s,d)}^I * (1.01)^{\sigma/(\sigma-1-\alpha)} \quad \text{for all s and d} \tag{4.84}$$

$$N_{sd}^N = N_{sd}^I * (1.01)^{(1-\sigma)/(\sigma-1-\alpha)} \quad \text{for all s and d} \tag{4.85}$$

$$P_{\bullet sd}^N = P_{\bullet sd}^I * (1.01)^{-1/(\sigma-1-\alpha)} \quad \text{for all s and d} \tag{4.86}$$

$$Q_{sd}^N = Q_{sd}^I \quad \text{for all s and d} \tag{4.87}$$

$$P_d^N = P_d^I \quad \text{for all d} \tag{4.88}$$

The validity of this new solution can be established by substituting into left and right hand sides of (T4.1)–(T4.11).

From (4.75), (4.77), (4.78) and (4.79) we see that the proportionate change in the H_ss has no effect on observables V, W, D and T. The F_{jr}s move uniformly, see (4.74). Thus if the F_{jr}^Is satisfied Balistreri et al.'s preferred structure, then the F_{jr}^Ns satisfy this structure with proportionate changes in Out_s and In_d.

With regard to Balistreri et al.'s estimating method described by (4.21)–(4.24), we now see that rescaling $\overline{H}_j$ for all j cannot affect the estimates of α and θ. With rescaled H's the optimal values for $V^e(s, d)$ can be achieved with the same values for α and θ, the same values for the variables with bars in (4.22), and with rescaled F_{jr}s.

Readers can check that (4.72)–(4.88) is not the only way to reset the values of the variables in Table 4.1 so that the observables, V, W, D and T, remain unchanged in response to a 1% change in the H_ss. For example, instead of (4.74), the F_{sd}s could increase by 1%. Then we could write down another solution for Table 4.1 with the original values of V, W, D and T. In this new solution, there would be no change in $\Phi_{\bullet sd}$ rather than no change in Q_{sd}. $P_{\bullet sd}$ would not change, N_{sd} and N_s would decrease by 1%, $Q_{\bullet sd}$ would increase by 1%, etc. We suspect that what this means for the Balistreri et al. estimating method is that a normalization must be imposed on Out_s in (4.24). However, on reading the article it wasn't clear to us how this was done.

References

Alaouze, C. M. (1976). Estimates of the Elasticity of Substitution Between Imported and Domestically Produced Intermediate Inputs. *IMPACT Preliminary Working Paper, No. OP-07*, mimeo (pp. 32). Available from the Centre of Policy Studies, Monash University.

Alaouze, C. M. (1977). Estimates of the Elasticity of Substitution Between Imported and Domestically Produced Goods Classified at the Input-Output Level of Aggregation. *IMPACT Working Paper, No. O-13* (pp. 32). Available at http://www.monash.edu.au/policy/elecpapr/O-13.htm.

Alaouze, C. M., Marsden J. S., & Zeitsch J. (1977). Estimates of the Elasticity of Substitution Between Imported and Domestically Produced Commodities at the Four Digit ASIC Level. *IMPACT Working Paper, No. O-11*, pp. 66, available at http://www.monash.edu.au/policy/elecpapr/o-11.htm.

Balistreri, E., & Rutherford, T. (2013). Computing general equilibrium theories of monopolistic competition and heterogeneous firms (Chap. 23). In P. B. Dixon & D. W. Jorgenson (Eds.), *Handbook of Computable General Equilibrium Modeling* (pp. 1513–1570). Amsterdam: Elsevier.

Balistreri, E. J., Hillberry, R. H., & Rutherford, T. F. (2011). Structural estimation and solution of international trade models with heterogeneous firms. *Journal of International Economics, 83*, 95–108.

Bernard, A. B., Eaton, J., Jensen, J. N., & Kortum, S. (2003). Plants and productivity in international trade. *American Economic Review, 93*(4), 1268–1290.

Blonigen, B., & Wilson, W. (1999). Explaining Armington: What determines substitutability between home and foreign goods. *The Canadian Journal of Economics/Revue canadienne d'Economique, 32*(1), 1–21.

Costinot, A., & Rodriguez-Clare, A. (2013). Trade theory with numbers: Quantifying the consequences of globalization. In G. Gopinath, E. Helpman, & K. Rogoff (Eds.), *Handbook of International Economics* (Vol. 4, pp. 197–261). Amsterdam: Elsevier.

Dimaranan, B. V., McDougall, R. A. (2002). *Global trade, assistance, and production: The GTAP 5 Data Base*. Center for Global Trade Analysis, Purdue University, March. Available at https://www.gtap.agecon.purdue.edu/databases/archives/v5/v5_doco.asp.

Dixon, P. B., Parmenter, B. R., Sutton, J., & Vincent, D. P. (1982). *ORANI: A multisectoral model of the Australian economy* (pp. xviii–372). Amsterdam: North-Holland.

Dixon, P. B., Parmenter, B. R., Powell, A. A., & Wilcoxen, P. J. (1992). *Notes and problems in applied general equilibrium economics* (pp. xvi–392). Amsterdam: North-Holland.

Gehlhar, M. (1998). Transport margins. (Chap. 11C). In R. A. McDougall, A. Elbehri & T. P. Truong (Eds.), *Global trade assistance and protection: The GTAP 4 Data Base*. Center for Global Trade Analysis, Purdue University. Available at https://www.gtap.agecon.purdue.edu/databases/v4/v4_doco.asp.

Head, K., & Ries, J. (2001). Increasing returns versus national product differentiation as an explanation for the pattern of U.S.–Canada trade. *American Economic Review, 91*(4), 858–876.

Hertel, T., Hummels, D., Ivanic, M., & Keeney, R. (2007). How confident can we be of CGE-based assessments of free trade agreements. *Economic Modelling, 24,* 611–635.

McDaniel, C. A., & Balistreri, E. J. (2003). A review of Armington trade substitution elasticities. *Economie Internationale, 2*(3), 301–313.

Narayanan, B., Aguiar, A. & McDougall R. (Eds.), (2012). *Global trade, assistance and production: the GTAP8 Data Base*. Center for Global Trade Analysis, Purdue University, https://www.gtap.agecon.purdue.edu/databases/V8/v8_doco.asp .

Shomos, A. (2005), "Armington elasticities for the MONASH and USAGE models", *Research Memorandum, Cat. No. GA-514*, Productivity Commission, Melbourne, September.

Zhang, X. G., & Verikios, G. (2003). *An alternative estimation of Armington elasticities for the GTAP model*. Melbourne: Research Memorandum GT 5 Productivity Commission.

Chapter 5
Melitz Equals Armington Plus Endogenous Productivity and Preferences

Abstract This chapter continues the exploration from Chap. 2 of the relationship between the Melitz and Armington models. We find that the principal results from a Melitz model can be obtained from an Amington model with additional equations that endogenize factor productivity for industries and preferences by households between goods obtained from different supplying regions. In short,

Melitz *equals* Armington plus endogenous productivity and preferences (M = A+)

This idea comes out of the algorithm devised by Balistreri and Rutherford (BR 2013) for solving general equilibrium models that contain Melitz sectors. As we describe in this chapter, the BR algorithm involves: solving Melitz sectors one at a time with guessed values of economy-wide variables; passing productivity and preference results from the Melitz sectoral computations to an Armington general equilibrium model; solving the Armington model and passing results for economy-wide variables back to the Melitz sectoral computations. We don't think an algorithmic approach such as this is necessary for solving Melitz general equilibrium models. Nevertheless the basic insight encapsulated in the (M = A+) equation is of considerable interest. It means that the results from a Melitz general equilibrium model for the effects of a trade reform can be interpreted as the sum of the effects in an Armington model of the reform and particular productivity and preference changes. With this interpretation, CGE modelers can draw on 40 years' experience with Armington models to help them understand results from Melitz models. We illustrate this in Chap. 6.

Keywords Decomposition algorithm · Balistreri · Rutherford · Melitz Armington · Result interpretation

As mentioned in Sect. 3.3, Balistreri and Rutherford (BR 2013) foresee dimensionality difficulties in solving a large-scale general equilibrium model with Melitz sectors. They point out that the Melitz model contains several endogenous country-by-country-by-sector variables (e.g. $\Phi_{\bullet sd}$, N_{sd}, $\Phi_{\min(s,d)}$ in Table 2.2 for each Melitz sector) which are either absent or exogenous in an Armington model.

© Springer Nature Singapore Pte Ltd. 2018
P. B. Dixon et al., *Trade Theory in Computable General Equilibrium Models*,
Advances in Applied General Equilibrium Modeling,
https://doi.org/10.1007/978-981-10-8325-9_5

They are also concerned that the increasing-returns-to-scale specification in Melitz (absent in Armington) can cause computational problems.

To overcome the computational problems that they perceive, Balistreri and Rutherford suggest a decomposition algorithm or "divide and conquer" approach. They start by solving each Melitz sector as an independent system of equations with the wage rate and demand for the sector's product in all countries (W_s and Q_d in Table 2.2) set according to an initial set of guesses. These Melitz computations generate estimates of sectoral productivity and preference variables which are transferred into an Armington multi-sectoral general equilibrium model. The Armington model is then solved to generate estimates of the wage rate and demand in all countries for the product of all sectors. These wage and demand estimates are fed back into the Melitz computations. A full solution of the general equilibrium model with Melitz sectors is obtained when wage rates and demand variables emerging from the Armington model coincide with those which were used in the immediately previous Melitz sectoral computations.

Balistreri and Rutherford compute in levels using GAMS software.[1] As reported in Chaps. 6 and 7, we have carried out computations using linear percentage-change representations of Melitz models implemented in GEMPACK software.[2] This experience shows that full-scale Melitz models can be solved relatively easily without resort to decomposition. Nevertheless, the Balistreri–Rutherford decomposition algorithm is of theoretical interest: it casts light on the relationship between a traditional Armington model and a Melitz model. It is also of practical interest to CGE modelers who use GAMS.

The chapter is organized as follows. In Sect. 5.1 we set out equations that turn the sectoral Melitz model described in Chap. 2 into a general equilibrium model. Section 5.2 describes the Armington auxiliary model used in the BR decomposition algorithm. While BR provide GAMS code for their algorithm, they give only a sketchy account of how it works. In Sect. 5.3 we explain it fully, with the underlying mathematics in Appendix 5.1. In Sect. 5.4 we focus on the theoretical relationship between Armington and Melitz exposed by Balistreri and Rutherford. We see this relationship as valuable in understanding simulation results from Melitz models.

5.1 Completing the Melitz General Equilibrium Model

Imagine that a commodity subscript c is added to all of the variables in the Melitz panel of Table 2.2. Also, we add an extra equation to define tariff revenue collected by country d on imports of commodity c from country s:

---

[1]See Bisschop and Meeraus (1982), Brooke et al. (1992) and Horridge et al. (2013).
[2]See Pearson (1988), Harrison et al. (2014), and Horridge et al. (2013).

$$R_{sd,c} = \left(T_{sd,c} - 1\right) \frac{P_{\bullet sd,c}}{T_{sd,c}} N_{sd,c} Q_{\bullet sd,c}. \tag{5.1}$$

Our Melitz model for sector c now consists of the Melitz versions of (T2.1)–(T2.12) with c's appended plus (5.1).

Next we add economy-wide equations. These define employment and GDP for each country:

$$LTOT_s = \sum_c L_{s,c} \tag{5.2}$$

$$GDP_d = W_d * LTOT_d + \sum_c \sum_s R_{sd,c}. \tag{5.3}$$

In (5.2), aggregate employment in country s is sectoral employment aggregated over all sectors c. In (5.3), GDP for country d is labor income (the only primary factor in our simple model) plus tariff revenue (the only indirect tax). With GDP in place, we can now add equations to determine the demand for commodity c in country d:

$$P_{d,c} Q_{d,c} = \mu_{d,c} * GDP_d. \tag{5.4}$$

In (5.4), $\mu_{d,c}$ is a non-negative parameter with $\sum_c \mu_{d,c} = 1$. Thus for simplicity we have assumed that the household in country d has a Cobb–Douglas utility function. By imposing (5.4) we are also assuming that the trade balance for each country is zero: aggregate expenditure on consumption in d equals d's GDP.

With (5.2)–(5.4) added to the equations for the Melitz sectoral models [(T2.1)–(T2.12) with c's appended plus (5.1), for c = 1, ..., n] we have a complete n-commodity Melitz general equilibrium model. Aggregate employment in each country can be specified exogenously. It is convenient to do this via the equation

$$LTOT_s = LX(s) \tag{5.5}$$

where LX(s) is the exogenously given level for country s. With given values for LX(s) our Melitz general equilibrium model can be solved in principle for all of the endogenous sectoral variables in the Melitz equations together with W_s, GDP_d, and $Q_{d,c}$. In performing a solution we need a numeraire (e.g. $W_1 = 1$) and correspondingly we need to delete a component from (5.4), e.g. the component for the last sector in the last country (Walras law).

An obvious decomposition approach to solving the Melitz general equilibrium model is: guess values for $Q_{d,c}$ and W_s for all c, d and s; solve the Melitz sectoral models for each c, one at a time; use (5.2)–(5.4) to compute the values implied by the sectoral models for $LTOT_s$, GDP_d, and $Q_{d,c}$; and then check for conflicts between the implied $LTOT_s$ values and the exogenously known values [LX(s)] and between the implied $Q_{d,c}$ values and those that were assumed in the Melitz sectoral models. If there are no conflicts then we have a solution to the Melitz general equilibrium model. If there are conflicts, then we must revise our guesses of $Q_{d,c}$ and W_s and resolve the Melitz sectoral models. The problem with this algorithm is that it does not offer a clear strategy for revising the guesses for $Q_{d,c}$ and W_s. The Balisteri–Rutherford algorithm overcomes this problem. As we will see, at the end of each iteration in their algorithm an Armington calculation suggests new values for $Q_{d,c}$ and W_s to be used as inputs to the Melitz sectoral models in the next iteration.

5.2 The Armington Auxiliary Model and the Evaluation of Its Productivity and Preference Variables from Melitz Sectoral Models

Table 5.1 sets out the Armington auxiliary model which can be used in the Balistreri–Rutherford decomposition algorithm to solve the Melitz general equilibrium model. In Table 5.1 we use "A" to denote Armington variable. Thus, PA(s,d,c) is the Armington version of the purchasers' price in country d of commodity c from country s.

The model in Table 5.1 is an Armington model for the special case, reflected in our simplified Melitz model, in which: labor is the only input to production; tariffs are the only indirect taxes; and households with Cobb–Douglas preferences are the only final demanders. Equation (T5.1) defines prices in terms of production costs and tariffs. Equation (T5.2) defines the average price of commodity c in country d as a CES function of the prices of commodity c from all sources. Equation (T5.3) is country d's demand function for c from s, derived from a CES cost-minimizing problem. Equation (T5.4) imposes market clearing for labor in country s. Equation (T5.5) defines tariff revenue collected by country d on imports[3] of c from s. Equation (T5.6) defines GDP in country d and (T5.7) determines overall demand for commodity c in country d under a Cobb–Douglas utility function.

If the values of the productivity, preference and tariff variables [$\Phi A(s, c)$, $\delta A(s, d, c)$ and $T_{sd,c}$] are known and we treat LX(s) as an exogenous variable, then the auxiliary model can be solved for the endogenous variables listed in the right hand panel of Table 5.1.[4] With this being a standard Armington model, the solution can be obtained relatively easily.

The model in Table 5.1 is the basis for Balistreri and Rutherford's Armington calculation mentioned at the end of Sect. 5.1. However, before we can see how this works, we need to connect the Melitz general equilibrium model with the Armington model. To do this, we add to the Melitz general equilibrium model

---

[3]We assume $T_{ss,c} = 1$ for all c and s.
[4]We would need a numeraire [e.g. WA(1) = 1] and we would need to delete one equation (Walras law).

Table 5.1 The Armington auxiliary model

Identifier	Equation	Dimension	Endogenous variable
(T5.1)	$PA(s,d,c) = \dfrac{WA(s) * T_{sd,c}}{\Phi A(s,c)}$	$r^2 * n$	$PA(s,d,c)$
(T5.2)	$PCA(d,c) = \left(\sum_s \delta A(s,d,c)^\sigma * PA(s,d,c)^{1-\sigma} \right)^{\frac{1}{1-\sigma}}$	$r * n$	$PCA(d,c)$
(T5.3)	$QA(s,d,c) = QCA(d,c) * \left(\delta A(s,d,c) * \dfrac{PCA(d,c)}{PA(s,d,c)} \right)^\sigma$	$r^2 * n$	$QA(s,d,c)$
(T5.4)	$LX(s) = \sum_{c,d} \left\{ \dfrac{QA(s,d,c)}{\Phi A(s,c)} \right\}$	r	$W(s)$
(T5.5)	$RA(s,d,c) = (T_{sd,c} - 1) * \left(\dfrac{QA(s,d,c) * WA(s)}{\Phi A(s,c)} \right)$	$r^2 * n$	$RA(s,d,c)$
(T5.6)	$GDPA(d) = WA(d) * LX(d) + \sum_{c,s} RA(s,d,c)$	r	$GDPA(d)$
(T5.7)	$PCA(d,c) * QCA(d,c) = \mu_{d,c} * GDPA(d)$	$r * n$	$QCA(d,c)$
	Total	$3 * r^2 n + 2 * r * r * n + 2 * r$	

Notation

r is the number of regions and n is the number of sectors or products

$PA(s,d,c)$ is the Armington version of the price in country d of commodity c from country s

$WA(s)$ is the Armington wage rate in country s

$T_{sd,c}$ is the power of the tariff in country d on c imported from s in both Melitz and Armington

$\Phi A(s,c)$ is Armington productivity in country s in the production of c

$PCA(d,c)$ is the average Armington price of c in d

$\delta A(s,d,c)$ is country d's preference variable for commodity c from s

$QA(s,d,c)$ is the Armington demand in country d for c from s

$QCA(d,c)$ is the Armington overall demand in country d for c

σ is the elasticity of substitution between varieties of the same commodity

$LX(s)$ is Armington total employment in country s, set exogenously

$RA(s,d,c)$ is the Armington tariff revenue collected in d on c from s

$GDPA(d)$ is the Armington GDP in country d

$\mu_{d,c}$ is the share of d's expenditure devoted to commodity c, $\mu_{d,c} > 0$ for all c and $\sum_c \mu_{d,c} = 1$

definitions of $\Phi A(s,c)$ and $\delta A(s,d,c)$. These definitions strip away complicating aspects of the Melitz model including multiple varieties and productivities in sector c in each country, fixed costs and imperfect competition. They define productivity and preferences as seen through the eyes of an Armington modeler. The definitions do not change the Melitz general equilibrium model: they simply hang off the end and can be evaluated recursively using variable values generated in the Melitz sectoral models. The definitions are as follows:

$$\Phi A(s,c) = \frac{\sum\limits_{d} Q_{\bullet sd,c} N_{sd,c}}{L_{s,c}} \tag{5.6}$$

[Productivity in sector c of country s defined as output divided by employment]

$$\delta A(s,d,c) = \left(\frac{\Phi A(s,c) * \frac{(P_{\bullet sd,c} Q_{\bullet sd,c} N_{sd,c} - R_{sd,c})}{W_s}}{Q_{d,c}} \right)^{\frac{1}{\sigma}} * \left(\frac{\left(\frac{W_s * T_{sd,c}}{\Phi A(s,c)} \right)}{\left(\frac{\sum_t P_{\bullet td,c} Q_{\bullet td,c} N_{td,c}}{Q_{d,c}} \right)} \right) \tag{5.7}$$

[Defines the preference variable in country d for good c from country s. Equation (5.7) can be understood as a rearrangement of the demand function for s, d,c set out in (T5.3). The numerator in the first fraction on the RHS of (5.7) is an Armington measure of the quantity of the s,d,c flow, i.e. labor productivity times labor input (which is the only input). The denominator in the first fraction is the total quantity of c absorbed in d. The numerator in the second fraction is an Armington measure of the purchasers' price in region d of commodity c from s, i.e. the wage rate in s inflated by the power of the tariff and deflated by productivity. The denominator in the second fraction is the average purchasers' price of commodity c in country d, i.e. the total value of purchases of c in d divided by total quantity.]

5.3   The Balistreri–Rutherford (BR) Algorithm

We now have enough apparatus to set out the BR algorithm for solving the Melitz general equilibrium model defined by the Melitz versions of (T2.1)–(T2.12) and (5.1)–(5.4):

Step 1   Guess values for $Q_{d,c}$ and W_d for all d and c.

Step 2   Solve the Melitz sectoral models [Melitz panel of Table 2.2 plus (5.1)] for each c, one at a time.

Step 3   Evaluate the Armington productivity and preference variables recursively using (5.6) and (5.7).

Step 4 Solve the Armington auxiliary model in Table 5.1 with $\Phi A(s, c)$ and $\delta A(s, d, c)$ set according to the values found in step 3 and $LX(s)$ treated as an exogenous variable set at the level required for the Melitz general equilibrium.

Step 5 Compare the values for $QCA(d, c)$ and $WA(d)$ for all d and c generated at step 4 with the guesses of $Q_{d,c}$ and W_d at step 1.

Step 6 If there are differences at step 5, return to step 1 and revise the guesses. Possible revision rules include:

$$Q_{d,c}^{(1,n+1)} = Q_{d,c}^{(1,n)} + \varepsilon * \left[QCA(d, c)^{(4,n)} - Q_{d,c}^{(1,n)} \right] \text{ and}$$
$$W_d^{(1,n+1)} = W_d^{(1,n)} + \varepsilon * \left[WA(d)^{(4,n)} - W_d^{(1,n)} \right]$$

where the superscript $(1,n)$ denotes guess used at step 1 in the nth iteration, the superscript $(4,n)$ denotes value emerging from step 4 in the nth iteration, and ε is a parameter between 0 and 1.

If there are no differences at step 5 (or the differences are sufficiently small), then the algorithm terminates. In this case, as shown in Appendix 5.1, we have found a solution to the Melitz general equilibrium model. This consists of: (a) the values of the Melitz sectoral variables found at step 2; (b) the $Q_{d,c}$ and W_d values guessed in step 1 (and confirmed in step 5); and (c) the values for $LTOT_s$ and GDP_d that can be computed from (5.2) and (5.3).

As well as demonstrating the validity of the BR algorithm, Appendix 5.1 shows for a converged Melitz–Armington solution (one that passes the no difference test at step 6) that the following conditions are satisfied:

$$R_{sd,c} = RA(s, d, c) \tag{5.8}$$

$$P_{d,c} = PCA(d, c) \tag{5.9}$$

$$P_{\bullet sd,c} N_{sd,c} Q_{\bullet sd,c} = PA(s, d, c) * QA(s, d, c). \tag{5.10}$$

These equations mean that the converged Armington results for tariff collections, prices of composite goods and values of commodity flows are the same as the Melitz results. In combination with (5.9), the convergence condition

$$Q_{d,c} = QCA(d, c) \tag{5.11}$$

implies that the Melitz and Armington results for the values of consumption of composite goods are the same:

$$P_{d,c} Q_{d,c} = PCA(d, c) * QCA(d, c). \tag{5.12}$$

If we define the percentage movement in country d's welfare by the movements in consumption of composite goods (the arguments of the household utility function), then the Melitz and Armington measures are, respectively,

$$\text{welfare}(d) = \sum_c Z(d, c) * q_{d,c} \tag{5.13}$$

and

$$\text{welfarea}(d) = \sum_c ZA(d, c) * qca(d, c) \tag{5.14}$$

where $q_{d,c}$ and $qca(d,c)$ are percentage changes in $Q_{d,c}$ and $QCA(d,c)$, and $Z(d,c)$ and $ZA(d,c)$ are consumption shares defined by

$$Z(d, c) = \frac{P_{d,c} Q_{d,c}}{\sum_e P_{d,e} Q_{d,e}} \tag{5.15}$$

and

$$ZA(d, c) = \frac{PCA(d, c) * QCA(d, c)}{\sum_e PCA(d, e) * QCA(d, e)}. \tag{5.16}$$

Via (5.11) and (5.12) it is clear that converged Armington welfare results are the same as Melitz results. This is important in Chap. 6 in which we use the Armington auxiliary model to decompose the Melitz welfare effects of a tariff change.

One confusion that arises in using the Armington auxiliary model to interpret and decompose Melitz results concerns measures of changes in trade volumes. In the Melitz model, the natural measure of the percentage change in the volume of commodity c sent from s to d is the percentage change in the number of units (the widget count) given by

$$\text{volume}_{sd,c} = n_{sd,c} + q_{\bullet sd,c} \tag{5.17}$$

where $n_{sd,c}$ and $q_{\bullet sd,c}$ are percentage changes in $N_{sd,c}$ and $Q_{\bullet sd,c}$. For Armington, the natural measure is

$$\text{volume } a(s, d, c) = qa(s, d, c) \tag{5.18}$$

where $qa(s,d,c)$ is the percentage change in $QA(s,d,c)$. From (5.10) we have

$$p_{\bullet sd,c} + n_{sd,c} + q_{\bullet sd,c} = pa(s, d, c) + qa(s, d, c) \tag{5.19}$$

where $p_{\bullet sd,c}$ and pa(s,d,c) are percentage changes in $P_{\bullet sd,c}$ and PA(s,d,c). Then using percentage change versions of (T5.1) and (T2.1, Melitz column) together with the convergence condition that

$$WA(s) = W_s, \qquad (5.20)$$

we find that

$$n_{sd,c} + q_{\bullet sd,c} = qa(s, d, c) - \phi a(s, c) + \phi_{\bullet sd,c} \qquad (5.21)$$

where $\phi a(s, c)$ and $\phi_{\bullet sd,c}$ are percentage changes in $\Phi A(s, c)$ and $\Phi_{\bullet sd,c}$. Because $\phi a(s, c)$ and $\phi_{\bullet sd,c}$ are not normally the same, (5.21) shows that the converged Armington and Melitz results for percentage changes in trade volumes are not normally the same. In Chap. 6, we interpret Melitz welfare results for the effects of a tariff shock as though these results arise from the Armington auxiliary model with tariff, productivity and preference shocks. When we are using the Armington auxiliary model as the explanatory device for Melitz results, it is appropriate to use Armington measures of percentage changes in trade volumes. For example, when we work out the efficiency effect of the tariff change as the welfare triangle (see Fig. 6.2), the Armington measure provides the base of the triangle.

5.4 Concluding Remarks: The Armington Model as a Tool for Interpreting Melitz Results

The solution to a Melitz general equilibrium model for the effects of a trade policy, for example, can be computed in an Armington model with policy shocks plus extra shocks for productivity and preferences. The extra shocks can be deduced from Melitz solutions by viewing Melitz results through Armington eyes. For example, Melitz produces an array of productivity results for the widget industry in country s, a different result for the typical firm on each s,d link. An Armington modeler sees the same productivity level for every widget firm in country s. What the analysis in this chapter shows is that the Armington modeler, accustomed to working only in industry averages, can obtain Melitz results by imposing average effects in an Armington model.

For the Melitz general equilibrium model described in this chapter, the specification of the productivity and preference variables that must be used in the Armington model to reveal Melitz solutions are specified in Eqs. (5.6) and (5.7). These specifications are relatively simple translations of results for Melitz sectoral variables into equivalent Armington variables. In (5.6), the productivity variable for country s's widget industry that must be used in the Armington model is the Melitz result for the production count in s divided by total input. The widget production count in s is the sum over shipments to each destination country d, calculated as the number shipped by the typical firm operating on the s,d link times the number of firms on the link. Total input covers labor used in current production and in setting up firms for production and for trade on links. In (5.7), the variable for d's preference for widgets from country s that must be used in the Armington model is deduced from Melitz results for quantities and prices of widgets sent from s to d. These quantities and prices are measured as though we were in an Armington world with no differences in productivity or fob prices across destinations. The Armington-equivalent quantity of widgets sent from s to d is the fob value deflated by s's wage rate and multiplied by average productivity in s's widget industry. The Armington-equivalent landed-duty-paid price for s's widgets in country d is the wage rate in country s divided by average productivity in s's widget industry and inflated by d's tariffs.

BR (2013) use the relationship between Melitz and Armington models explained in this chapter as the basis for an algorithm for solving Melitz general equilibrium models. As illustrated in Chaps. 6 and 7, we think there are better computational approaches to solving Melitz models. But the relationship between Melitz and Armington exposed by the BR algorithm is important. It means that for interpreting Melitz results, CGE modelers can use 40 years' experience in interpreting results from models with Armington specifications of international trade. This experience includes understanding the effects in an Armington framework of changes in tariffs $[T_{sd,c}]$, changes in productivity $[\Phi A(s, c)]$ and changes in preferences $[\delta A(s,d,c)]$.

Appendix 5.1: Establishing the Validity of the Balistreri–Rutherford Decomposition Algorithm

A BR Solution

We define a BR solution as a list of values of:

- Melitz sectoral variables [those in (T2.1)–(T2.12) together with (5.1) for all commodities c];
- Melitz economy-wide variables [$LTOT_s$, GDP_d and W_s for all countries s and d]; and
- Armington variables [those in Table 5.1];

that jointly satisfy the Melitz versions of (T2.1)–(T2.12) plus (5.1), the economy-wide Melitz Eqs. (5.2) and (5.3), the Armington equations (T5.1)–(T5.7), and the Armington productivity and preference Eqs. (5.6) and (5.7).

If we implement steps 1 to 4 of the algorithm set out in Sect. 5.3, and then use (5.2) and (5.3) to calculate $LTOT_s$ and GDP_d, what emerges is a BR solution. We will have found variable values that satisfy (T2.1)–(T2.12) plus (5.1), (5.6) and (5.7), (T5.1)–(T5.7) and (5.2) and (5.3). But notice that a BR solution does not reveal a Melitz general equilibrium: it does not necessarily satisfy (5.4) and (5.5).

A Converged BR Solution

We define a *converged* BR solution as a BR solution with two additional properties: (5.11) and (5.20). We show that the Melitz variables in a converged BR solution form a Melitz general equilibrium. To do this all that is necessary is to establish that a BR solution that satisfies (5.11) and (5.20) also satisfies (5.4) and (5.5).

Strategy for Demonstrating that a Converged BR Solution Reveals a Melitz General Equilibrium: Proving That a Converged Solution Satisfies (5.4) and (5.5)

We will start by showing that a converged BR solution satisfies (5.5). On the way to doing this we show that (5.8) and (5.9) are valid. Then, on the way to establishing (5.4) we will show that

$$\text{GDPA}(d) = \text{GDP}_d \tag{5.22}$$

After establishing that a converged BR solution satisfies (5.4) and (5.5) and thereby establishing the validity of the BR algorithm, we demonstrate (5.10).

Establishing (5.5) via (5.8) and (5.9)

The first step in deriving (5.8) is to rearrange (5.1) as

$$T_{sd,c} - 1 = \frac{R_{sd,c}}{\left(P_{\bullet sd,c}Q_{\bullet sd,c}N_{sd,c} - R_{sd,c}\right)}. \tag{5.23}$$

Then substituting from (5.23) and (T5.3) into (T5.5) gives

$$RA(s, d, c) = \left(\frac{R_{sd,c}}{\left(P_{\bullet sd,c}Q_{\bullet sd,c}N_{sd,c} - R_{sd,c}\right)}\right) \\ * \left(\frac{QCA(d,c) * \left(\delta A(s,d,c) * \frac{PCA(d,c)}{PA(s,d,c)}\right)^{\sigma} * WA(s)}{\Phi A(s,c)}\right) \tag{5.24}$$

Using (5.7) we obtain

$$RA(s, d, c) = \left(\frac{R_{sd,c}}{\left(P_{\bullet sd,c}Q_{\bullet sd,c}N_{sd,c} - R_{sd,c}\right)}\right) * QCA(d,c) * \frac{WA(s)}{\Phi A(s,c)} * \\ \left(\left(\frac{\Phi A(s,c) * \frac{\left(P_{\bullet sd,c}Q_{\bullet sd,c}N_{sd} - R_{sd,c}\right)}{W_s}}{Q_{d,c}}\right)^{\frac{1}{\sigma}} * \left(\frac{\left(\frac{W_s * T_{sd,c}}{\Phi A(s,c)}\right)}{\left(\frac{\sum_t P_{\bullet td,c}Q_{\bullet td,c}N_{td,c}}{Q_{d,c}}\right)}\right) * \frac{PCA(d,c)}{PA(s,d,c)}\right)^{\sigma} \tag{5.25}$$

Using (T5.1) and the properties of a converged solution, that is (5.11) and (5.20), we can simplify (5.25) to

$$RA(s, d, c) = R_{sd,c} * \left(\frac{PCA(d, c)}{\frac{\sum_t P_{\bullet td,c} Q_{\bullet td,c} N_{td,c}}{Q_{d,c}}} \right)^{\sigma}. \tag{5.26}$$

Now we work on the bracketed term on the right-hand side of (5.26). From (T5.2), (5.7) and (T5.1), we have

$$PCA(d, c)^{1-\sigma} =$$

$$\sum_s \left(\frac{\Phi A(s, c) * \frac{(P_{\bullet sd,c} Q_{\bullet sd,c} N_{sd,c} - R_{sd,c})}{W_s}}{Q_{d,c}} \right) * \left(\frac{\left(\frac{W_s * T_{sd,c}}{\Phi A(s, c)}\right)}{\frac{\sum_t P_{\bullet td,c} Q_{\bullet td,c} N_{td,c}}{Q_{d,c}}} \right)^{\sigma} * \left(\frac{WA(s) * T_{sd,c}}{\Phi A(s, c)} \right)^{1-\sigma} \tag{5.27}$$

Using (5.20) and simplifying gives

$$PCA(d, c)^{1-\sigma} =$$

$$\sum_s \left(\frac{\Phi A(s, c) * \frac{(P_{\bullet sd,c} Q_{\bullet sd,c} N_{sd,c} - R_{sd,c})}{W_s}}{Q_{d,c}} \right) * \frac{\left(\frac{W_s * T_{sd,c}}{\Phi A(s, c)}\right)}{\left(\frac{\sum_t P_{\bullet td,c} Q_{\bullet td,c} N_{td,c}}{Q_{d,c}}\right)^{\sigma}} \tag{5.28}$$

Further simplifying and using (5.23) gives

$$PCA(d, c) = \sum_s \frac{P_{\bullet sd,c} Q_{\bullet sd,c} N_{sd,c}}{Q_{d,c}}. \tag{5.29}$$

Then from (5.26) and (5.29) we get (5.8).

To derive (5.9) we use (T2.3) to eliminate $\delta_{sd,c}^{\sigma}$ from (T2.2). This gives

$$P_{d,c} = \left(\sum_s N_{sd,c} \frac{Q_{\bullet sd,c}}{Q_{d,c}} \left(\frac{P_{\bullet sd,c}}{P_{d,c}} \right)^{\sigma} P_{\bullet sd,c}^{1-\sigma} \right)^{\frac{1}{(1-\sigma)}} \tag{5.30}$$

which simplifies to

$$P_{d,c} = \sum_s \frac{N_{sd,c} Q_{\bullet sd,c} P_{\bullet sd,c}}{Q_{d,c}}. \tag{5.31}$$

Comparing (5.31) and (5.29) establishes (5.9).

Now we can move to the derivation of (5.5). Substituting from (T5.3) and (5.7) into (T5.4) gives

$$LX(s) =$$

$$\sum_{c,d} \frac{QCA(d,c)}{\Phi A(s,c)} * \left(\left(\frac{\Phi A(s,c) * \frac{(P_{\bullet sd,c} Q_{\bullet sd,c} N_{sd,c} - R_{sd,c})}{W_s}}{Q_{d,c}} \right)^{\frac{1}{\sigma}} * \frac{\left(\frac{W_s * T_{sd,c}}{\Phi A(s,c)} \right)}{\left(\frac{\sum_t P_{\bullet td,c} Q_{\bullet td,c} N_{td,c}}{Q_{d,c}} \right)} * \frac{PCA(d,c)}{PA(s,d,c)} \right)^{\sigma} \tag{5.32}$$

Using (T5.1), (5.29) and (5.11) and simplifying gives

$$LX(s) = \sum_{c,d} \frac{(P_{\bullet sd,s} Q_{\bullet sd,c} N_{sd,c} - R_{sd,c})}{W_s}. \tag{5.33}$$

Now we eliminate $R_{sd,c}$ via (5.1):

$$LX(s) = \sum_{c,d} \frac{\left(P_{\bullet sd,c} Q_{\bullet sd,c} N_{sd,c} - (T_{sd,c} - 1) \frac{P_{\bullet sd,c}}{T_{sd,c}} N_{sd,c} Q_{\bullet sd,c} \right)}{W_s}$$

$$= \sum_{c,d} \frac{P_{\bullet sd,c} Q_{\bullet sd,c} N_{sd,c}}{W_s T_{sd,c}}. \tag{5.34}$$

From the Melitz versions of (T2.9), (T2.5) and (T2.6), we have

$$0 = \sum_d N_{sd,c} \left(\frac{P_{\bullet sd,c}}{T_{sd,c}} - \frac{W_s}{\Phi_{\bullet sd,c}} \right) Q_{\bullet sd,c} - \sum_d N_{sd,c} F_{sd,c} W_s - N_{s,c} H_{s,c} W_s. \tag{5.35}$$

Using (5.35) we can eliminate the F and H terms from (T2.7). Then, adding over c, we obtain

$$\sum_c L_{s,c} = \sum_{c,d} \frac{N_{sd,c} Q_{\bullet sd,c}}{\Phi_{\bullet sd,c}} + \sum_{c,d} \frac{N_{sd,c}}{W_s} \left(\frac{P_{\bullet sd,c}}{T_{sd,c}} - \frac{W_s}{\Phi_{\bullet sd,c}} \right) Q_{\bullet sd,c}. \tag{5.36}$$

Using (T2.1) gives

$$\sum_c L_{s,c} = \sum_{c,d} \frac{N_{sd,c}Q_{\bullet sd,c}}{\Phi_{\bullet sd,c}} + \sum_{c,d} \frac{N_{sd,c}}{W_s}\left(\frac{P_{\bullet sd,c}}{\sigma T_{sd,c}}\right)Q_{\bullet sd,c} \tag{5.37}$$

which can be rearranged via (T2.1) as

$$\sum_c L_{s,c} = \sum_{c,d} \frac{P_{\bullet sd,c}Q_{\bullet sd,c}N_{sd,c}}{W_s T_{sd,c}}. \tag{5.38}$$

Comparing (5.34) and (5.38) and using (5.2) we see that (5.5) holds.

Establishing (5.4) by first deriving equation (5.22)
Substituting from (5.20), (5.5) and (5.8) into (T5.6) gives:

$$\text{GDPA}(d) = W_d * \text{LTOT}_d + \sum_{c,s} R_{sd,c} \tag{5.39}$$

Then from (5.3) we obtain (5.22). Now substituting (5.9), (5.11) and (5.22) into (T5.7) gives (5.4).

Establishing (5.10)
Substituting from (5.7), (5.11) and (5.9) into (T5.3) gives

$$QA(s,d,c) = Q_{d,c} * \left[\left(\frac{\Phi A(s,c) * \dfrac{(P_{\bullet sd,c}Q_{\bullet sd,c}N_{sd,c} - R_{sd,c})}{W_s}}{Q_{d,c}}\right)^{\frac{1}{\sigma}} \right.$$
$$\left. * \left(\frac{\left(\dfrac{W_s * T_{sd,c}}{\Phi A(s,c)}\right)}{\left(\dfrac{\sum_t P_{\bullet td,c}Q_{\bullet td,c}N_{td,c}}{Q_{d,c}}\right)}\right) * \frac{P_{d,c}}{PA(s,d,c)}\right]^{\sigma} \tag{5.40}$$

Then using (5.23), (5.20) and (T5.1) we can rewrite (5.40) as

$$QA(s,d,c) = Q_{d,c}$$
$$* \left(\left(\frac{\dfrac{(P_{\bullet sd,c}Q_{\bullet sd,c}N_{sd,c})}{PA(s,d,c)}}{Q_{d,c}}\right)^{\frac{1}{\sigma}} * \left(\frac{PA(s,d,c)}{\left(\dfrac{\sum_t P_{\bullet td,c}Q_{\bullet td,c}N_{td,c}}{Q_{d,c}}\right)}\right) * \frac{P_{d,c}}{PA(s,d,c)}\right)^{\sigma}$$
$$\tag{5.41}$$

Now using (5.31) we can simplify (5.41):

$$QA(s, d, c) = \frac{\left(P_{\bullet sd,c} Q_{\bullet sd,c} N_{sd,c}\right)}{PA(s, d, c)} \tag{5.42}$$

which gives us (5.10).

References

Balistreri, E., & Rutherford, T. (2013). Computing general equilibrium theories of monopolistic competition and heterogeneous firms (Chapter 23). In P. B. Dixon & D. W. Jorgenson (Eds.), *Handbook of computable general equilibrium modeling* (pp. 1513–1570). Amsterdam: Elsevier.

Bisschop, J., & Meeraus, A. (1982). On the development of a general algebraic modeling system in a strategic planning environment. *Mathematical Programming Study, 20,* 1–19.

Brooke, A., Meeraus, A., & Kendrick, D. (1992). *Release 2.25: GAMS a user's guide.* San Francisco: The Scientific Press.

Harrison, W. J., Horridge, J. M., Jerie, M., & Pearson, K. R. (2014). *GEMPACK manual,* GEMPACK Software, ISBN 978-1-921654-34-3. Available at http://www.copsmodels.com/gpmanual.htm.

Horridge, J. M., Meeraus, A., Pearson, K., & Rutherford, T. (2013). Software platforms: GAMS and GEMPACK (Chap. 20). In P. B. Dixon & D. W. Jorgenson (Eds.), *Handbook of computable general equilibrium modeling* (pp. 1331–1382). Amsterdam: Elsevier.

Pearson, K. R. (1988). Automating the computation of solutions of large economic models. *Economic Modelling, 5*(4), 385–395.

Chapter 6
Illustrative GEMPACK Computations in a General Equilibrium Model with Melitz Sectors

Abstract One way to learn about the theoretical properties of a model is to construct and apply a simple numerical version. This is also a good preparation for creating policy-relevant models. Here we describe MelitzGE, a simplified Melitz general equilibrium model implemented with stylized data. Using MelitzGE we start by conducting simulations for which the results can be known a priori. Test simulations such as these check the coding of models. They can also expose theoretical properties. For example, a MelitzGE test simulation of the effects of a uniform 1% world-wide increase in employment shows a uniform increase in consumption of more than 1%, determined by the substitution elasticity σ. Sorting out why this is so helps us understand how love of variety and scale operate in Melitz. Next we conduct tariff simulations. Using the Balistreri-Rutherford decomposition discussed in Chap. 5, we find that Melitz love-of-variety and productivity effects tend to cancel out leaving welfare determined by phenomena familiar from Armington: terms-of-trade and efficiency effects. Recognition that these effects depend on tariff levels and trade-flow sensitivity to tariff changes leads to an investigation of the equivalence between Armington and Melitz models when calibrated to produce similar trade sensitivities. The GEMPACK code for our computations is in an appendix. As illustrated in this chapter and the next, GEMPACK is ideal software for Melitz-style CGE modelling. Nevertheless, readers will not need to be familiar with GEMPACK or follow the GEMPACK code to understand the chapter.

Keywords Test simulations · Melitz in GEMPACK · Welfare decomposition Armington-Melitz equivalence

Electronic supplementary material Readers can access the GEMPACK programs for running the simulations reported in this chapter at https://doi.org/10.1007/978-981-10-8325-9_6.

In this chapter we construct and apply a numerical version of the Melitz general equilibrium model specified by Eqs. (T2.1)–(T2.12) in Table 2.2 together with Eqs. (5.1)–(5.4) in Sect. 5.1. We refer to this model as MelitzGE.

The construction of the model is described in Sect. 6.1. The database for the model is stylized. We wait until Chap. 7 before implementing a real-world general equilibrium model with Melitz features. Building a simple numerical model with stylized but representative data and conducting exploratory simulations deepens our understanding of the properties of the Melitz model and provides a platform for the more ambitious work undertaken in Chap. 7.

In Sects. 6.2–6.5 we report results from four sets of MelitzGE simulations. The first set, in Sect. 6.2, are test simulations designed mainly to check the validity of our coding. We also use these simulations to demonstrate a point from Sect. 3.3: intuition gained from envelope theorems and from thinking of results as reflecting the behaviour of a single optimizing agent can be useful in interpreting results.

The second set is concerned with the effects of tariff increases. The results are described in Sect. 6.3. We start with results for standard variables that appear in every CGE model such as GDP, exports, imports and the terms of trade. Then we focus on Melitz variables such as the number and average productivity of firms on each link. Section 6.4 continues the analysis of the tariff results concentrating on welfare. We use ideas from the Balistreri and Rutherford algorithm described in Chap. 5 to show that Melitz tariff results can be interpreted as Armington tariff results with the addition of the effects of shocks to productivity and preferences. This leads to a decomposition of tariff-induced MelitzGE welfare effects into contributions from changes in: employment; efficiency (tax-carrying flows); terms of trade; production technology (average productivity in industries); and conversion technology (variety effects). The last two contributions are specific to Melitz. They don't appear in Armington models. We find that these Melitz contributions tend to cancel out, a phenomenon that we attribute to the envelope theorem discussed in Sect. 3.3.

The third set of results, in Sect. 6.5, is again about tariffs. We compare results from MelitzGE with those from an Armington model built on the MelitzGE database. When the Melitz inter-variety substitution elasticity and the Armington inter-country substitution elasticity are set equal (both on 3.8) we find that the trade-flow contractions in Melitz from a given tariff increase are much larger than those in Armington. This explains differences between Melitz and Armington welfare results. By setting the Armington inter-country elasticity at a higher value than the Melitz inter-variety elasticity we produce Armington results for trade flows that closely approximate Melitz results. Once the trade-flow results are brought into line, so are the welfare results.

The analysis in this chapter suggests an approximate equivalence between Melitz and Armington for the effects of tariff changes. In the concluding remarks, Sect. 6.6, we review the findings of some other authors on the equivalence proposition.

6.1 Setting Up and Solving a Melitz CGE Model

To set up and solve MelitzGE and the related Armington model, referred to as the Armington auxiliary model, we used the GEMPACK code presented with annotations in Appendix 6.1. In computing solutions of equations that describe a general equilibrium, GEMPACK starts from an initial solution and then uses a system of linear equations in percentage changes or changes in variables to calculate the movements in the endogenous variables away from their initial values in response to movements in exogenous variables away from their initial values. To fully capture non-linearities in the equation system, GEMPACK computations are conducted in a series of steps. In the first step, the exogenous variables are moved a fraction of the way along the path from their initial values to their desired final values. This gives a new solution for the endogenous variables which is relatively free of linearization error provided that the step size (fraction) is not too big. In the second step GEMPACK calculates the effects on this new solution of another movement in the exogenous variables along the path towards the desired final values. With the movements in the exogenous variables broken into a sufficient number of steps, GEMPACK arrives at an accurate solution for the endogenous variables at the given final values of the exogenous variables.[1]

Familiarity with GEMPACK is not essential for following the arguments in this chapter. Nevertheless, readers will find it informative to refer to Appendix 6.1. To help non-GEMPACK users obtain an overview of the code in Appendix 6.1, we have provided Box 6.1.

The code in Appendix 6.1 is for an n-sector, r-country version of the MelitzGE model. The GEMPACK representation of the MelitzGE equations can be seen in part A6.1.5 of the appendix. This is a linear representation of the Melitz versions of (T2.1)–(T2.12) and (5.1)–(5.4). Part A6.1.5 also includes other equations defining variables that are helpful in analysing results. For each country, these equations define movements in: the balance of trade; real exports; real imports; real consumption; real GDP in expenditure and income terms for which results should always be identical; the average propensity to consume each commodity; welfare determined by consumption of composite commodities [$Q_{d,c}$ in Eq. (5.4)]; and the wage rate relative to the world average.

---

[1]Johansen (1960) formulated what is now recognized as the first CGE model. His solution method was a 1-step version of the GEMPACK method. The original description of the theory underlying the multi-step GEMPACK method is in Dixon et al. (1982, Sect. 8 and Chap. 5). For more recent expositions see Dixon et al. (2013, Sect. 2.4) and Horridge et al. (2013). The GEMPACK software was initially created by Pearson (1988). For information on GEMPACK see https://www.copsmodels.com/gempack.htm.

Box 6.1. Introduction to the GEMPACK Solution Strategy

Here is an example to help non-GEMPACK users to get an overview of what is going on in Appendix 6.1. We illustrate key GEMPACK ideas: initial solution, coefficients, reads, formulas, variables, updates and linear equations.

Assume we have a model with 3 variables (X_1, X_2, and X_3) connected by 2 equations:

$$X_1 * X_2 - X_3^2 = 0 \tag{1}$$

$$2 * X_1 - X_2 - 1 = 0 \tag{2}$$

Assume that from data or otherwise we know that X_1 has initial value 1. We can tell GEMPACK about this by a read statement: **Read** X_1 from a data file.

Then GEMPACK can calculate the rest of the initial solution recursively from formulas:

Formula $X_2 = 2 * X_1 - 1 = 1$

Formula $X_3 = (X_1 * X_2)^{0.5} = 1$

(assume only positive X_3 values are relevant)

GEMPACK users derive a system of linear equations in percentage changes of variables by totally differentiating the LHSs of (1) and (2) and putting the results equal to zero. The logic is that we start from a solution, so to get to another solution we should leave the values of the LHSs unchanged. In GEMPACK the model (1) and (2) can be written as linear **equations**:

$$X_1 * X_2 * [x_1 + x_2] - 2 * X_3^2 * x_3 = 0 \tag{3}$$

$$2 * X_1 * x_1 - X_2 * x_2 = 0 \tag{4}$$

where x_i is the percentage change in X_i. GEMPACK interprets x_i as a **variable** and $X_1 * X_2$, X_3^2, X_1 and X_2 as **coefficients**. At initial values of the coefficients, (3) and (4) can be written as:

$$\begin{pmatrix} 1 & 1 & -2 \\ 2 & -1 & 0 \end{pmatrix} * \begin{pmatrix} x_1 \\ x_2 \\ x_3 \end{pmatrix} = 0 \tag{5}$$

Assume that x_3 is chosen to be exogenous. Then GEMPACK solves (5) for x_1 and x_2 as

$$\begin{pmatrix} x_1 \\ x_2 \end{pmatrix} = -\begin{pmatrix} 1 & 1 \\ 2 & -1 \end{pmatrix}^{-1} * \begin{pmatrix} -2 \\ 0 \end{pmatrix} * x_3 = \begin{pmatrix} 2/3 \\ 4/3 \end{pmatrix} * x_3 \qquad (6)$$

Assume that we are interested in the effects of 30% increase in X_3. From (6) we can obtain the 1-step solution: $x_1 = 20\%$ and $x_2 = 40\%$. A little bit of work with (1) and (2) shows that the true solution is $x_1^{\text{true}} = 20.26$ and $x_2^{\text{true}} = 40.53$. GEMPACK can get closer to this true solution in a 2-step procedure. In the first step we use (6) to find the effects on X_1 and X_2 of increasing X_3 from 1 to 1.15. According to (6), X_1 and X_2 move to 1.10 and 1.20. GEMPACK updates the coefficients to reflect the new values of X_1, X_2, X_3 either by the formulas or by **update** statements and then reforms (5) but with (X_1, X_2, X_3) set on (1.10, 1.20, 1.15), giving

$$\begin{pmatrix} 13.2 & 1.32 & -2.645 \\ 2.20 & -1.20 & 0 \end{pmatrix} * \begin{pmatrix} x_1 \\ x_2 \\ x_3 \end{pmatrix} = 0 \qquad (7)$$

leading to

$$\begin{pmatrix} x_1 \\ x_2 \end{pmatrix} = -\begin{pmatrix} 1.32 & 1.32 \\ 2.20 & -1.20 \end{pmatrix}^{-1} * \begin{pmatrix} -2.645 \\ 0 \end{pmatrix} * x_3 = \begin{pmatrix} 0.707219 \\ 1.296569 \end{pmatrix} * x_3 \qquad (8)$$

Now GEMPACK uses (8) to compute the effects on X_1 and X_2 of moving X_3 from 1.15 to 1.30, a percentage increase of 13.04%. Equation (8) gives the step-2 percentage increases in X_1 and X_2 as 9.2246 and 16.9118. Combining the step-1 and step 2 increases, GEMPACK now computes the total increases in X_1 and X_2 as 20.1471 [$=100 * (1.10 * 1.092246 - 1)$] and 40.2941 [$=100 * (1.20 * 1.169118 - 1)$]. The 2-step solution is more accurate than the 1-step solution. GEMPACK obtains further increases in accuracy with more steps.

Further equations are in part A6.1.10. These are linear representations of: (5.6) and (5.7) defining Armington variables for productivity and preferences; and (T5.1)–(T5.7) specifying the Armington auxiliary model. Part A6.1.10 also contains equations that use Armington variables in defining movements in: nominal GDP; expenditure and income measures of real GDP (for which results should be identical); employment; real exports; export prices; real imports; import prices; and average world wages. The last four equations in part A6.1.10 are used in transferring results for average wages, employment and average propensities to consume between MelitzGE and Armington auxiliary. The roles of these equations are explained in the discussion of closures at the end of Appendix 6.1.

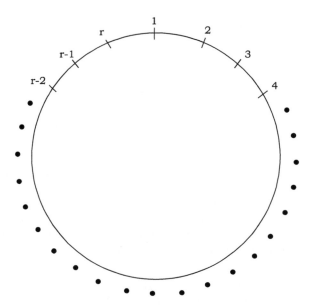

Fig. 6.1 Location of countries 1 to r

The final group of equations in the GEMPACK code are in part A6.1.11. These equations calculate the welfare decomposition explained in Sect. 6.4.

The code is set up for a special case in which the $n * r$ sectors are identical in the initial solution, facing identical demand and cost conditions. Initially, for all sectors/commodities (c) and countries (s or d): $W_s = 1$ (same wage rate in all countries); $T_{sd,c} = 1$ (zero tariffs); $H_{s,c} = H$ (same fixed setup costs in all sectors); $g_{s,c}(\Phi) = \alpha \Phi^{-\alpha-1}, \Phi \geq 1$ (same Pareto distribution of productivities in all sectors); $\delta_{sd,c} = 1$ (no country preference biases in any sector); $\mu_{d,c} = 1/n$ (equal expenditure shares on all commodities); the substitution elasticity σ is the same across all commodities; and $N_{s,c} = Q_{d,c} = 1$ (two harmless normalizations).

The countries can be thought of as located at equal distances on the circumference of a circle (Fig. 6.1), with set up costs, $F_{sd,c}$, being determined by the shortest distance on the circle between s and d. Following Balistreri and Rutherford (2013), we set α at 4.6 and σ at 3.8 giving $\beta = 1.398$ [see (2.27)]. Then, in the initial situation, we assume that a firm k needs a productivity level of at least 1.1 ($\Phi_k \geq 1.1$) for it to operate in its own country (non-zero sales on the ss-link). At the other extreme, we assume that the minimum productivity level required for a firm to operate on all links is 2. With these assumptions and with the countries numbered from 1 to r, r even, we compute initial values for $\Phi_{min(s,d,c)}$ according to:

$$\Phi_{min(s,d,c)} = 1.1 + \frac{(2.0 - 1.1)}{r} * 2 * MIN\{|s - d|, r - |s - d|\} \quad \text{for all s, d and c.}$$

$$(6.1)$$

Under (6.1) the $\Phi_{min(s,d,c)}$'s for country s are spread evenly from 1.1 (for d equal to s) to 2 (for the country or countries furthest from s on the circle). With the initial values of Φ_{min} set in this way we determined the initial values recursively for: $\Phi_{\bullet sd,c}$ via (T2.11); $N_{sd,c}$ via (T2.8); $P_{\bullet sd,c}$ via (T2.1); $P_{d,c}$ via (T2.2); $Q_{\bullet sd,c}$ via (T2.3); $Q_{min(s,d,c)}$ via (T2.12); $F_{sd,c}$ via (T2.10); $Q_{sd,c}$ via (T2.4); $\Pi_{\bullet sd,c}$ via (T2.5); $H_{s,c}$ via (T2.6) and (T2.9); and $L_{s,c}$ via (T2.7). Readers who are following the GEMPACK code in Appendix 6.1 can find these recursive evaluations in part A6.1.2.

Identical sectors and countries is a special case. However, we do not use this feature to simplify or speed up our calculations. Thus we think that the GEMPACK experience reported in this chapter is a reasonable guide to how the software would perform in an empirically specified model. The most obvious qualification is that our illustrative model lacks intermediate inputs. Their inclusion increases dimensionality. Nevertheless, available GEMPACK experience with empirically specified imperfect competition models suggests that intermediate inputs do not cause major computational problems, see for example Horridge (1987), Abayasiri-Silva and Horridge (1998), Swaminathan and Hertel (1996) and Akgul et al. (2016), as well as our own experience reported in Chap. 7.

Although the computations in this chapter are for a special case, we think this case is reasonably representative of a real world situation. In the 2-country n-commodity version, around which our discussion is based, the initial solution implies for each country that: exports (and imports) are 25.4% of GDP; fixed setup costs $\left(\sum_c W_s H_{s,c} N_{s,c} \right)$ are 16% of GDP; and fixed costs on trade links $\left(\sum_c \sum_{d \neq s} W_s F_{sd,c} N_{sd,c} \right)$ are 10% of the fob value of exports, see Table 6.1.

6.2 Test Simulations and Interpreting Results

Table 6.2 contains results from four MelitzGE test simulations. These are simulations for which we know the correct results a priori. Test simulations are important in applied general equilibrium modelling because they offer the only reasonably foolproof way of checking the coding of a model. In addition, designing and thinking about test simulations is often a valuable part of understanding a model.

We conduct the test simulations with a 2-country, 2-commodity version of MelitzGE, that is r = n = 2. The closure (set of exogenous variables) is the same in all four simulations. The exogenous variables are: the average wage rate across countries, which acts as the numeraire; aggregate employment in each country; consumer preferences over sources of commodity c [$\delta_{sd,c}$]; tariff rates; setup costs for firms [$H_{s,c}$]; setup costs for trade on every link [$F_{sd,c}$]; and the Cobb-Douglas preference coefficients [$\mu_{d,c}$].[2]

---

[2]For d = 2 we allow uniform percentage endogenous adjustment in $\mu_{d,c}$ across c. This is equivalent to eliminating an equation in accordance with Walras law.

Table 6.1 Selected items from the MelitzGE 2-commodity/2-country database (the data are the same for both commodities c and both countries s)

Data item	Value
Wage rate in country s, W_s	1
Labor requirement for setting up a c-producing firm in country s, $H_{s,c}$	0.14887
Labor requirements for setting up a c-firm on the sd link	
$F_{sd,c}$, s = d	0.11065
$F_{sd,c}$, s ≠ d	0.59010
Number of c firms in country s, $N_{s,c}$	1
Number of c firms operating on the sd link	
$N_{sd,c}$, s = d	0.64505
$N_{sd,c}$, s ≠ d	0.04123
Total employment in country s, $LTOT_s$	1.85880
Quantity of labor used in setting up c-firms in country s, $H_{s,c} * N_{s,c}$	0.14887
Quantity of labor used in establishing c-firms on sd link	
$F_{sd,c} * N_{sd,c}$, s = d	0.07137
$F_{sd,c} * N_{sd,c}$, s ≠ d	0.02433
Fixed cost labor used by c-firms in country s, $H_{s,c} * N_{s,c} + \sum_{d=1}^{2} F_{sd,c} * N_{sd,c}$	0.24457
Value of GDP	1.85880
Value of consumption	1.85880
Value of exports	0.47259
Value of imports	0.47259

In the first test simulation we impose a 1% increase in the numeraire, the average wage rate across countries. The expected result, and the result shown in the first column of Table 6.2, is zero effect on all real variables (quantities) and a 1% increase in all nominal variables (prices and values).

In the second test simulation we apply 1% shocks to fixed setup costs for firms in both countries producing commodity 1 and to fixed costs for trading commodity 1 on all links ($H_{d,c}$ and $F_{sd,c}$ for c = 1 and all s and d). As shown in column 2 of Table 6.2, a 1% increase in the H's and F's for commodity 1 has no effect on observable quantities and values:

- employment by commodity and country shows zero effect;
- the price of composite commodity 1 in each country rises by 0.35600% offset by a decline in consumption in each country of 0.35474% leaving the potentially observable *value* of consumption of commodity 1 in each country unchanged; and
- the number of commodity-1 firms on each link decreases by 0.99010%, the price charged by a typical firm on each link is unchanged and the quantity it ships increases by 1%, implying zero effect on the potentially observable *values* of commodity-1 trade on each link.

These results confirm the argument in Sect. 4.1 and Appendix 4.4 that in calibrating a Melitz model (setting parameter values) it is legitimate to assign for each

Table 6.2 Test simulations with MelitzGE (percentage changes)

Selected variables	Nominal homogeneity (1)	Scaling fixed costs (2)	Scaling consumption (3)	Increased scale (4)
Exogenous variables				
World average wage rate	1.0	0.0	0.0	0.0
Fixed costs, start up and links				
$H_{s,1}$ for all s	0.0	1.0	0.0	0.0
$H_{s,2}$ for all s	0.0	0.0	0.0	0.0
$F_{sd,1}$ for all s, d	0.0	1.0	0.0	0.0
$F_{sd,2}$ for all s, d	0.0	0.0	0.0	0.0
Preference variables				
$\delta_{s2,1}$ for all s	0.0	0.0	0.73588	0.0
All other δ's	0.0	0.0	0.0	0.0
Employment by country				
$LTOT_s$ for all s	0.0	0.0	0.0	1.0
Endogenous variables				
Price of composites				
$P_{1,1}$	1.0	0.35600	0.0	−0.35474
$P_{1,2}$	1.0	0.0	0.0	−0.35474
$P_{2,1}$	1.0	0.35600	−0.99010	−0.35474
$P_{2,2}$	1.0	0.0	0.0	−0.35474
Typical link prices $P_{\bullet sd,c}$ for all s, d, c	1.0	0.0	0.0	0.0
Number of firms				
$N_{d,1}$ for all d	0.0	−0.99010	0.0	1.0
$N_{d,2}$ for all d	0.0	0.0	0.0	1.0
Number of firms on link				
$N_{sd,1}$ for all s, d	0.0	−0.99010	0.0	1.0
$N_{sd,2}$ for all s, d	0.0	0.0	0.0	1.0
Employment by commodity $L_{s,c}$ for all s, c	0.0	0.0	0.0	1.0
Consumption by country and com				
$Q_{1,1}$	0.0	−0.35474	0.0	1.35956
$Q_{1,2}$	0.0	0.0	0.0	1.35956
$Q_{2,1}$	0.0	−0.35474	1.0	1.35956
$Q_{2,2}$	0.0	0.0	0.0	1.35956
Trade by typical firm				
$Q_{\bullet sd,1}$ for all s, d	0.0	1.0	0.0	0.0
$Q_{\bullet sd,2}$ for all s, d	0.0	0.0	0.0	0.0
Cons. by com, src, and country				
$Q_{sd,1}$ for all s, d	0.0	−0.35474	0.0	1.35956
$Q_{sd,2}$ for all s, d	0.0	0.0	0.0	1.35956
Welfare by country				
welfare (1)	0.0	−0.17753	0.0	1.35956
welfare (2)	0.0	−0.17753	0.49876	1.35956

commodity an arbitrary value to the H in one country: this merely affects the scaling of the H's for the other countries. For any commodity, rescaling the H's doesn't affect the fit of the model to observable quantities and values. Similarly, for each commodity, it is legitimate to assign arbitrary values to the diagonal F's, $F_{dd,c}$: this merely affects the scaling of the $F_{sd,c}$ for $s \neq d$.

As distinct from calibration, in simulation proportionate movements in the H's and F's matter. For example, column 2 of Table 6.2 shows that a 1% increase in the H's and F's for commodity 1 reduces welfare in both countries. The percentage change in the welfare of country d arising from a shock is measured in MelitzGE by a weighted average of the percentage changes in d's consumption of each composite commodity ($Q_{d,c}$, for all c) with the weights being expenditure shares. We will return to the welfare effects of changes in H's and F's later in this section where we explain the quantitative result in column 2, a welfare reduction in each country of 0.17753%.

The simulation in the third column of Table 6.2 illustrates another calibration idea: that the initial consumption quantities of composite commodities ($Q_{d,c}$ for all d and c) are arbitrary. The simulation shows that scaling country 2's preference coefficients for commodity 1 from all sources ($\delta_{s2,1}$ for all s) increases country 2's consumption of composite commodity 1 ($Q_{2,1}$) with a corresponding reduction in its price ($P_{2,1}$) and no change in the potentially observable value of expenditure by country 2 on commodity 1 ($P_{2,1}Q_{2,1}$).[3] Again, calibration should not be confused with simulation. In simulation, a uniform percentage increase in $\delta_{s2,1}$ over all s represents an improved ability in country 2 to turn units of commodity 1 from different sources into units of composite commodity 1, and is thus welfare enhancing.

The final simulation in Table 6.2 shows the effects of a 1% increase in employment in both countries. People imbued with constant-return-to-scale ideas would expect this simulation to generate a 1% increase in all real variables with zero effect on prices. However, as can be seen from column 4, consumption of commodities identified by source ($Q_{sd,c}$ for all s, d and c), consumption of composite commodities ($Q_{d,c}$ for all d and c) and welfare in both countries increase by 1.35956%, and the price of composite commodities falls by 0.35474%. With 1% more resources (labor) in both countries, MelitzGE shows a 1% increase in the number of firms for each commodity ($N_{d,c}$) and the number of firms on each trade link ($N_{sd,c}$). There is no change in the sales of typical firms on links ($Q_{\bullet sd,c}$). Consequently the count (number of widgets) for each commodity on each link increases by 1%. But more firms means more varieties, generating a "love-of-variety" benefit. In the Melitz world, even though country d's count for commodity c from country s increases by 1%, the resulting effective consumption

---

[3]We simulated the effects of a 0.73588% increase in the $\delta_{s2,1}$'s. We chose this number in anticipation (confirmed in the simulation) that with σ equal to 3.8, $Q_{2,1}$ would increase by 1%. This can be worked out from (T2.2) and (T2.3): scaling the $\delta_{s2,1}$'s by $1.01^{\wedge}((\sigma - 1)/\sigma)$ multiplies $P_{2,1}$ by the factor 1/1.01, multiplies $Q_{2,1}$ by the factor of 1.01 and changes none of the other Melitz variables in Table 2.2.

in d of c from s ($Q_{sd,c}$) increases by 1.35956% [=100 $*$ {1.01^(σ/(σ − 1)) − 1} = 100 $*$ {1.01^(3.8/2.8) − 1}, see (T2.4)] generating a similar percentage increase in d's consumption of composite c. With more varieties, any given demand for a composite commodity can be satisfied at lower cost. Thus, $P_{d,c}$ falls (by 0.35474%) for all d and c.

Interpreting Results: Envelope Theorems and an Optimizing Agent

In Chap. 3 we demonstrated an equivalence between a Melitz general equilibrium model and a cost-minimizing problem and suggested that this may be useful in result interpretation. The equivalence implies that envelope theorems and intuition based on single-agent behaviour may be applicable. We use simulation 2 in Table 6.2 to illustrate both these ideas.

The envelope theorem gives the expectation that a 1% increase in the commodity-1 H's and F's (as in simulation 2) would reduce welfare by an amount equivalent to that from a loss of labor in each country of 1% of its total fixed-cost labor for commodity 1. Referring to the data items for MelitzGE in Table 6.1, we see that total fixed-cost labor for commodity 1 in each country is 0.24457 units. The loss of 1% of this fixed-cost labor represents a loss in total labor in each country of 0.131574% (=100 $*$ 0.0024457/1.85880). In simulation 4 in Table 6.2, we found that a 1% increase in labor in both countries induces, through a variety effect, an increase in welfare of more than 1%, 1.35956%. Thus we would expect the welfare effect for each country in simulation 2 of Table 6.2 to be approximately −0.17888% (=−0.131574 $*$ 1.35956). This is close to the results shown for simulation 2 in the last two rows of Table 6.2.

Next, we think about the results in column 2 of Table 6.2 from the point of view of a single optimizing agent. With increases in fixed costs, we would expect a planner in charge of worldwide commodity-1 production to reduce the number of commodity-1 firms and increase output per firm. This is what we see in column 2 of Table 6.2. The number of commodity-1 firms in each country [$N_{d,1}$] and the number operating on each trade link [$N_{sd,1}$] fall by 0.99010%. At the same time, the typical commodity-1 firm on each trade link increases its sales on the link [$Q_{\bullet sd,1}$] by 1%. As with any increase in costs we would expect our planner to increase prices and for consumers to reduce demand. Again, this is what we see in column 2. The price to consumers per unit of composite commodity 1 [$P_{d,1}$] rises by 0.35600% and demand [$Q_{d,1}$] falls by 0.35474%.

6.3   The Effects of a Tariff Increase in the MelitzGE Model

In this and Sects. 6.4 and 6.5, we analyse some MelitzGE results for the effects of increases in tariffs. We continue to use the 2-country, 2-commodity version of MelitzGE, with the same exogenous variables as in Sect. 6.2: the average wage rate across countries, which acts as the numeraire; aggregate employment in each country; consumer preferences over sources of commodity c; tariff rates; setup inputs for firms in each country; setup inputs for trade on links; and the Cobb-Douglas preference coefficients.

Table 6.3 reports results for three experiments. In the first, country 2 increases its tariffs on all imports from an initial level of zero to 10%, that is $T_{12,c}$ increases from 1 to 1.10 for all c. Experiments 2 and 3 give results for the effects of the imposition by country 2 of tariff rates of 23 and 65%. In this section we concentrate on the first experiment. In Sects. 6.4 and 6.5 we look at all three experiments and the relationships between them.

The imposition of a 10% tariff by country 2 causes a sharp contraction in trade. The volume of country 1's exports declines by 20.648% and the volume of country 1's imports declines by 25.046%. Despite the differences in volume movements between exports and imports, country 1's trade remains balanced: country 1 suffers a decline in its terms of trade with the price of its imports rising by 6.011% and the price of its exports rising by 0.135%. The terms-of-trade decline for country 1 explains why its consumption declines relative to GDP (-1.321% relative to -0.017%) and why its wage rate declines relative to the worldwide average wage rate (-2.502%). The import/export results for country 2 are the complement of those for country 1. GDP in country 2 declines, but unlike country 1, country 2's consumption rises relative to GDP (1.044% compared with -0.230%) reflecting terms-of-trade improvement. At least at a qualitative level, none of these results owes anything to the Melitz aspects of MelitzGE. They will all be familiar to CGE modelers who work in the Armington tradition.

By contrast, the next two blocks of results in the first panel of Table 6.3 deliver Melitz insights. With trade now being a less attractive means for creating variety, both countries increase the number of varieties of commodity c that they provide to the domestic market: $N_{11,c}$ increases by 6.307% and $N_{22,c}$ increases by 7.681%. The productivity in country 1 of the typical firm servicing the domestic link and its sales on that link both decline by 1.321%. For country 2 the corresponding number is a decline of 1.596%.

On export markets, variety (number of firms) declines. $N_{21,c}$ declines by 22.529% and $N_{12,c}$ declines by 18.501%. Export volumes shipped by typical firms increase. The number of units of commodity c sent by the typical firm on the 2-to-1 link increases by 5.706% and the number of units sent by the typical firm on the

Table 6.3 MelitzGE results for the effects of tariffs imposed by country 2 (percentage changes)

Shocked exogenous variables, %Δ in:	$t_{12,c} = 10$ for all c		$t_{12,c} = 23$ for all c		$t_{12,c} = 65$ for all c	
Endogenous variables	Country d = 1	Country d = 2	Country d = 1	Country d = 2	Country d = 1	Country d = 2
Real GDP[a]	−0.017	−0.230	−0.060	−0.962	−0.220	−3.856
Real consumption[a]	−1.321	1.044	−2.550	1.399	−4.546	−0.036
Volume of exports[a]	−20.648	−25.046	−40.529	−47.417	−73.634	−80.279
Volume of imports[a]	−25.046	−20.648	−47.417	−40.529	−80.279	−73.634
Price of exports[a]	0.135	6.011	0.220	13.350	−0.630	32.851
Price of imports[a]	6.011	0.135	13.350	0.220	32.851	−0.630
Wage rate relative to average world rate[a]	−2.502	2.567	−5.389	5.696	−12.650	14.482
$N_{1d,c}$ for all c, number of c-firms on 1d link	6.307	−18.501	12.615	−37.003	23.866	−70.006
$N_{2d,c}$ for all c, number of c-firms on 2d link	−22.529	7.681	−43.610	14.867	−77.114	26.290
$Q_{\bullet 1d,c}$ for all c, typical c-firm flow on 1d link	−1.321	4.548	−2.550	10.567	−4.546	29.923
$Q_{\bullet 2d,c}$ for all c, typical c-firm flow on 2d link	5.706	−1.596	13.262	−2.968	37.793	−4.948
$N_{d,c}$ for all c, c-firms set up in d	0.000	0.000	0.000	0.000	0.000	0.000
Productivity of typical c-firm on sd link						
$\Phi_{\bullet 1d,c}$ for all c, on 1d link	−1.321	4.548	−2.550	10.567	−4.546	29.923
$\Phi_{\bullet 2d,c}$ for all c, on 2d link	5.706	−1.596	13.262	−2.968	37.793	−4.948
Welfare decomposition						
Welfare (d)	−1.321	1.044	−2.550	1.399	−4.546	−0.036
Made up of contributions from changes in:						
Employment	0.000	0.000	0.000	0.000	0.000	0.000
Tax-carrying flows	0.000	−0.246	0.000	−1.018	0.000	−4.016
Terms of trade	−1.304	1.276	−2.490	2.378	−4.333	3.932
Production technology or productivity	−2.651	−3.287	−5.681	−6.925	−12.556	−14.596
Conversion technology or preferences	2.635	3.301	5.622	6.965	12.342	14.644

[a]All of these variables are calculated using converged results from the Armington auxiliary model discussed in Chap. 5. For example, the percentage change in real consumption for country d, which is the same as the percentage change in d's welfare, is calculated as an expenditure weighted average of percentage movements in d's consumption of composite commodities, QCA(d, c) over all c, see (5.14). This is the same as the Melitz measure of the percentage change in welfare, see (5.13). The percentage change in the volume of imports for country d is a cif value-weighted average of the percentage changes in QA(s, d, c) over all c and $s \neq d$. The percentage change in the price indexes for exports and imports are calculated from percentage changes in values deflated by percentage changes in volumes

1-to-2 link increases by 4.548%. The productivity levels of typical firms on these export links also increase by 5.706 and 4.548%.

These results are standard for Melitz. They imply that trade barriers reduce the average size and productivity of firms servicing their own domestic markets; increase the number of domestic varieties in each country's domestic market; increase the average size and productivity of firms servicing international markets; and reduce the number of varieties that are traded internationally.

As mentioned earlier, country 2's tariffs cause trade to contract: country 1's exports decline by 20.648% and country 2's by 25.046%. The note at the end of Table 6.3 explains that these are Armington measures. For these measures, all shipments (domestic and export) of commodity c from country d are treated as though they are produced by firms with the same productivity level, $\Phi A(d, c)$. Alternatively, trade flows can be measured in count terms. In these terms, country 1's exports $(N_{12,c} * Q_{\bullet 12,c})$ decline by 14.8% [=100 * ((1 − 0.18501) * (1 + 0.04548) − 1)] and country 2's exports $(N_{21,c} * Q_{\bullet 21,c})$ decline by 18.1% [=100 * ((1 − 0.22529) * (1 + 0.05706) − 1)]. The count measures of the percentage contractions in trade volumes are less than those implied by the converged results from the Armington auxiliary model reported in Table 6.3. With the average productivity of trading firms increasing relative of non-trading firms, $\phi_{\bullet sd,c} > \phi a(s, c)$ for $d \neq s$. Via (5.21), this implies that the percentage reduction in the count volume on the sd link is less than that in the Armington volume. We focus mainly on Armington measures. This facilitates our explanation in Sect. 6.4 of Melitz welfare results using a decomposition formula based on the Armington auxiliary model. We return to the problem of volume measures in Chap. 7 in which we distinguish between count units and quality-adjusted (or effective) units.

A rather curious result in Table 6.3 is that the number of c-firms in country d $(N_{d, c})$ is unaffected by country 2's tariffs. This result is derived in Appendix 6.2 using Table 2.2.

6.4   Decomposing MelitzGE Welfare Results via an Armington Model

Theory

In Chap. 5 we demonstrated that Melitz results are equivalent to Armington results with extra shocks to productivity and preferences. Using this idea, we now set out a decomposition equation for interpreting the welfare effects of a tariff change in MelitzGE and apply it to the results in Table 6.3 (see bottom blocks).

As in Chap. 5, we define the percentage change in welfare in country d in MelitzGE as a weighted average of the percentage changes in d's consumption of composite commodities:

$$\text{welfare}(d) = \sum_c Z(d, c) * q_{d,c} \quad \text{for all } d, \tag{6.2}$$

where

welfare(d) is the percentage change in d's welfare;
$q_{d,c}$ is the percentage change in d's consumption of composite commodity c (that is the percentage change in $Q_{d,c}$); and
Z(d, c) is the share of d's consumption expenditure devote to c, that is

$$Z(d, c) = \left(\frac{P_{d,c} Q_{d,c}}{\sum_j P_{d,j} Q_{d,j}} \right) \quad \text{for all } c \text{ and } d. \tag{6.3}$$

Recognizing that MelitzGE results for welfare can be generated by the Armington auxiliary model (Table 5.1) with movements in productivity $[\Phi A(s, c)]$ and preferences $[\delta A(s, d, c)]$ given by (5.6) and (5.7), we can disaggregate MelitzGE results for welfare(d) into five Armington components. These are shown for the two country case[4] in Box 6.2 as the contributions to welfare of changes in: employment; tax-carrying flows; the terms of trade; production technology; and conversion technology or preferences. The algebra underlying Box 6.2 is given in Appendix 6.3. Here, we provide an intuitive explanation of the five components.

To start with, we interpret the decomposition equation as referring to small changes in variables. In this case we don't have to worry about movements in the levels variables, PA(s, d, c), QA(s, d, c) etc. We can imagine that these levels are fixed at their starting values. We will consider large changes later in this section.

The LHS of the decomposition equation is 100 times the change in welfare. The first term on the RHS is 100 times the contribution to the change in welfare of the change in employment. With labor in the Armington model being paid according to the value of its marginal product, an $x\%$ increase in employment in country d [lx(d) = x] generates an expansion in the quantity of GDP (holding prices at their initial levels) of the wage rate [W(d)] times the increase in employment [0.01 * LX(d) * lx(d)]. With prices held constant, this is also the contribution of the expansion in employment to welfare because, in our simplified model, the percentage change in the quantity of GDP is the same as that in the quantity of consumption which by definition is the same as the percentage change in welfare.

---

[4]The equation in Box 6.2 is easily generalized to the r-country case.

Box 6.2. Armington Decomposition of Melitz Welfare

$$\left(\sum_c \sum_s PA(s,d,c) * QA(s,d,c) \right) * \text{welfare}(d)$$

$$= WA(d) * LX(d) * lx(d)$$

[changes in employment]

$$+ \sum_c \sum_s \frac{PA(s,d,c) * QA(s,d,c)}{T_{sd,c}} * (T_{sd,c} - 1) * qa(s,d,c)$$

[changes in tax-carrying flows]

$$+ \left\{ \begin{array}{l} \sum_c \frac{PA(d,F,c) * QA(d,F,c)}{T_{dF,c}} * (pa(d,F,c) - t_{dF,c}) \\ - \sum_c \frac{PA(F,d,c) * QA(F,d,c)}{T_{Fd,c}} * (pa(F,d,c) - t_{Fd,c}) \end{array} \right\}$$

[changes in the terms of trade]

$$+ \sum_c \sum_j \frac{PA(d,j,c) * QA(d,j,c)}{T_{dj,c}} * \phi a(d,c)$$

[changes in production technology or productivity]

$$+ \left(\frac{\sigma}{\sigma - 1} \right) * \sum_c \sum_s PA(s,d,c) * QA(s,d,c) * \widehat{\delta}a(s,d,c)$$

$$\left[\begin{array}{l} \text{changes in preferencesor the efficiency with which commodity c from different sources} \\ \text{can be converted into composite units of c for consumption in d} \end{array} \right]$$

Notation: The decomposition refers to welfare for country d. Country F (foreign) is the other country. Uppercase symbols are defined in Table 5.1. Lowercase symbols are percentage changes in the variables denoted by the corresponding uppercase symbols, for example, pa(F, d, c) is the percentage change in PA(F, d, c). An exception is $\widehat{\delta}a(s,d,c)$. This is the percentage change in $\delta a(s,d,c)$.

The second term on the RHS of the decomposition equation is the contribution to welfare in country d of changes in tax-carrying flows. This is the general equilibrium version of the consumer and producer surplus rectangles and triangles in familiar partial equilibrium demand and supply diagrams (e.g. Fig. 6.2). Country d gains welfare if there is an expansion in its absorption of commodity c from

Tariff-inclusive price

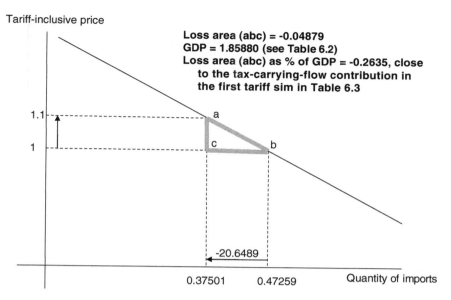

Fig. 6.2 Country 2's demand for imports: back-of-the-envelope calculation of the welfare contribution of changes in tax-carrying flows in the first simulation in Table 6.3

source s [that is, qa(s, d, c) > 0] and this flow is taxed by country d. The gain in welfare arises because d's users of c from s (commodity s, c) value an extra unit at the *tax-inclusive* price [PA(s, d, c)] but it costs country d only the *tax-exclusive* price to provide an extra unit of s, c. The welfare gain per unit of extra s, c is the gap between the tax-inclusive and tax-exclusive prices which, as reflected in the second term of the decomposition formula, is PA(s, d, c) $* (T_{sd,c} - 1)/T_{sd,c}$.

The third term is the terms-of-trade effect. A terms-of-trade improvement, that is an increase in fob export prices relative to cif import prices, enables country d to convert any given volume of exports into an increased volume of welfare-enhancing imports. The percentage movement in d's fob export price for commodity c is given by pa(d, F, c)–$t_{dF,c}$. In measuring d's welfare this percentage movement is weighted by the ratio of the fob value of the d, F, c flow to the value of d's total consumption. Similarly, the percentage movement in d's cif import price for commodity c is given by pa(F, d, c)–$t_{Fd,c}$. In measuring d's welfare this is weighted by the ratio of the cif value of the F, d, c flow to the value of d's total consumption.

The fourth term is the contribution to d's welfare of changes in production technology. Country d's welfare is improved if it can produce more output per unit of labor input. If d's productivity in the production of commodity c improves by $x\%$ [$\phi a(d, c) = x$], then $x\%$ of the labor devoted to commodity c can be released to other productive uses without affecting d's production of c. From a welfare point of view, this is equivalent to an increase in employment. Quantitatively, the welfare effect is the value of $x\%$ of the labor devoted to c. With labor being the only input, this is $x\%$ of the tax-exclusive value of the output of c in country d.

The fifth term in the decomposition equation is the contribution to d's welfare of changes in conversion technology or preferences [changes in the $\delta A(s, d, c)$s]. This term is less familiar to CGE modelers than the previous terms. It appears in the welfare decomposition equation because increases in the $\delta A(s, d, c)$s improve the ability of country d to convert units of commodity c from different sources into welfare-carrying units of composite-commodity c. This can be understood by recalling that (T5.2) and (T5.3) in Table 5.1 imply that composite units of commodity c are "produced" for households in country d by the CES technology:

$$QCA(d, c) = \left[\sum_s \delta A(s, d, c) QA(s, d, c)^{(\sigma-1)/\sigma} \right]^{\sigma/(\sigma-1)}. \qquad (6.4)$$

This means that increases in $\delta A(s, d, c)$ allow more composite commodity, $QCA(d, c)$, to be generated for any given levels of underlying Armington commodities, $QA(s, d, c)$, or equivalently, that less units of the underlying commodities are required to generate any given level of the composite commodity. Via the δA's, the Armington auxiliary model captures love-of-variety effects generated in the Melitz model, effects which change the ability of any given volume of Armington commodities to satisfy consumer requirements.

To derive the fifth term, a good starting point is (T5.2). In percentage-change form (T5.2) can be written as[5]

---

[5]Recall that lowercase symbols denote percentage changes in corresponding upper case variables. We make an exception for δA since δ is already a lowercase symbol. We denote the percentage change in δA by $\widehat{\delta}a$.

$$\text{pca}(d, c) = \frac{1}{1 - \sigma} \sum_s \left(\frac{\delta A(s, d, c)^\sigma * PA(s, d, c)^{1-\sigma}}{PCA(d, c)^{1-\sigma}} \right) * \left(\sigma * \widehat{\delta a}(s, d, c) + (1 - \sigma) * \text{pa}(s, d, c) \right).$$

(6.5)

Thus, a 1% increase in $\delta A(s, d, c)$ has an *impact* percentage effect on the cost of creating a unit of composite c in country d given by

$$\text{pca}(d, c)|_{\widehat{\delta a}(s,d,c)=1} = -\left(\frac{\sigma}{\sigma - 1} \right) * \left(\frac{\delta A(s, d, c)^\sigma * PA(s, d, c)^{1-\sigma}}{PCA(d, c)^{1-\sigma}} \right)$$

(6.6)

Via (T5.3) this can be written as

$$\text{pca}(d, c)|_{\widehat{\delta a}(s,d,c)=1} = -\left(\frac{\sigma}{\sigma - 1} \right) * \left(\frac{PA(s, d, c) * QA(s, d, c)}{PCA(d, c) * QCA(d, c)} \right)$$

(6.7)

which is negative (recall that $\sigma > 1$). The significance of a reduction in the cost of creating units of composite c for country d's welfare depends on the share of c in d's total consumption. Combining this idea with (6.7) leads to the fifth term in the decomposition equation.

As mentioned earlier, with the levels variables fixed at their initial values, our decomposition equation accurately produces the change in welfare caused by small shocks to the exogenous variables in MelitzGE. With large shocks, we need to allow for changes in the levels variables. In GEMPACK computations (see Box 6.1) this is done by applying the shocks to the exogenous variables in n steps. In the first step we apply 1/n-th of the required changes in the exogenous variables. If n is large we can work out accurately the change in welfare in the first step and the five contributions identified on the RHS of the decomposition equation. Then we update the levels variables according to the changes from the first step. In the second step we again apply 1/n-th of the required changes in the exogenous variables. We work out the welfare effects in this second step and the five contributions using the decomposition equation with updated levels variables. Proceeding in this way, we can use the decomposition equation to calculate accurately the welfare effect of the total shocks to the exogenous variables. The contribution of each of the five components is the sum of its contribution across the n steps.[6]

---

[6]Adding up contributions from successive steps is the idea underlying GEMPACK decomposition calculations, see Harrison et al. (2000).

Results

In the bottom blocks in Table 6.3 we use the equation from Box 6.2 to decompose the welfare effects of the increases in country 2's tariffs.

The most striking aspect of the welfare decomposition results is the offsetting nature of the production-technology and conversion-technology contributions (components 4 and 5). For both countries in the three tariff experiments, the production-technology contribution is negative, and is closely offset by a positive conversion-technology contribution. The production- and conversion-technology contributions are what Melitz adds to an Armington welfare calculation. Because these contributions offset, it appears that the Armington calculation of the welfare effects of a tariff change is not misleading, even in a world in which Melitz specifications are valid.

We suspect that this striking result is another implication of the envelope theorem. As demonstrated in Chap. 3, with tariffs at zero, a Melitz model generates an optimal trade-off in the widgets market between keeping costs down through long-production runs and meeting consumer demand for variety. The envelope theorem suggests that marginal shifts in this trade-off (e.g. shorter production runs but more varieties) away from the optimum will have little effect on welfare. Thus, although the imposition of tariffs causes the cost/variety trade-off in each country to change, this change does not have a significant effect on welfare. In both countries, restriction of trade through the imposition of a tariff by country 2 causes reduced productivity (higher costs) offset by increased variety. In both countries, a relatively large number of small, domestic-market-only, low-productivity firms replace imports from a relatively small number of high-productivity foreign firms. For example, by combining data in Table 6.1 with results for country 1 in the 10% experiment, we can see that the changes in N_{11c} and N_{21c} are 0.04068 (=0.64505 * 0.06307) and −0.00929 (=0.04123 * −0.22529), implying an increase of 4.6% [=100 * (0.04068 − 0.00929)/(0.64505 + 0.04123)] in the number of varieties available to households in country 1. At the same time, the emergence of low-productivity firms lowers average productivity in country 1.

The cancelling out of the two technology effects leaves welfare in our MelitzGE tariff simulations determined by factors that have been familiar to trade economists since the 1950s or earlier[7]: the terms-of-trade effect and the efficiency or tax-carrying-flows effect.

For country 2, the welfare outcome of an increase in tariffs from zero to 10% is dominated by the terms-of-trade effect: a 1.276 contribution to a total welfare effect of 1.044%. By imposing a 10% tariff, country 2 improves its terms of trade by 5.9% (6.011% increase in the price of its exports compared with 0.135% increase in the

---

[7]See for example Corden (1957) and Johnson (1960).

price of its imports). With exports (and imports) being about 22.4% of GDP,[8] a 5.9% improvement in the terms of trade is equivalent to a GDP gain of 1.32%, close to the terms-of-trade welfare contribution shown for country 2 in the first tariff simulation. The tax-carrying-flow effect or the familiar welfare triangle from text-book partial equilibrium diagrams provides a small offset, −0.246%, to country 2's terms-of-trade gain. Again, the magnitude of this effect is easily understood via a simple calculation, see Fig. 6.2 and the data in Table 6.1.

Consistent with the theory of the optimal tariff,[9] as country 2 increases its tariffs, the negative welfare contribution from tax-carrying flows increases much more rapidly than the positive welfare contribution from the terms of trade. By the time country 2's tariffs have reached 65% (third simulation in Table 6.3), the tax-carrying-flow effect has more than cancelled out the terms-of-trade effect. This, together with a small positive contribution from the combined technology components leaves the net welfare effect for country 2 slightly negative (−0.036%). By conducting a series of simulations in which we varied the tariff imposed by country 2, we found that the optimal tariff for country 2 in the absence of retaliation by country 1 is 23% (second simulation in Table 6.3).

For country 1, the terms-of-trade movement accounts for almost the entire welfare effect in all three simulations: there are no employment effects because employment is held constant and there are no tax-carrying-flow effects because country 1 has no taxes. The terms-of-trade effects for country 1 are the opposite of those for country 2.

6.5 Is a Melitz Model Equivalent to an Armington Model with a Higher Substitution Elasticity?

That the welfare results computed in the previous section depend almost entirely on Armington mechanisms (terms-of-trade and efficiency effects) suggested to us that results from a Melitz model might be more generally equivalent to those from an Armington model.

Initially we tested this idea by comparing tariff results from Melitz and Armington models built with identical databases and with identical values for the substitution parameter σ, $\sigma = 3.8$. Table 6.4 gives the results for this exercise. The Melitz results in Table 6.4 are the same as those in Table 6.3: they refer to the effects of unilateral tariff increases by country 2 computed with the 2-country, 2-commodity version of MelitzGE. The Armington results were computed by the

---

[8]With the tariffs at zero, exports are 25.42% of country 2's GDP. With the imposition by country 2 of 10% tariffs, the export share for country 2 falls. In results not shown here we found that the export share falls to 19.32%. Thus 22.37% is the halfway share as tariff rates move from 0 to 10.
[9]See for example, Dixon and Rimmer (2010).

Table 6.4 Percentage effects of tariffs imposed by country 2: Melitz and Armington results with σ = 3.8 in both models

Shocked exogenous variables	Melitz with σ = 3.8 $t_{12,c} = 10$, all c		Armington with σ = 3.8 $t_{12,c} = 10$, all c		Melitz with σ = 3.8 $t_{12,c} = 23$, all c		Armington with σ = 3.8 $t_{12,c} = 23$, all c		Melitz with σ = 3.8 $t_{12,c} = 65$ for all c		Armington with σ = 3.8 $t_{12,c} = 65$ for all c	
Endogenous variables	Country d = 1	Country d = 2	Country d = 1	Country d = 2	Country d = 1	Country d = 2	Country d = 1	Country d = 2	Country d = 1	Country d = 2	Country d = 1	Country d = 2
Volume of exports	−20.648	−25.046	−10.583	−15.165	−40.529	−47.417	−22.106	−30.580	−73.634	−80.279	−47.365	−60.325
Volume of imports	−25.046	−20.648	−15.165	−10.583	−47.417	−40.529	−30.580	−22.106	−80.279	−73.634	−60.325	−47.365
Welfare(d)	−1.321	1.044	−1.258	1.102	−2.550	1.399	−2.562	1.876	−4.546	−0.036	−5.206	1.958
Made up of contributions from changes in:												
Employment	0.000	0.000	0.000	0.000	0.000	0.000	0.000	0.000	0.000	0.000	0.000	0.000
Tax-carrying flows	0.000	−0.246	0.000	−0.126	0.000	−1.018	0.000	−0.556	0.000	−4.016	0.000	−2.671
Terms of trade	−1.304	1.276	−1.258	1.227	−2.490	2.378	−2.562	2.432	−4.333	3.932	−5.206	4.629
Production technology, productivity	−2.651	−3.287	0.0	0.0	−5.681	−6.925	0.0	0.0	−12.556	−14.596	0.0	0.0
Conversion technology, preferences	2.635	3.301	0.0	0.0	5.622	6.965	0.0	0.0	12.342	14.644	0.0	0.0

model and closure set out in Table 5.1. Only the tariffs for country 2 were shocked: δA and ΦA were left unchanged.

For the 10% tariff shock, the welfare effects in Table 6.4 given by the Melitz and Armington models are quite similar (−1.321 and −1.258% for country 1 and 1.044 and 1.102 for country 2). The welfare effects for country 1 generated by the two models remain close as the tariff shock is increased (−2.550 and −2.562% for the 23% tariff shock, and −4.546 and −5.206 for the 65% tariff shock). However, welfare effects for country 2 generated by the two models separate as the tariff shock increases. With the tariff shock at 65%, Melitz shows a welfare reduction of 0.036% for country 2 whereas Armington shows a welfare gain of 1.958%.

By looking at the welfare contributions, we see that Melitz and Armington produce similar terms-of-trade effects. For example, with the tariff shock at 23%, the Melitz terms-of-trade contributions to welfare in the two countries are −2.490 and 2.378%, similar to the Armington contributions of −2.562 and 2.432%. That Melitz and Armington give similar terms-of-trade contributions explains why Melitz and Armington give similar welfare results for country 1: for Melitz, the total welfare effect for country 1 is approximately the terms-of-trade contribution and for Armington it is exactly the terms-of-trade contribution.

Given the similarity in the Melitz and Armington terms-of-trade contributions and the approximate cancelling out in Melitz of the productivity and preference contributions, we see that the differences between the Melitz and Armington welfare results for country 2 must be caused mainly by differences in the tax-carrying-flow contributions. For the 23% tariff experiment, differences in the tax-carrying-flow contributions (−1.018 and −0.556) account for 0.462 percentage points of the total difference in the welfare results of 0.477 percentage points (=1.876 − 1.399). For the 65% tariff experiment, differences in the tax-carrying-flow contributions (−4.016 and −2.671) account for 1.345 percentage points of the total difference in the welfare results of 1.994 percentage points (=1.9958 + 0.036).

Why do the Melitz and Armington tax-carrying-flow contributions for country 2 in Table 6.4 differ? In particular, why are the Melitz contributions in absolute terms so much larger than the Armington contributions? The answer can be seen in Fig. 6.2 and the import results for country 2 in Table 6.4. Figure 6.2 shows for the imposition of a given tariff that the welfare contribution from tax-carrying flows depends on the extent to which imports are inhibited. Table 6.4 shows in each experiment that country 2's imports fall much more sharply for Melitz than for Armington (20.648% compared with 10.583% for the 10% tariff experiment, 40.529% compared with 22.106% for the 23% tariff experiment, and 73.634% compared with 47.365% for the 65% tariff experiment).

This suggests that by adopting a higher substitution elasticity in the Armington model, and thereby making trade flows in Armington more sensitive to tariff increases, we might be able to bring the Armington results for welfare into line with the Melitz results. Table 6.5 compares Armington results with the *inter-country* substitution elasticity set at 7.0 with Melitz results with the *inter-variety* substitution elasticity set at 3.8. These two models generate similar trade flow results and therefore similar tax-carrying-flow contributions to country 2's welfare (−0.246

Table 6.5 Percentage effects of tariffs imposed by country 2: Melitz results with $\sigma = 3.8$ compared with Armington results with $\sigma = 7.0$

	Melitz with $\sigma = 3.8$		Armington with $\sigma = 7.0$		Melitz with $\sigma = 3.8$		Armington with $\sigma = 7.0$		Melitz with $\sigma = 3.8$		Armington with $\sigma = 7.0$	
Shocked exogenous variables	$t_{12,c} = 10$, all c		$t_{12,c} = 10$, all c		$t_{12,c} = 23$, all c		$t_{12,c} = 23$, all c		$t_{12,c} = 65$ for all c		$t_{12,c} = 65$ for all c	
Endogenous variables	Country d = 1	Country d = 2	Country d = 1	Country d = 2	Country d = 1	Country d = 2	Country d = 1	Country d = 2	Country d = 1	Country d = 2	Country d = 1	Country d = 2
Volume of exports	−20.648	−25.046	−10.583	−15.165	−40.529	−47.417	−22.106	−30.580	−73.634	−80.279	−47.365	−60.325
Volume of imports	−25.046	−20.648	−15.165	−10.583	−47.417	−40.529	−30.580	−22.106	−80.279	−73.634	−60.325	−47.365
Welfare(d)	−1.321	1.044	−1.258	1.102	−2.550	1.399	−2.562	1.876	−4.546	−0.036	−5.206	1.958
Made up of contributions from changes in:												
Employment	0.000	0.000	0.000	0.000	0.000	0.000	0.000	0.000	0.000	0.000	0.000	0.000
Tax-carrying flows	0.000	−0.246	0.000	−0.126	0.000	−1.018	0.000	−0.556	0.000	−4.016	0.000	−2.671
Terms of trade	−1.304	1.276	−1.258	1.227	−2.490	2.378	−2.562	2.432	−4.333	3.932	−5.206	4.629
Production technology, productivity	−2.651	−3.287	0.0	0.0	−5.681	−6.925	0.0	0.0	−12.556	−14.596	0.0	0.0
Conversion technology, preferences	2.635	3.301	0.0	0.0	5.622	6.965	0.0	0.0	12.342	14.644	0.0	0.0

compared with −0.244, −1.018 compared with −0.997, and −4.016 compared with −3.784). The adoption of a higher substitution elasticity for Armington does not significantly affect the Armington terms-of-trade contributions. These contributions depend mainly on the size of the tariff shock, not the sensitivity of trade flows to the shock. Thus, by bringing the Armington trade-flow results into line with the Melitz trade-flow results, we substantially close the gaps between the Melitz welfare results and the Armington welfare results. For example, for the 65% tariff experiment in Table 6.5, the difference between the Melitz and Armington welfare results for country 2 is 0.380 percentage points (=0.416 − 0.036), down from 1.994 percentage points in Table 6.4 (=1.958 + 0.036).

It is tempting to interpret the results in Table 6.4 as meaning that Armington leads to under estimates of the restrictiveness of tariffs relative to Melitz. However, we don't think that such an interpretation is legitimate. To us, Table 6.4 demonstrates that $\sigma = 3.8$ in a Melitz model doesn't mean the same thing as $\sigma = 3.8$ in an Armington model. A Melitz model recognizes substitution possibilities between varieties produced within a country. These substitution possibilities are in addition to the inter-country possibilities recognized by Armington. Consequently, it seems reasonable to expect a Melitz model with a relatively low inter-variety substitution elasticity (e.g. 3.8) to exhibit comparable trade-flow sensitivity to tariff shocks as an Armington model with a relatively high inter-country substitution elasticity (e.g. 7.0).

In comparing unobservable implications (e.g. welfare effects) from competing models we should parameterize the models so that they give the same results for observable outcomes. Potentially, it is possible to observe the response of trade flows to tariff changes. Let's assume for the sake of argument that MelitzGE with $\sigma = 3.8$ correctly produces these responses. Table 6.5 demonstrates in the simplified framework of MelitzGE that we can build an Armington model on the same database[10] as that of the Melitz model which also correctly produces the trade flow responses. And when we do this, the Armington model shows similar welfare results as the Melitz model.

Table 6.5 gives us a tentative yes answer to the question posed in the heading to this section. However, we should emphasize that this answer is tentative. The version of MelitzGE that we have implemented is effectively a 1-sector model (all the sectors are identical in terms of costs and demands). While it is possible to adjust one instrument, the inter-country substitution elasticity, in a 2-country, 1-sector Armington model to reconcile the model's results with those from a Melitz model, Balistreri et al. (2010, p. 87) doubt that this can be generalized. They say

One might think that the Armington elasticity of substitution, σ_A, can be set to match the trade reactions in the Melitz model ... but this is not the case. If we adjust σ_A to match some of the Melitz model trade flows the errors on the other flows in the bilateral matrix become larger.

---

[10]By database we mean values of trade flows, outputs, wage rates and employment.

The quantitative and policy significance of Balistreri et al.'s objection should be treated as open issues.

6.6 Concluding Remarks

In this chapter we have described MelitzGE and implemented it with fictitious data. The aim was to deepen understanding of Melitz theory and provide a platform for Chap. 7 in which we convert a large, policy-oriented CGE model from Armington to Melitz.

In solving MelitzGE, we used GEMPACK software which works with linear equations expressed in percentage changes of variables. Previous Melitz computations have been carried out with GAMS software relying on non-linear levels representations of equations. The GEMPACK approach proved highly efficient and simplified the solution of Melitz models.[11] Using GEMPACK we are able to avoid Balistreri and Rutherford's iterative decomposition approach which generates Melitz solutions by iterating between Melitz and Armington models. Nevertheless, the idea underlying Balistreri and Rutherford's decomposition approach is highly suggestive. Using their idea we were able to decompose Melitz results for the welfare effects of a tariff change into five components computed via an Armington model. This decomposition allowed us to identify the offsetting nature of the productivity and variety contributions[12] to welfare that Melitz adds to Armington.

We anticipated the productivity/variety offset on the basis of the analysis in Chap. 3 which established that if tariffs are zero, then Melitz models imply that the number and size of widget firms in each country and widget trade between countries is optimal for satisfying any given levels of widget demands by country. We interpret the productivity/variety offset as an implication of optimality and the consequent applicability of the envelope theorem. The role of the envelope theorem was apparent both in the formal test simulations in Sect. 6.2 and the illustrative tariff simulations in Sects. 6.3–6.5.

Taken literally, the envelope theorem explains the cancelling out of the Melitz productivity and variety effects in tariff simulations only if the initial situation is optimal and the tariff shocks are small. It is an empirical question as to whether the Melitz productivity/variety effects will cancel out if the initial situation is distorted by non-zero tariffs and other taxes or the tariff shocks are large.

---

[11]Here we report GEMPACK computations with a 2-country, 2-sector version of MelitzGE. GEMPACK experience with high-dimension versions of MelitzGE is described in Dixon et al. (2016). Chapter 7 confirms that GEMPACK is suitable software for solving large-scale Melitz models. Also see earlier GEMPACK-based papers on imperfect competition cited in Sect. 6.1.

[12]In this chapter we also refer to variety contributions as preference contributions and conversion-technology contributions.

The envelope theorem has proved a valuable guide in many CGE calculations, the bulk of which start from a distorted equilibrium and are concerned with non-negligible shocks. We suspect that with the introduction of Melitz features, the envelope theorem will go on being a useful guide. Evidence of this can be seen in Table 6.3. Compare vertical panels 2 and 3 which show the effects of moving from one distorted position to another: from a position with a 23% tariff to a position with a 65% tariff. The comparison reveals that despite starting from a distorted position (23% tariff) the insight from the envelope theorem continues to apply: the movements in the productivity and preference terms continue to approximately offset. Nevertheless, we need to keep an open mind on this issue. If a model embraces distortions that impinge directly on the productivity/variety trade off, then it is possible that Melitz might capture legitimate welfare changes from a tariff reform that are missed by Armington. This could happen for example for tariff cuts in an industry in which small-scale domestic production is subsidized. Also, as we find in Chap. 7 there can be significant Melitz-related effects in a model in which resources can move between Melitz and non-Melitz industries.

The approximate equivalence that we found in Sect. 6.5 between Melitz and Armington tariff simulations depends on the productivity/variety offset and on being able to calibrate the Armington inter-country substitution elasticity and the Melitz inter-variety substitution elasticity so that the two models imply equal sensitivity of trade flows to tariff shocks. Consideration by other authors of equivalence or otherwise between Melitz and Armington results has produced mixed findings. Arkolakis et al. (2012, p. 118) reached conclusions broadly compatible with the calculations in Table 6.5. They state that

> Within the class of trade models considered in this paper [which included Armington and Melitz], the number of sources of gains from trade varies, but conditional on observed trade data, the total size of the gains from trade does not.

In other words, Arkolakis et al. are saying that over a fairly broad class of models if a shock gives the same trade response then it also gives the same welfare outcomes. This conclusion is disputed by Balistreri and Rutherford (2013, p. 1542):

> The strong equivalence results suggested by Arkolakis et al. (2008, 2012) are not supported in our empirical model. For us, this indicates that the real world complexities accommodated in CGE models are, indeed, important.

However, it appears that Balistreri and Rutherford did not compare Armington and Melitz results across comparable experiments, that is, experiments in which the Armington elasticities are adjusted so that the trade responses across models are the same. Put another way, we suspect that the Balistreri and Rutherford comparison is more like that in Table 6.4 than that in Table 6.5.

Zhai (2008, p. 593) reports an Armington/Melitz comparison in which he explicitly recognizes the need to equalize trade responses but finds significantly different welfare responses:

> To ensure the new model [a Melitz model] generates additional gains from trade expansion in comparison with the conventional model [an Armington model], I raise the Armington elasticies in the standard Armington CGE model by 33 per cent and run the tariff reduction simulation. Compared to the Melitz CGE model, the Armington CGE model with high elasticities predicts similar expansion in global real exports, but 23 per cent lower global welfare gains.

Zhai does not explain why his Melitz calculations give larger welfare effects than the comparable Armington calculations, but we note that he does not fully implement the Melitz model:

> I abstract from the dynamic parts of the Melitz model by assuming no entry and exit of firms …. (Zhai 2008, p. 585).

This introduces pure profits in Zhai's version of the Melitz model that are not present in either the original Melitz model or Zhai's version of the Armington model. An extra distortion, in the form of pure profits, in Zhai's Melitz model but not in his Armington model casts doubt on the legitimacy of the welfare comparison across the two models.

The Melitz/Armington comparisons by Arkolakis et al. (2012) and those in this chapter are based on special assumptions. The formal analysis in Arkolakis et al. is confined to the effects on country j's welfare of shocks to the price of imports from country i in 1-sector, 1-factor-of-production, n-country models with iceberg trade costs. We also assume that there is only one factor of production in each of n countries although we do allow for revenue-generating tariffs and focus on the effects on country j's welfare emanating from j's own trade policy. Nevertheless, strong statements are not warranted concerning the empirical relevance of welfare equivalence between Armington and Melitz models. On the other hand, strong non-equivalence statements are equally unwarranted. For example it is premature to accept uncritically that:

> … Balistreri, Hillberry and Rutherford (2011) show that adding firm heterogeneity to standard computable general equilibrium models of trade raises the gains from trade liberalization by a factor of four. Empirical confirmation of the gains from trade predicted by models with heterogeneous firms represents one of the truly significant advances in the field of international economics. Melitz and Trefler (2012, p. 114)

Further work with empirically-based Melitz CGE models will be required to resolve the equivalence issue. Chapter 7 is a contribution towards that end.

Appendix 6.1: GEMPACK Program and Closures for the MelitzGE and Armington Auxiliary Models

This appendix contains the GEMPACK code for solving the MelitzGE and the Armington auxiliary models. Readers can download the code and zipped up simulations for this chapter using the Electronic Supplementary Material, see footnote at the opening page of this chapter.

At the end of the appendix, we list the exogenous variables for three closures together with explanatory notes. The first closure is suitable for computing linked MelitzGE and Armington auxiliary solutions such as those in Table 6.4. The second closure is suitable for computing de-linked MelitzGE and Armington auxiliary solutions such as those in Table 6.5. The third closure can be used for experimenting with the Balistreri-Rutherford algorithm (see Sect. 5.3).

GEMPACK code

```
! **************************************************************************** !
! The MelitzGE model                              !
! **************************************************************************** !


File   SETS # Commodities and countries # ;
File   DATA # Other data e.g. parameter values #;

Set CNT # Set of regions # read elements from file SETS header "CNT";
Set COM # Set of commodities # read elements from file SETS header "COM";

! A6.1.1  DECLARATION OF COEFFICIENTS FOR MELITZGE                    !
Coefficient
(Parameter) NUMREG # Number of regions or countries #;
(Parameter) SIGMA # Substitution elasticity between varieties #;
(All,c,COM)(All,s,CNT)(All,d,CNT) C_F(c,s,d) # Labor required to setup a c-firm for trade on the sd-link #;
(All,c,COM)(All,s,CNT)(All,d,CNT) C_T(c,s,d) # Power of tariff on c imposed by d on flows from s #;
(All,s,CNT) C_W(s) # Wage rate in region s #;
(All,c,COM)(All,s,CNT)(All,d,CNT) C_PIT(c,s,d) # Profits on the sd-link by the typical c-firm on sd-link #;
(All,c,COM)(All,s,CNT)(All,d,CNT) C_DELTA(c,s,d) # d's preference for c from s #;
(All,c,COM)(All,s,CNT)(All,d,CNT) C_PHI_MIN(c,s,d) # Marginal prod'ty of min. prod'ty c firm on sd-link #;
(All,c,COM)(All,s,CNT)(All,d,CNT) C_N(c,s,d) # Number of firms in region s sending c on the sd-link #;
(All,c,COM)(All,s,CNT) C_ND(c,s) # Number of c-producing firms in region s #;
(All,c,COM)(All,s,CNT)(All,d,CNT) C_PHIT(c,s,d) # Marginal productivity of a typical c firm on sd-link #;
(All,c,COM)(All,s,CNT)(All,d,CNT) C_PT(c,s,d) # Tariff-inclusive price of c by typical firm on sd-link #;
(All,c,COM)(All,d,CNT) C_P(c,d) # Price of the c-composite in region d #;
(Parameter) ALPHA # Parameter in Pareto distribution of firm productivities #;
(Parameter) BETA # Ratio typical prod'ty on link to minimum, determined by sigma and alpha, see (A2.1.7) #;
(All,c,COM)(All,d,CNT) C_QD(c,d) # Demand for composite c in region d # ;
(All,c,COM)(All,s,CNT)(All,d,CNT) C_Q(c,s,d) # The CES aggregate quantity of c sent on the sd-link # ;
(All,c,COM)(All,s,CNT)(All,d,CNT) C_QT(c,s,d) # Quantity sent by typical c-producing firm on the sd-link #;
(All,c,COM)(All,s,CNT)(All,d,CNT) C_Q_MIN(c,s,d) # Quantity sent by min. prod'ty c-firm on the sd-link #;
(All,c,COM)(All,s,CNT) C_H(c,s) # Labor input to setup a c-firm in region s # ;
(All,c,COM)(All,s,CNT) C_L(c,s) # Employment in the c-industry in region s # ;
(Parameter) LB_C_PHI_MIN # Min. productivity for a firm to have non-zero production in initial situation # ;
(Parameter) UB_C_PHI_MIN # Minimum productivity of firms that trade on all links in initial situation #;
(all,c,COM)(All,s,CNT)(All,d,CNT) C_R(c,s,d) # Share of region d's expenditure on c that is sourced from s #;
(All,c,COM)(All,d,CNT) C_RBot(c,d)  # Denominator in the evaluation of C_R #;
(All,c,COM)(All,s,CNT)(All,d,CNT) C_REV(c,s,d) # Tariff revenue on sd-link # ;
(All,d,CNT) C_LTOT(d) # Aggregate employment in region d # ;
(All,d,CNT) C_GDP(d) # Nominal GDP in region d #;
(All,c,COM)(All,d,CNT) C_MU(c,d) # share of d's expenditure devoted to commodity c # ;
(All,d,CNT) C_BTS(d) # Bal of trade surplus: GDP less consumption, same as exports (fob) less imports (cif)#;
```

! A6.1.2 SETTING INITIAL VALUES FOR THE COEFFICIENTS IN MELITZGE AND DETERMINING
INITIAL LEVELS SOLUTION !

Read
SIGMA **from file** DATA **Header** *"SGMA";! 3.8 is value used by Balistreri and Rutherford (2013)!*
ALPHA **from file** DATA **Header** *"ALFA";! 4.6 is value used by Balistreri and Rutherford (2013)!*
UB_C_PHI_MIN **from file** DATA **Header** *"UBMN"*;

Formula
(**initial**) NUMREG = **sum**(c,CNT, 1) ;
(**initial**) (**All**,s,CNT) C_W(s) = 1.0 ;
(**initial**) (**All**,c,COM)(**All**,s,CNT)(**All**,d,CNT) C_T(c,s,d) = 1.0 ;
(**initial**) (**All**,c,COM)(**All**,s,CNT)(**All**,d,CNT) C_DELTA(c,s,d) = 1.0 ;
(**initial**) LB_C_PHI_MIN = 1.1 ;

(**initial**)(**All**,c,COM)(**All**,s,CNT)(**All**,d,CNT) *!See equation (6.1)!* C_PHI_MIN(c,s,d) =
          LB_C_PHI_MIN + (UB_C_PHI_MIN - LB_C_PHI_MIN)*2*(1.0/NUMREG)*
          min{**ABS**($Pos(s,CNT)-$Pos(d,CNT)), NUMREG-**ABS**[$Pos(s,CNT)-$Pos(d,CNT)]} ;
(**initial**) (**All**,c,COM)(**All**,s,CNT) C_ND(c,s) = 1.0 ;
(**initial**) (**All**,c,COM)(**All**,d,CNT) C_QD(c,d) = 1.0 ;

! Starting from values for SIGMA, C_W, C_T, C_DELTA, C_PHI_MIN, C_ND, ALPHA and C_QD, we
compute values for the other parameters and coefficients in Table 2.2 in a recursive sequence.
We also evaluate coefficients appearing in additional MelitzGE equations (5.1) to (5.4)   !

!Equation (A1.7)! (**Initial**) BETA = [ALPHA/(ALPHA - SIGMA + 1)]^(1/(SIGMA-1));
!Melitz (T2.11)! (**Initial**) (**All**,c,COM)(**All**,s,CNT)(**All**,d,CNT) C_PHIT(c,s,d)= BETA*C_PHI_MIN(c,s,d);
!Melitz (T2.8)! (**Initial**) (**All**,c,COM)(**All**,s,CNT)(**All**,d,CNT) C_N(c,s,d) =
                         [C_PHI_MIN(c,s,d)^(-ALPHA)]*C_ND(c,s);
!Melitz (T2.1)! (**Initial**) (**All**,c,COM)(**All**,s,CNT)(**All**,d,CNT)
                    C_PT(c,s,d) = [C_W(s)*C_T(c,s,d)/C_PHIT(c,s,d)]*SIGMA/(SIGMA-1);
!Melitz (T2.2)! (**Initial**) (**All**,c,COM)(**All**,d,CNT) C_P(c,d) =
             sum(s,CNT, C_N(c,s,d)*(C_DELTA(c,s,d)^SIGMA)*C_PT(c,s,d)^(1-SIGMA))^(1/(1-SIGMA));
!Meltiz (T2.3)! (**Initial**) (**All**,c,COM)(**All**,s,CNT)(**All**,d,CNT) C_QT(c,s,d) =
                    C_QD(c,d)*(C_DELTA(c,s,d)^SIGMA)*[C_P(c,d)/C_PT(c,s,d)]^SIGMA ;
!Melitz (T2.12)!(**Initial**)(**All**,c,COM)(**All**,s,CNT)(**All**,d,CNT) C_Q_MIN(c,s,d)=C_QT(c,s,d)/(BETA^SIGMA);
!Melitz (T2.10)! (**Initial**) (**All**,c,COM)(**All**,s,CNT)(**All**,d,CNT) C_F(c,s,d) =
                    (1/(SIGMA-1))*[1/C_PHI_MIN(c,s,d)]*C_Q_MIN(c,s,d);
!Melitz (T2.4)! (**Initial**) (**All**,c,COM)(**All**,s,CNT)(**All**,d,CNT) C_Q(c,s,d) =
                    C_QT(c,s,d)*C_N(c,s,d)^[SIGMA/(SIGMA-1)];
!Melitz (T2.5)! (**Initial**) (**All**,c,COM)(**All**,s,CNT)(**All**,d,CNT) C_PIT(c,s,d) =
             (C_PT(c,s,d)/C_T(c,s,d) - C_W(s)/C_PHIT(c,s,d))*C_QT(c,s,d) - C_F(c,s,d)*C_W(s);
!Melitz (T2.6 & T2.9)!(**Initial**) (**All**,c,COM)(**All**,s,CNT) C_H(c,s) =
                    Sum(d,CNT, C_N(c,s,d)*C_PIT(c,s,d))/[C_ND(c,s)*C_W(s)];
!Melitz (T2.7)!(**Initial**)(**All**,c,COM)(**All**,s,CNT) C_L(c,s) =
             Sum(d,CNT,C_N(c,s,d)*C_QT(c,s,d)/C_PHIT(c,s,d))
             +**Sum**(d,CNT,C_N(c,s,d)*C_F(c,s,d))+C_ND(c,s)*C_H(c,s);
!Melitz (5.1)! (**Initial**) (**All**,c,COM)(**All**,s,CNT)(**All**,d,CNT) C_REV(c,s,d) =
             (C_T(c,s,d)-1)*(C_W(s)/C_PHIT(c,s,d))*(SIGMA/(SIGMA-1))*C_N(c,s,d)*C_QT(c,s,d);
!Melitz (5.2)! (**Initial**) (**All**,d,CNT) C_LTOT(d) = **sum**(c,COM, C_L(c,d)) ;
!Melitz (5.3)! (**Initial**) (**All**,d,CNT) C_GDP(d) =
                    sum(c,COM, C_W(d)*C_L(c,d)) + **sum**(c,COM, **sum**(s,CNT, C_REV(c,s,d)));

!Melitz (5.4)! **(Initial) (All**,c,COM)**(All**,d,CNT) C_MU(c,d) = C_QD(c,d)*C_P(c,d)/C_GDP(d) ;

! Other useful coefficients !
(Initial) (All,d,CNT) C_BTS(d) = C_GDP(d) - **sum**(c,COM, C_P(c,d)*C_QD(c,d));
(All,c,COM)**(All**,d,CNT) C_RBot(c,d) =
Sum(s,CNT, C_N(c,s,d)*(C_DELTA(c,s,d)^SIGMA)*(C_PT(c,s,d)^(1-SIGMA)));
(All,c,COM)**(All**,s,CNT)**(All**,d,CNT) C_R(c,s,d) =
    [C_N(c,s,d)*(C_DELTA(c,s,d)^SIGMA)*(C_PT(c,s,d)^(1-SIGMA))]/C_Rbot(c,d);

! A6.1.3 DECLARATION OF VARIABLES FOR MELITZGE   !

Variable
(All,c,COM)**(All**,s,CNT)**(All**,d,CNT) p_tsd(c,s,d) *# Tariff-inclusive price of c by typical firm on sd-link #*;
(All,s,CNT) w(s) *# Wage rate in region s #*;
(All,c,COM)**(All**,s,CNT)**(All**,d,CNT) t(c,s,d) *# Power of tariff on c imposed by d on flows from s #*;
(All,c,COM)**(All**,s,CNT)**(All**,d,CNT) phi_tsd(c,s,d) *# Marginal productivity of a typical c firm on sd-link #*;
(All,c,COM)**(All**,d,CNT) p_d(c,d) *# Price of the c-composite in region d #* ;
(All,c,COM)**(All**,s,CNT)**(All**,d,CNT) q_tsd(c,s,d) *# Quantity sent by typical c-producing firm on the sd-link #*;
(All,c,COM)**(All**,s,CNT)**(All**,d,CNT) n_sd(c,s,d) *# Number of firms in region s sending c on the sd-link #*;
(All,c,COM)**(All**,d,CNT) q_d(c,d) *# Quantity of composite c consumed region d #* ;
(All,c,COM)**(All**,s,CNT)**(All**,d,CNT) q_sd(c,s,d) *# CES aggregate quantity of c sent on the sd-link #* ;
(All,c,COM)**(All**,s,CNT)**(All**,d,CNT) pi_tsd(c,s,d) *# Profits on the sd-link of typical c-firm on sd-link #*;
(All,c,COM)**(All**,s,CNT)**(All**,d,CNT) delta(c,s,d) *# d's preference for c from s #*;
(All,c,COM)**(All**,s,CNT)**(All**,d,CNT) f_sd(c,s,d) *# Labor required to setup a c-firm for trade on the sd-link #*;
(All,c,COM)**(All**,s,CNT) nd(c,s) *# Number of c-producing firms in region s #*;
(All,c,COM)**(All**,s,CNT) h(c,s) *# Labor input to setup a c-firm in region s #* ;
(All,c,COM)**(All**,s,CNT) l(c,s) *# Employment in the c-industry in region s #*;
(All,c,COM)**(All**,s,CNT)**(All**,d,CNT) phi_min(c,s,d) *# Marginal prod'ty of min. prod'ty c firm on sd-link #*;
(All,c,COM)**(All**,s,CNT)**(All**,d,CNT) q_min(c,s,d) *# Quantity sent by min. prod'ty c-firm on the sd-link #*;
(All,d,CNT) gdp(d) *# GDP for region d #* ;
(Change)(All,d,CNT) d_bts(d) *# Balance of trade surplus #*;
(All,d,CNT) ltot(d) *# Aggregate employment in region d #* ;
(change)(All,c,COM)**(All**,s,CNT)**(All**,d,CNT) d_rev(c,s,d) *# Tariff revenue on sd-link #* ;
(All,c,COM)**(All**,d,CNT) mu(c,d) *# Share of d's expenditure devoted to commodity c #* ;
(All,c,COM)**(All**,d,CNT) f_mu(c,d) *# Matrix shifter on mu #* ;
(All,d,CNT) ff_mu(d) *# Vector shifter on mu #* ;
ave_wage *# Average worldwide wage rate #*;
(All,s,CNT) welfare(s) *# Welfare, sum over composite goods in utility function (no source dimesion) #*;
(All,d,CNT) expvol(d) *# Export volume, count measure #*;
(All,d,CNT) impvol(d) *# Import volume, count measure #*;
(All,d,CNT) cr(d) *# Real consumption measured by adding over commodities by source #*;
(All,d,CNT) gdprealexp(d) *# Real GDP, expenditure measure #*;
(All,d,CNT) gdprealinc(d) *# Real GDP, income measure #*;
(All,s,CNT) rel_wage(s) *# Wage in s relative to world average #* ;

!A6.1.4 UPDATES FOR MELITZGE COEFFICIENTS   !

Update
(All,c,COM)**(All**,s,CNT)**(All**,d,CNT) C_T(c,s,d) = t(c,s,d);
(All,s,CNT) C_W(s) = w(s);
(All,c,COM)**(All**,s,CNT)**(All**,d,CNT) C_DELTA(c,s,d)= delta(c,s,d);
(All,c,COM)**(All**,s,CNT)**(All**,d,CNT) C_PHI_MIN(c,s,d)= phi_min(c,s,d);

(**All**,c,COM)(**All**,s,CNT) C_ND(c,s) = nd(c,s);
(**All**,c,COM)(**All**,d,CNT) C_QD(c,d) = q_d(c,d);
(**All**,c,COM)(**All**,s,CNT)(**All**,d,CNT) C_F(c,s,d) = f_sd(c,s,d) ;
(**All**,c,COM)(**All**,s,CNT)(**All**,d,CNT) C_PIT(c,s,d) = pi_tsd(c,s,d) ;
(**All**,c,COM)(**All**,s,CNT)(**All**,d,CNT) C_N(c,s,d) = n_sd(c,s,d) ;
(**All**,c,COM)(**All**,s,CNT)(**All**,d,CNT) C_PHIT(c,s,d) = phi_tsd(c,s,d) ;
(**All**,c,COM)(**All**,s,CNT)(**All**,d,CNT) C_PT(c,s,d) = p_tsd(c,s,d) ;
(**All**,c,COM)(**All**,d,CNT) C_P(c,d) = p_d(c,d) ;
(**All**,c,COM)(**All**,s,CNT)(**All**,d,CNT) C_Q(c,s,d) = q_sd(c,s,d) ;
(**All**,c,COM)(**All**,s,CNT)(**All**,d,CNT) C_QT(c,s,d) = q_tsd(c,s,d) ;
(**All**,c,COM)(**All**,s,CNT)(**All**,d,CNT) C_Q_MIN(c,s,d) = q_min(c,s,d) ;
(**All**,c,COM)(**All**,s,CNT) C_H(c,s) = h(c,s) ;
(**All**,c,COM)(**All**,s,CNT) C_L(c,s) = l(c,s) ;
(**change**) (**All**,c,COM)(**All**,s,CNT)(**All**,d,CNT) C_REV(c,s,d) = d_rev(c,s,d) ;
(**All**,d,CNT) C_LTOT(d) = ltot(d) ;
(**All**,d,CNT) C_GDP(d) = gdp(d) ;
(**All**,c,COM)(**All**,d,CNT) C_MU(c,d) = mu(c,d) ;
(**change**) (**All**,d,CNT) C_BTS(d) = d_bts(d) ;

! A6.1.5 MELITZGE EQUATIONS, PERCENTAGE CHANGE AND CHANGE VERSIONS   !

! Percentage change forms for the MelitzGE equations from Table 2.2 !
Equation E_p_tsd *# Melitz equation (T2.1) #*
(**All**,c,COM)(**All**,s,CNT)(**All**,d,CNT) p_tsd(c,s,d) = w(s) + t(c,s,d)-phi_tsd(c,s,d);
Equation E_p_d *# Melitz equation (T2.2) #*
(**All**,c,COM)(**All**,d,CNT) p_d(c,d) =
    (1/(1-SIGMA))* **Sum**(s, CNT, C_R(c,s,d)*[n_sd(c,s,d)+SIGMA*delta(c,s,d)+(1-SIGMA)*p_tsd(c,s,d)]);
Equation E_q_tsd *# Melitz equation (T2.3) #*
(**All**,c,COM)(**All**,s,CNT)(**All**,d,CNT) q_tsd(c,s,d) = [q_d(c,d) + SIGMA*(p_d(c,d) + delta(c,s,d) - p_tsd(c,s,d))];
Equation E_q_sd *# Melitz equation (T2.4) #*
(**All**,c,COM)(**All**,s,CNT)(**All**,d,CNT) q_sd(c,s,d) = (SIGMA/(SIGMA - 1))*n_sd(c,s,d) + q_tsd(c,s,d) ;
Equation E_pi_tsd *# Melitz equation (T2.5) #*
(**All**,c,COM)(**All**,s,CNT)(**All**,d,CNT) C_PIT(c,s,d)*pi_tsd(c,s,d) =
    [C_PT(c,s,d)*C_QT(c,s,d)/C_T(c,s,d)]*[p_tsd(c,s,d) + q_tsd(c,s,d)-t(c,s,d)]
    - [C_W(s)*C_QT(c,s,d)/C_PHIT(c,s,d)]*[w(s) + q_tsd(c,s,d) - phi_tsd(c,s,d)]
    - [C_F(c,s,d)*C_W(s)]*(f_sd(c,s,d)+w(s));
Equation E_nd *# Melitz equation (T2.6 and T2.9) #*
(**All**,c,COM)(**All**,s,CNT) C_ND(c,s)*C_H(c,s)*C_W(s)*[nd(c,s) + h(c,s)+ w(s)] =
    Sum(d,CNT, C_N(c,s,d)*C_PIT(c,s,d)*[n_sd(c,s,d)+pi_tsd(c,s,d)]);
Equation E_l *# Melitz equation (T2.7) #*
(**All**,c,COM)(**All**,s,CNT) C_L(c,s)*l(c,s) =
    sum(d,CNT,[C_N(c,s,d)*C_QT(c,s,d)/C_PHIT(c,s,d)]*[n_sd(c,s,d)+q_tsd(c,s,d) -phi_tsd(c,s,d)])
    + **sum**(d,CNT, C_N(c,s,d)*C_F(c,s,d)*[n_sd(c,s,d)+f_sd(c,s,d)]) + C_ND(c,s)*C_H(c,s)*[nd(c,s) + h(c,s)];
Equation E_n_sd *# Melitz equation (T2.8) #*
(**All**,c,COM)(**All**,s,CNT)(**All**,d,CNT) n_sd(c,s,d) = nd(c,s) -ALPHA*phi_min(c,s,d);
Equation E_phi_min *# Meltiz equation (T2.10) #*
(**All**,c,COM)(**All**,s,CNT)(**All**,d,CNT) phi_min(c,s,d)+f_sd(c,s,d) = q_min(c,s,d);
Equation E_phi_tsd *# Melitz equation (T2.11) #*
(**All**,c,COM)(**All**,s,CNT)(**All**,d,CNT) phi_tsd(c,s,d) =phi_min(c,s,d);
Equation E_q_min *# Meltiz equation (T2.12) #*
(**All**,c,COM)(**All**,s,CNT)(**All**,d,CNT) q_min(c,s,d) = q_tsd(c,s,d);

! Percentage change and change forms for the MelitzGE equations (5.1) to (5.4) !

Equation E_rev *# Equation (5.1) #*

(**All**,c,COM)(**All**,d,CNT)(**All**,r,CNT)

100*d_rev(c,d,r) = [SIGMA/(SIGMA-1)]*C_T(c,d,r)*(C_W(d)/C_PHIT(c,d,r))*C_N(c,d,r)

        C_QT(c,d,r)[t(c,d,r) +w(d) +n_sd(c,d,r)+q_tsd(c,d,r) -phi_tsd(c,d,r)]

       - [SIGMA/(SIGMA-1)]*(C_W(d)/C_PHIT(c,d,r))*C_N(c,d,r)*C_QT(c,d,r)

        *[w(d) +n_sd(c,d,r)+q_tsd(c,d,r) -phi_tsd(c,d,r)];

Equation E_w *# Equation (5.2) #*

(**All**,s,CNT) C_LTOT(s)*ltot(s) = **sum**(c,COM, C_L(c,s)*l(c,s)) ;

Equation E_gdp *# Equation (5.3) #*

(**All**,d,CNT) C_GDP(d)*gdp(d) =

        Sum{c,COM, C_W(d)*C_L(c,d)*(w(d)+l(c,d))} + **Sum**(c,COM, **Sum**(s,CNT, 100*d_rev(c,s,d)));

Equation E_q_d *# Equation (5.4) #*

(**All**,c,COM)(**All**,d,CNT) p_d(c,d) + q_d(c,d) = mu(c,d) + gdp(d) ;

! Other useful equations in percentage change & change forms for MelitzGE   !

Equation E_bts *# Balance of trade surplus: GDP - Absorption #*

(**All**,d,CNT) 100*d_bts(d) = C_GDP(d)*gdp(d) - **Sum**(c,COM, (C_P(c,d)*C_QD(c,d))*[p_d(c,d) + q_d(c,d)] };

Equation E_expvol *# Export volume, count measure #*

(**All**,d,CNT) **Sum**{c,COM,**Sum**(r,CNT:r **ne** d, C_PT(c,d,r)*C_QT(c,d,r)*C_N(c,d,r)/C_T(c,d,r))}*expvol(d) =

Sum{c,COM,**Sum**(r,CNT:r **ne** d, C_PT(c,d,r)*C_QT(c,d,r)*C_N(c,d,r)/C_T(c,d,r)*[q_tsd(c,d,r)+n_sd(c,d,r)])};

Equation E_impvol *# Import volume, count measure #*

(**All**,d,CNT) **Sum**{c,COM,**Sum**(s,CNT:s **ne** d, C_PT(c,s,d)*C_QT(c,s,d)*C_N(c,s,d)/C_T(c,s,d))}*impvol(d) =

Sum{c,COM,**Sum**(s,CNT:s **ne** d,C_PT(c,s,d)*C_QT(c,s,d)*C_N(c,s,d)/C_T(c,s,d)*[q_tsd(c,s,d)+n_sd(c,s,d)])};

Equation E_cr *# Real consumption measured by adding over quantities of coms by source (no variety effect) #*

(**All**,d,CNT) **Sum**{c,COM, **Sum**(s,CNT, C_PT(c,s,d)*C_QT(c,s,d)*C_N(c,s,d))}*cr(d) =

    Sum{c,COM, **Sum**(s,CNT, C_PT(c,s,d)*C_QT(c,s,d)*C_N(c,s,d)*[n_sd(c,s,d)+q_tsd(c,s,d)])};

Equation E_gdprealexp *# Real GDP, expenditure measure #*

(**All**,d,CNT)

C_GDP(d)*gdprealexp(d)=**Sum**{c,COM,**Sum**(s,CNT,C_PT(c,s,d)*C_QT(c,s,d)*C_N(c,s,d))}*cr(d)

   +**sum**{c,COM,**Sum**(r,CNT:r **ne** d, C_PT(c,d,r)*C_QT(c,d,r)*C_N(c,d,r)/C_T(c,d,r))}*expvol(d)

   -**sum**{c,COM, **Sum**(s,CNT:s **ne** d, C_PT(c,s,d)*C_QT(c,s,d)*C_N(c,s,d)/C_T(c,s,d))}*impvol(d);

Equation E_gdprealinc *# Real GDP, income measure #*

(**All**,d,CNT) C_GDP(d)*gdprealinc(d)=**Sum**{c,COM,C_W(d)*C_L(c,d)*l(c,d)}

 +**Sum**(c,COM,**Sum**(s,CNT:s **ne** d,

  [C_PT(c,s,d)*C_N(c,s,d)*C_QT(c,s,d)*(C_T(c,s,d)-1)/C_T(c,s,d)]*[n_sd(c,s,d)+q_tsd(c,s,d)]))

 + **Sum**(c,COM, **Sum**(r,CNT, [C_N(c,d,r)*C_QT(c,d,r)*C_PT(c,d,r)/C_T(c,d,r)]*phi_tsd(c,d,r))) ;

Equation E_mu *# Allows movements in total consumption to GDP ratio in d: useful for Walras' law #*

(**All**,c,COM)(**All**,d,CNT) mu(c,d) =ff_mu(d) + f_mu(c,d);

Equation E_welfare *# Welfare: sum over composite goods in the utility function (takes account of variety) #*

(**All**,d,CNT) **Sum**{cc,COM, C_P(cc,d)*C_QD(cc,d)}*welfare(d) =

        Sum{c,COM,C_P(c,d)*C_QD(c,d)*q_d(c,d)};

Equation E_rel_wage *# Wage in s relative to world average #*

(**All**,s,CNT) w(s) = ave_wage +rel_wage(s);

Equation E_ave_wage *# average world-wide wage rate#*

Sum(tt,CNT, C_LTOT(tt))*ave_wage = **sum**(s,CNT, C_LTOT(s)*w(s));

```
! ********************************************************************** !
!   The Armington auxiliary model                                       !
! ********************************************************************** !
```

! A6.1.6 DECLARATION OF COEFFICIENTS FOR ARMINGTON AUXILIARY MODEL   !

Coefficient
(Parameter) SIGMAA # *Substitution elasticity between commodities from different countries, Armington#*;
(All,d,CNT) C_WA(d) # *Wage rate in region d, Armington #*;
(All,c,COM)**(All**,d,CNT) C_QDA(c,d) # *Demand in d for composite c, Armington #*;
(All,d,CNT) C_LX(d) # *Aggregate employment in region d, Armington #*;
(All,c,COM)**(All**,s,CNT) C_PHIA(c,s) # *Productivity, industry c region s, Armington #*;
(All,c,COM)**(All**,s,CNT)**(All**,d,CNT) C_QA(c,s,d) # *Quantity of c sent from s to d, Armington #*;
(All,c,COM)**(All**,s,CNT)**(All**,d,CNT) C_PA(c,s,d) # *Price to consumers in d of c sent from s, Armington #*;
(All,c,COM)**(All**,d,CNT) C_PCA(c,d) # *Price of composite c to consumers in d, Armington # *;
(All,c,COM)**(All**,s,CNT)**(All**,d,CNT) C_DELTAA(c,s,d) # *Regions d's preference for c from s, Armington #*;
(All,c,COM)**(All**,s,CNT)**(All**,d,CNT) C_REVA(c,s,d) # *Tariff revenue on c sent from s to d, Armington # *;
(All,d,CNT) C_GDPA(d) # *Income side GDP in region d, Armington # *;
(all,c,COM)**(All**,s,CNT)**(All**,d,CNT) C_SHA(c,s,d) # *Share of d's expenditure on c that is sourced from s # *;
(All,c,COM)**(All**,d,CNT) C_SHBotA(c,d) # *Used in forming C_SHA #*;
(All,r,CNT) C_GDPEXPA(r) # *GDP expenditure, Armington #*;
(All,c,COM)**(All**,s,CNT) C_LA(c,s) # *Employment in industry c country s, Armington #*;

! A6.1.7 SETTING INITIAL VALUES FOR THE COEFFICIENTS IN ARMINGTON AUXILIARY
           AND DETERMINING INITIAL LEVELS SOLUTION   !

Read SIGMAA **from file** DATA **Header** *"SGAA"*;*! Same as Melitz SIGMA value in decomposition simulations !*

! Aligns initial solution for Armington with that for Melitz !
Formula
(Initial) (All,d,CNT) C_WA(d) =C_W(d);
(initial) (All,c,COM)**(All**,d,CNT) C_QDA(c,d) = C_QD(c,d) ;
(initial) (All,d,CNT) C_LX(d) = C_LTOT(d) ;

! Sets Armington values for productivity and preferences consistent with Melitz !
Formula
*!Equation (5.6)!***(Initial)(All**,c,COM)**(All**,s,CNT)
C_PHIA(c,s)=**Sum**(d,CNT,C_QT(c,s,d)*C_N(c,s,d))/C_L(c,s);
*!Equation (5.7)!***(Initial)(All**,c,COM)**(All**,s,CNT)**(All**,d,CNT) C_DELTAA(c,s,d) =
{[C_PHIA(c,s)*{[C_PT(c,s,d)*C_QT(c,s,d)*C_N(c,s,d) - C_REV(c,s,d)]/C_W(s)}/C_QD(c,d)]^(1/SIGMAA)}
*{[C_W(s)*C_T(c,s,d)/C_PHIA(c,s)]/[sum{r,CNT, C_PT(c,r,d)*C_QT(c,r,d)*C_N(c,r,d)}/C_QD(c,d)]};

! Completing the initial solution for the Armington model !
!Equation (T5.1)! **(Initial)(All**,c,COM)**(All**,s,CNT)**(All**,d,CNT) C_PA(c,s,d) =
                    C_WA(s)*C_T(c,s,d)/C_PHIA(c,s);
*!Equation (T5.2)!***(Initial)(All**,c,COM)**(All**,d,CNT) C_PCA(c,d) =
                    [sum{s,CNT, (C_DELTAA(c,s,d)^SIGMAA)*(C_PA(c,s,d)^(1-SIGMAA))}]^(1/(1-SIGMAA));
!Equation (T5.3)! **(Initial)(All**,c,COM)**(All**,s,CNT)**(All**,d,CNT) C_QA(c,s,d) =
                    C_QDA(c,d)*[C_DELTAA(c,s,d)*C_PCA(c,d)/C_PA(c,s,d)]^SIGMAA;
!Equation (T5.5)! **(Initial)(All**,c,COM)**(All**,s,CNT)**(All**,d,CNT) C_REVA(c,s,d) =
                    {C_T(c,s,d)-1}*{C_QA(c,s,d)*C_WA(s)/C_PHIA(c,s)};
!Equation (T5.6)! **(Initial)(All**,d,CNT) C_GDPA(d) =
                    C_WA(d)*C_LX(d)+**Sum**(c,COM, **sum**(s,CNT, C_REVA(c,s,d)));
```
```

! *Other useful coefficients for Armington* !
(**All**,c,COM)(**All**,d,CNT) C_SHBotA(c,d) = C_PCA(c,d)*C_QDA(c,d);
(**All**,c,COM)(**All**,s,CNT)(**All**,d,CNT) C_SHA(c,s,d)= C_PA(c,s,d)*C_QA(c,s,d)/ C_SHBotA(c,d);

(**Initial**)(**All**,d,CNT) C_GDPEXPA(d) = **Sum**{c,COM, C_PCA(c,d)*C_QDA(c,d)}
  + **Sum**{c,COM, **Sum**(tt,CNT:tt **ne** d, [C_PA(c,d,tt)/C_T(c,d,tt)]*C_QA(c,d,tt))}
  - **Sum**{c,COM, **Sum**(s,CNT:s **ne** d, [C_PA(c,s,d)/C_T(c,s,d)]*C_QA(c,s,d))} ;
(**Initial**)(**All**,c,COM)(**All**,s,CNT) C_LA(c,s) = **Sum**(d,CNT, C_QA(c,s,d))/C_PHIA(c,s);

! *A6.1.8 DECLARATION OF VARIABLES FOR ARMINGTON AUXILIARY*   !
Variable
(**All**,d,CNT) wa(d) # *Wage rate in region d, Armington* #;
(**All**,c,COM)(**All**,d,CNT) q_da(c,d) # *Demand in d for composite c, Armington* #;
(**All**,c,COM)(**All**,s,CNT)(**All**,d,CNT) qa(c,s,d) # *Quantity of c sent from s to d, Armington* #;
(**All**,c,COM)(**All**,s,CNT)(**All**,d,CNT) pa(c,s,d) # *Price to consumers in d of c sent from s, Armington* # ;
(**All**,c,COM)(**All**,d,CNT) pca(c,d) # *Price of composite c to consumers in d, Armington* # ;
(**change**)(**All**,c,COM)(**All**,s,CNT)(**All**,d,CNT) d_reva(c,s,d) #*Tariff revenue on c sent from s to d, Armington*#;
(**All**,d,CNT) gdpa(d) # *GDP in region d, Armington* # ;
(**All**,c,COM)(**All**,s,CNT) phia(c,s) # *Productivity, industry c region s, Armington* # ;
(**All**,c,COM)(**All**,s,CNT)(**All**,d,CNT) deltaa(c,s,d) # *d's preference coefficient for c from s, Armington* #;
(**All**,d,CNT) lx(d) # *Employment in d, Armington* #;
(**All**,c,COM)(**All**,d,CNT) mua(c,d) # *Share of d's expenditure devoted to c, Armington* # ;
(**All**,c,COM)(**All**,s,CNT) slack_phia(c,s) # *Endogenize to set phia independently of Melitz* # ;
(**All**,c,COM)(**All**,s,CNT)(**All**,d,CNT) sl_deltaa(c,s,d) # *Endogenize to set deltaa independently of Melitz* #;
(**All**,d,CNT) f_lx(d) # *Exogenize to equalize Armington & Melitz aggregate employment* #;
(**All**,c,COM)(**All**,d,CNT) f_muan(c,d) # *Matrix shifter on mua* # ;
(**All**,d,CNT) ff_mua(d) # *Vector shifter on mua* # ;
(**All**,c,COM)(**All**,d,CNT) f3_mua(c,d) #*Exog if Armington mua must move with Melitz mu, in decomp sims*#;
(**All**,c,COM)(**All**,d,CNT) f2_mua(c,d) #*Exog to insulate Armington mua from Melitz mu, in B&R algorithm*#;
(**All**,r,CNT) gdprealexpa(r) # *GDP real expenditure, Armington* #;
(**All**,r,CNT) gdprealinca(r) # *GDP real income, Armington* # ;
(**All**,d,CNT) gdpexpa(d) # *Nominal GDP expenditure side, Armington* #;
(**All**,c,COM)(**All**,s,CNT) la(c,s) # *Employment in industry c in country s* #;
(**all**,d,CNT) exportsa(d) # *quantity of exports, Armington* #;
(**all**,d,CNT) pexportsa(d) # *price of exports fob, Armington* #;
(**all**,d,CNT) importsa(d) # *quantity of imports, Armington* #;
(**all**,d,CNT) pimportsa(d) # *price of imports cif, Armington* #;
ave_wagea # *Average worldwide wage,Armington* #;
f_ave_wagea # *Ratio, average world-wide wage in Armington relative to Melitz* #;

! *A6.1.9 UPDATES FOR ARMINGTON AUXILIARY COEFFICIENTS*   !
Update
(**All**,d,CNT) C_WA(d)=wa(d);
(**All**,c,COM)(**All**,d,CNT) C_QDA(c,d) = q_da(c,d);
(**All**,c,COM)(**All**,s,CNT) C_PHIA(c,s) = phia(c,s);
(**All**,c,COM)(**All**,s,CNT)(**All**,d,CNT) C_QA(c,s,d) = qa(c,s,d);
(**All**,c,COM)(**All**,s,CNT)(**All**,d,CNT) C_PA(c,s,d) = pa(c,s,d);
(**All**,c,COM)(**All**,d,CNT) C_PCA(c,d) = pca(c,d);
(**All**,c,COM)(**All**,s,CNT)(**All**,d,CNT) C_DELTAA(c,s,d) = deltaa(c,s,d);
(**Change**) (**All**,c,COM)(**All**,s,CNT)(**All**,d,CNT) C_REVA(c,s,d)=d_reva(c,s,d);
(**All**,d,CNT) C_GDPA(d) = gdpa(d);
(**All**,s,CNT) C_LX(s)= lx(s);
(**All**,d,CNT) C_GDPEXPA(d) = gdpexpa(d) ;
(**All**,c,COM)(**All**,s,CNT) C_LA(c,s) = la(c,s);

! A6.1.10 ARMINGTON AUXILIARY EQUATIONS, PERCENTAGE CHANGE AND CHANGE VERSIONS!

Equation E_phia *# Equation (5.6), slack_phia is exo to link Armington and Melitz #*
(**All**,c,COM)(**All**,s,CNT)phia(c,s) = [1/**sum**(dd,CNT, C_QT(c,s,dd)*C_N(c,s,dd))]
    *sum(d,CNT, C_QT(c,s,d)*C_N(c,s,d)*[q_tsd(c,s,d) + n_sd(c,s,d)]) - l(c,s) +slack_phia(c,s);

Equation E_deltaa *# Equation (5.7), sl_deltaa is exo to link Armington and Melitz #*
(**All**,c,COM)(**All**,s,CNT)(**All**,d,CNT) deltaa(c,s,d) =(1/SIGMA)* (1/{C_PHIA(c,s)
    *[C_PT(c,s,d)*C_QT(c,s,d)*C_N(c,s,d) - C_REV(c,s,d)]/C_W(s)})
    *{[C_PHIA(c,s)*C_PT(c,s,d)*C_QT(c,s,d)*C_N(c,s,d)/C_W(s)]
    *[phia(c,s)+p_tsd(c,s,d)+q_tsd(c,s,d) + n_sd(c,s,d)- w(s)]
  -[C_PHIA(c,s)* C_REV(c,s,d)/C_W(s)]* (phia(c,s) -w(s))-100*[C_PHIA(c,s)/C_W(s)]* (d_rev(c,s,d))}
    +(1- 1/SIGMA)*q_d(c,d) + [w(s)+t(c,s,d)-phia(c,s)]
  -[1/**Sum**(r,CNT,C_PT(c,r,d)*C_QT(c,r,d)*C_N(c,r,d))]***Sum**(k,CNT,C_PT(c,k,d)*C_QT(c,k,d)*C_N(c,k,d)
    *[p_tsd(c,k,d)+q_tsd(c,k,d) + n_sd(c,k,d)])   + sl_deltaa(c,s,d);

! Armington model from Table 5.1 in percentage change form !

Equation E_pa *# Equation (T5.1) #*
(**All**,c,COM)(**All**,s,CNT)(**All**,d,CNT) pa(c,s,d) = wa(s) + t(c,s,d) - phia(c,s) ;

Equation E_pca *# Equation (T5.2) #*
(**All**,c,COM)(**All**,d,CNT) pca(c,d) =
    (1/(1-SIGMAA))*{**sum**(s,CNT, C_SHA(c,s,d)*[SIGMAA*deltaa(c,s,d) + (1-SIGMAA)*(pa(c,s,d))])};

Equation E_qa *# Equation (T5.3) #*
(**All**,c,COM)(**All**,s,CNT)(**All**,d,CNT) qa(c,s,d) = q_da(c,d) + SIGMAA*[deltaa(c,s,d) + pca(c,d) - pa(c,s,d)];

Equation E_wa *# Equation (T5.4) #*
(**All**,s,CNT) C_LX(s)*lx(s) = **sum**(c,COM, **sum**(d,CNT,[C_QA(c,s,d)/C_PHIA(c,s)]*[qa(c,s,d) - phia(c,s)]));

Equation E_d_reva *# Equation (T5.5) #*
(**All**,c,COM)(**All**,s,CNT)(**All**,d,CNT) 100*d_reva(c,s,d) = C_T(c,s,d)*C_QA(c,s,d)*C_WA(s)*(1/C_PHIA(c,s))
    *[t(c,s,d)+qa(c,s,d)+wa(s)-phia(c,s)] - C_QA(c,s,d)*C_WA(s)/C_PHIA(c,s)*[qa(c,s,d)+wa(s)-phia(c,s)];

Equation E_gdpa *# Equation (T5.6) #*
(**All**,d,CNT) C_GDPA(d)*gdpa(d) = [C_WA(d)*C_LX(d)]*[wa(d)+lx(d)] +
100***sum**(c,COM,**Sum**(s,CNT,d_reva(c,s,d)));

Equation E_q_da *# Equation (T5.7) #*
(**All**,c,COM)(**All**,d,CNT) pca(c,d) + q_da(c,d) = mua(c,d) + gdpa(d) ;

! Other useful equations for the Armington model including definitions of macro variables !

Equation E_gdpexpa *# GDP nominal expenditure, Armington #*
(**All**,d,CNT) C_GDPEXPA(d)*gdpexpa(d) = **Sum**{c,COM, C_PCA(c,d)*C_QDA(c,d)*[pca(c,d)+q_da(c,d)]}
+ **Sum**{c,COM,**Sum**(tt,CNT:tt **ne** d,[C_PA(c,d,tt)/C_T(c,d,tt)]*C_QA(c,d,tt)*[pa(c,d,tt)-t(c,d,tt)+qa(c,d,tt)])}
- **Sum**{c,COM, **Sum**(s,CNT:s **ne** d,[C_PA(c,s,d)/C_T(c,s,d)]*C_QA(c,s,d)*[pa(c,s,d)-t(c,s,d)+qa(c,s,d)])} ;

Equation E_gdprealexpa *# GDP real expenditure, Armington #*
(**All**,d,CNT) C_GDPEXPA(d)*gdprealexpa(d) =**Sum**{c,COM, C_PCA(c,d)*C_QDA(c,d)*q_da(c,d)}
    + **Sum**{c,COM,**Sum**(tt,CNT:tt **ne** d, [C_PA(c,d,tt)/C_T(c,d,tt)]*C_QA(c,d,tt)*qa(c,d,tt))}
   - **Sum**{c,COM, **Sum**(s,CNT:s **ne** d, [C_PA(c,s,d)/C_T(c,s,d)]*C_QA(c,s,d)*qa(c,s,d))} ;

Equation E_gdprealinca *# GDP real income, Armington #*
(**All**,d,CNT) C_GDPA(d)*gdprealinca(d) =C_LTOT(d)*C_WA(d)*lx(d)
    + **Sum**(c,COM, **Sum**(s,CNT, [C_T(c,s,d)-1]*[C_PA(c,s,d)/C_T(c,s,d)]*C_QA(c,s,d)*qa(c,s,d)))
    + SIGMAA/(SIGMAA-1)***Sum**(c,COM, **Sum**(s,CNT,C_PA(c,s,d)*C_QA(c,s,d)*deltaa(c,s,d)))
    + **Sum**(c,COM, {**Sum**(tt,CNT, [C_PA(c,d,tt)/C_T(c,d,tt)]*C_QA(c,d,tt))}*phia(c,d)) ;

Equation E_la *# Employment by industry and country #*
(**All**,c,COM)(**All**,s,CNT) C_LA(c,s)*la(c,s) = **Sum**(d,CNT, (C_QA(c,s,d)/C_PHIA(c,s))*(qa(c,s,d) - phia(c,s)));

Equation E_exportsa *# quantity of exports #*
(**All**,d,CNT) exportsa(d) = (1/**Sum**{c,COM, **Sum**(tt,CNT:tt **ne** d, [C_PA(c,d,tt)/C_T(c,d,tt)]*C_QA(c,d,tt))})
    ***Sum**{c,COM, **Sum**(tt,CNT:tt **ne** d, [C_PA(c,d,tt)/C_T(c,d,tt)]*C_QA(c,d,tt)*qa(c,d,tt))} ;

Equation E_pexportsa *# price of exports fob #*
(**All**,d,CNT) pexportsa(d) = (1/**Sum**{c,COM, **Sum**(tt,CNT:tt **ne** d, [C_PA(c,d,tt)/C_T(c,d,tt)]*C_QA(c,d,tt))})
    ***Sum**{c,COM, **Sum**(tt,CNT:tt **ne** d, [C_PA(c,d,tt)/C_T(c,d,tt)]*C_QA(c,d,tt)*[w(d)-phia(c,d)])} ;

Equation E_importsa # *quantity of imports* #
(**all**,d,CNT) importsa(d) = (1/**Sum**{c,COM, **Sum**(s,CNT:s **ne** d, [C_PA(c,s,d)/C_T(c,s,d)]*C_QA(c,s,d))})
   * **Sum**{c,COM, **Sum**(s,CNT:s **ne** d, [C_PA(c,s,d)/C_T(c,s,d)]*C_QA(c,s,d)*qa(c,s,d))} ;
Equation E_pimportsa # *price of imports cif* #
(**all**,d,CNT) pimportsa(d) = (1/**Sum**{c,COM, **Sum**(s,CNT:s **ne** d, [C_PA(c,s,d)/C_T(c,s,d)]*C_QA(c,s,d))})
   * **Sum**{c,COM, **Sum**(s,CNT:s **ne** d, [C_PA(c,s,d)/C_T(c,s,d)]*C_QA(c,s,d)*[w(s)-phia(c,s)])} ;
Equation E_ave_wagea # *average world-wide wage rate, Armington* #
 Sum(tt,CNT, C_LX(tt))*ave_wagea = **Sum**(s,CNT, C_LX(s)*wa(s));
Equation E_f_ave_wagea # *Ratio of Armington world-wide wage rate to Melitz* #
 ave_wagea = ave_wage + f_ave_wagea;
Equation E_f_lx # *f_lx is exo to transfer aggregate employment from Melitz to Armington* #
(**All**,d,CNT) lx(d) = ltot(d) + f_lx(d);
Equation E_mua # *This & next eqn allow mua to move with mu or be set independ. Also accomodates Walras* #
(**All**,c,COM)(**All**,d,CNT) mua(c,d) = f_muan(c,d)+f2_mua(c,d) +ff_mua(d);
Equation E_f2_mua # *f2_mua exog to insulate Armington mua's from Melitz mu's, in B&R algorithm* #
(**All**,c,COM)(**All**,d,CNT) f2_mua(c,d) =mu(c,d)+f3_mua(c,d) ;

! *A6.1.11 ARMINGTON DECOMPOSITION OF MELITZ WELFARE, see Box 6.2* !
Coefficient (**All**,d,CNT) WELFAREINDEX(d) # *Welfare index* #;

Formula (initial) (**All**,d,CNT) WELFAREINDEX(d) = 1.0 ;

Variable
(**All**,d,CNT) welfarea(d) # *Welfare, calculated in Armington model* #;
(**change**) (**All**,d,CNT) cont_toft(d) # *Welfare contribution, terms of trade* #;
(**change**) (**All**,d,CNT) cont_prim(d) # *Welfare contribution, primary factors* #;
(**change**) (**All**,d,CNT) cont_tcf(d) # *Welfare contribution, tax-carrying flows* #;
(**change**) (**All**,d,CNT) cont_techmix(d) # *Welfare contribution, variety* #;
(**change**) (**All**,d,CNT) cont_techprod(d) # *Welfare contribution, production technology* #;
(**change**) (**All**,d,CNT) cont_total(d) # *Total of welfare contributions* #;

Update (**All**,d,CNT) WELFAREINDEX(d) = welfare(d) ;

Equation E_welfarea # *Welfare, calculated in Armington as real consumption* #
(**All**,d,CNT) welfarea(d) =
   (1/**Sum**{cc,COM,C_PCA(cc,d)*C_QDA(cc,d)})***Sum**{c,COM,C_PCA(c,d)*C_QDA(c,d)*q_da(c,d)};
Equation E_cont_toft # *Welfare contribution, terms of trade* #
(**All**,d,CNT) cont_toft(d) = WELFAREINDEX(d)*(1/**sum**{cc,COM, C_PCA(cc,d)*C_QD(cc,d)})
      *{**Sum**{c,COM, **Sum**(tt,CNT:tt **ne** d, [C_PA(c,d,tt)/C_T(c,d,tt)]*C_QA(c,d,tt)*(wa(d)-phia(c,d)))}
      - **Sum**{c,COM,**Sum**(s,CNT:s **ne** d, [C_PA(c,s,d)/C_T(c,s,d)]*C_QA(c,s,d)*(wa(s)-phia(c,s)))} } ;
Equation E_cont_prim # *Welfare contribution, primary factors* #
(**All**,d,CNT) cont_prim(d)= WELFAREINDEX(d)*(1/**Sum**{cc,COM, C_PCA(cc,d)*C_QD(cc,d)})
          *{**Sum**{c,COM, C_W(d)*C_LA(c,d)*la(c,d)}};
Equation E_cont_tcf # *Welfare contribution, tax-carrying flows* #
(**All**,d,CNT) cont_tcf(d)= WELFAREINDEX(d)*(1/**Sum**{cc,COM, C_PCA(cc,d)*C_QD(cc,d)})
         * **Sum**(c,COM, **Sum**(s,CNT,[C_T(c,s,d)-1]*[C_PA(c,s,d)/C_T(c,s,d)]*C_QA(c,s,d)*qa(c,s,d)));
Equation E_cont_techmix # *Welfare contribution, variety* #
(**All**,d,CNT) cont_techmix(d)=WELFAREINDEX(d)*(1/**Sum**{cc,COM,
C_PCA(cc,d)*C_QD(cc,d)})*SIGMAA/(SIGMAA-1)
          * **Sum**(c,COM, **Sum**(s,CNT, C_PA(c,s,d)*C_QA(c,s,d)*deltaa(c,s,d)));
Equation E_cont_techprod # *Welfare contribution, production technology* #
(**All**,d,CNT) cont_techprod(d) = WELFAREINDEX(d)*(1/**Sum**{cc,COM, C_PCA(cc,d)*C_QD(cc,d)})
         * **Sum**(c,COM, {**Sum**(tt,CNT,[C_PA(c,d,tt)/C_T(c,d,tt)]*C_QA(c,d,tt))}*phia(c,d));
Equation E_cont_total # *Total of welfare contributions* #
(**All**,d,CNT) cont_total(d) = cont_toft(d) + cont_prim(d) + cont_tcf(d) + cont_techmix(d) + cont_techprod(d);

Closures

Table 6.6 lists three closures (exogenous variables) for the MelitzGE and Armington auxiliary models.

The first closure was used for generating the results in Table 6.4 including the Armington decomposition of Melitz welfare results. Under this closure the Melitz-implied productivity and preference effects of tariff changes or other shocks are calculated via Eqs. (5.6) and (5.7) and passed to the Armington model. This is done automatically in the GEMPACK code by treating slack_phia and sl_deltaa as exogenous and unshocked variables (rows 9 and 10, first closure in Table 6.6 and equations E_phia and E_deltaa in part A6.1.10 of the GEMPACK code). By treating ave_wage and f_ave_wagea as exogenous we ensure that the numeraires in the Melitz and Armington models are the same (see equation E_f_ave_wagea in part A6.1.10). By treating f_lx as exogenous and unshocked, we adopt the same movements in employment by country in the two models (see E_f_lx in part A6.1.10). The treatments of f_mu, ff_mu("CNT1"), f_muan, ff_mua("CNT1) and

Table 6.6 Closures for MelitzGE and Armington auxiliary models

		Linked as in Table 6.4	Unlinked as in Table 6.5	B&R algorithm
MelitzGE variables				
1	Labor market	ltot	ltot	w
2	Consumer preferences	delta	delta	delta
3	Powers of tariffs	t	t	t
4	Tradelink setup inputs	f_sd	f_sd	f_sd
5	Inputs to set up a firm	h	h	h
6	Consumption of composite coms	f_mu	f_mu	q_d
7	Cons of composites and Walras	ff_mu("*CNT1*")	ff_mu("*CNT1*")	ff_mu("*CNT1*")
8	Numeraire and cons of composites	ave_wage	ave_wage	ff_mu("*CNT2*")
Armington auxiliary variables				
9	Industry productivity	slack_phia	phia	slack_phia
10	Preferences or conversion tech	sl_deltaa	deltaa	sl_deltaa
11	Consumption of composite coms	f_muan	f_muan	f_muan
12	Cons of composites and Walras	ff_mua ("*CNT1*")	ff_mua ("*CNT1*")	ff_mua ("*CNT1*")
13	Connects Melitz and Armington cons	f3_mua	f3_mua	f2_mua
14	Connects M and A numeraires	f_ave_wagea	f_ave_wagea	ave_wagea
15	Connects M and A employment	f_lx	f_lx	lx

f3_mua as exogenous and unshocked variables in the first closure ensure that the Melitz and Armington models have the same consumption propensities out of GDP (E_mu, E_mua and E_f2_mua in parts A6.1.5 and A6.1.10) while having sufficient flexibility to accommodate Walras' law [ff_mu("CNT2") and ff_mua("CNT2") are endogenously determined at zero].

The second closure in Table 6.6 was used for the comparison in Table 6.5 of Melitz and Armington tariff results generated with the Armington inter-country substitution elasticity set at a higher value than the Melitz inter-variety substitution elasticity (7.0 compared with 3.8). This second closure differs from the previous one only in the Armington treatments of productivity and preferences (rows 9 and 10). For the Melitz-Armington comparison we applied no shocks to the Armington productivity and preference variables. We wanted to see how closely a stand-alone Armington model could reproduce Melitz results. Consequently, in the second closure in Table 6.6, the productivity and preference variables (phia and deltaa) are exogenous and were uninformed by Melitz (unshocked) in the comparison simulation.

The third closure in Table 6.6 can be used to investigate the workings of the Balistreri-Rutherford (B&R) algorithm. In this closure, Melitz economy-wide variables [wage rates and consumption of composite commodities, w(d) and q_d(c, d) for all c and d] are exogenous. Correspondingly, the Melitz versions of aggregate employment in each country [ltot(d) for all d] and the shift variables on consumption propensities [f_mu] are endogenous. With exogenous treatment of the wage rate in each country, the average world-wide wage rate [ave_wage] must be endogenous. Correspondingly, ff_mu("CNT2") becomes exogenous: sufficient flexibility to accommodate Walras' law is provided by the endogenization of f_mu.

In the Armington part of the closure for the B&R algorithm, slack_phia and sl_deltaa are exogenous. Consequently the Armington model receives results from Melitz that inform its productivity and preference movements. By contrast, the treatment of f2_mua as an exogenous variable in place of f3_mua isolates the Armington determination of average propensities from the Melitz determination (see E_f2_mua and E_mua in part A6.1.10). Aggregate employment for each country in Armington [lx(d) for all d] is exogenous, determined independently of Melitz employment [f_lx is endogenous in E_f_lx, see part A6.1.10 in the GEMPACK code]. Similarly, the numeraire for Armington, ave_wagea, is set independently of Melitz [f_ave_wagea in E_f_ave_wagea is endogenous, see part A6.1.10].

To gain understanding of the B&R algorithm we used the third closure in Table 6.6 in a sequence of simulations with t(c, "CNT1", "CNT2") equal to 10 for all c, together with guessed shocks for w(d) and q_d(c, d) for all c, d. The other exogenous variables were unshocked and the substitution elasticities SIGMA and SIGMAA were set at 3.8. Following the steps in Sect. 5.3 we reproduced the results from the first panel of Table 6.3. In the first step we guessed w(d) and q_d(c, d) at zero. This produced results for Melitz variables. Consistent with the B&R algorithm, we could have paused at this stage and used Eqs. (5.6) and (5.7) to generate productivity and preference shocks to be applied in Armington. However with slack_phia and sl_deltaa exogenous, this happens automatically. Moving to step 5 we compared the Armington outcomes for wa(d) and q-da(c, d) with the guessed input values for w(d) and q_d(c, d). Then following step 6, we made new guesses for w(d) and q_d(c, d) and returned to step 1. In making the new guesses we found that a low value for ε was necessary ($\varepsilon = 0.25$). With higher values there was a tendency to create explosive cobwebs. With $\varepsilon = 0.25$, we achieved convergence but rather slowly.

Appendix 6.2: Showing that an Increase in Country 2's Tariffs Doesn't Affect the Number of Firms in Either Country

In the tariff simulations reported in Sect. 6.3 we increased $T_{12,c}$ for all c by the same percentage. This resulted in changes in the number of c-firms operating on all international links, $N_{12,c}$ and $N_{21,c}$, but curiously no change that the number of c-firms in either country s, $N_{s,c}$. In this appendix we show why $N_{s,c}$ is constant. As it turns out this is not a fundamental or robust result. It depends on special data setup assumptions.

In demonstrating that $N_{s,c}$ is constant for all s and c under the conditions imposed in Sect. 6.3, we start by combining the Melitz versions of (T2.6) and (T2.9):

$$0 = \sum_d N_{sd,c} \Pi_{\bullet sd,c} - N_{s,c} H_{s,c} W_s. \tag{6.8}$$

Now using (T2.1) and (T2.5) we obtain

$$0 = \sum_d N_{sd,c} \left[W_s \left(\frac{1}{(\sigma - 1)} \right) \frac{Q_{\bullet sd,c}}{\Phi_{\bullet sd,c}} - W_s * F_{sd,c} \right] - N_{s,c} H_{s,c} W_s \tag{6.9}$$

Next we note that $Q_{\bullet sd,c}/\Phi_{\bullet sd,c}$, is constant. This result can be derived as follows. From (T2.11) and (T2.12) we see that $Q_{\bullet sd,c}/\Phi_{\bullet sd,c}$ equals $\beta^{\sigma-1} * Q_{\min(s,d),c}/\Phi_{\min(s,d),c}$. With $F_{sd,c}$ fixed, (T2.10) implies that $Q_{\min(s,d),c}/\Phi_{\min(s,d),c}$ is fixed and hence $Q_{\bullet sd,c}/\Phi_{\bullet sd,c}$ is fixed.

Eliminating W_s in (6.9) and using the fixity of $Q_{\bullet sd,c}/\Phi_{\bullet sd,c}$, $F_{sd,c}$ and $H_{s,c}$, we create a change version:

$$0 = \sum_d N_{sd,c} \left[\left(\frac{1}{(\sigma - 1)} \right) \frac{Q_{\bullet sd,c}}{\Phi_{\bullet sd,c}} * n_{sd,c} - F_{sd,c} * n_{sd,c} \right] - N_{s,c} H_{s,c} * n_{s,c} \tag{6.10}$$

where $n_{sd,c}$ and $n_{s,c}$ are percentage changes in $N_{sd,c}$ and $N_{s,c}$. With aggregate employment fixed in each country, the symmetry of industries 1 and 2 implies that employment in each industry is fixed. Thus, from (T2.7) we obtain

$$0 = \sum_d \frac{N_{sd,c} Q_{\bullet sd,c}}{\Phi_{\bullet sd,c}} * n_{sd,c} + \sum_d N_{sd,c} F_{sd,c} * n_{sd,c} + N_{s,c} H_{s,c} * n_{s,c}. \qquad (6.11)$$

Adding (6.10) and (6.11) yields

$$0 = \sum_d \frac{N_{sd,c} Q_{\bullet sd,c}}{\Phi_{\bullet sd,c}} * n_{sd,c}. \qquad (6.12)$$

Combining (6.12) and (6.11) implies that

$$N_{s,c} H_{s,c} * n_{s,c} = - \sum_d N_{sd,c} F_{sd,c} * n_{sd,c}. \qquad (6.13)$$

Substituting from (T2.10), (T2.11) and (T2.12) into (6.13) gives

$$N_{s,c} H_{s,c} * n_{s,c} = - \frac{1}{(\sigma - 1) * \beta^{\sigma-1}} * \sum_d N_{sd,c} * \frac{Q_{\bullet sd,c}}{\Phi_{\bullet sd,c}} n_{sd,c} \qquad (6.14)$$

and combining (6.12) and (6.14) gives

$$n_{s,c} = 0 \quad \text{for all s and c.} \qquad (6.15)$$

This result is an artefact of the particular data setup of MelitzGE. It depends on identical data for industries 1 and 2 in country s. It was this assumption, combined with the constancy of aggregate employment in country s, that led to the constancy of employment in each industry in country s, enabling us to derive (6.11) which eventually led to (6.15).

Appendix 6.3: Deriving the Armington Decomposition of Melitz Welfare

We derive the formula in Box 6.2. This formula uses results from the Armington auxiliary model to decompose welfare results generated by MelitzGE.

Chapter 5 (particularly Appendix 5.1) explains that a solution to the MelitzGE model specified by the Melitz versions of (T2.1)–(T2.12) and by (5.1)–(5.4) is contained in a converged BR solution. This means that MelitzGE solutions for welfare can be computed via the Armington auxiliary model specified by (T5.1)–(T5.7) providing we: (a) adopt the same numeraire and substitution values in the Armington model as in the Melitz model; (b) set the Armington industry-productivity and preference variables according to (5.6) and (5.7); and (c) assume the same level of aggregate employment in each country in the Armington model as required for the MelizGE model, that is:

$$LX(d) = LTOT_d \quad \text{for all d.} \tag{6.16}$$

In Chap. 5 we found that MelitzGE results for the percentage change in the welfare of country d can be computed according to[13]

$$\text{welfare (d)} = \sum_c ZA(d, c) * qca(d, c) \quad \text{for all d,} \tag{6.17}$$

where qca(d, c) is the percentage change in QCA(d, c) computed in the Armington model satisfying (a)–(c) and ZA(d, c) is the Armington share of d's expenditure devoted to commodity c. With Cobb-Douglas preferences, ZA(d, c) is a parameter and is the same as $\mu_{d,c}$ in Table 5.1.

Continuing to assume that (a)–(c) are satisfied, we work with the Armington model in Table 5.1 to derive the decomposition equation in Box 6.2. Using the notational conventions explained at the foot of Box 6.2, we start by writing Table 5.1 in percentage change and change form as:

$$pa(s, d, c) = wa(s) + t_{sd,c} - \phi a(s, c) \tag{6.18}$$

$$pca(d, c) = \sum_s SA(s, d, c) * pa(s, d, c) + \frac{\sigma}{1-\sigma} * \sum_s SA(s, d, c) * \widehat{\delta}a(s, d, c) \tag{6.19}$$

$$qa(s, d, c) = qca(d, c) + \sigma * \widehat{\delta}a(s, d, c) + \sigma(pca(d, c) - pa(s, d, c)) \tag{6.20}$$

$$LX(s) * lx(s) = \sum_{c,d} \left\{ \frac{QA(s, d, c)}{\Phi A(s, c)} * (qa(s, d, c) - \phi a(s, c)) \right\} \tag{6.21}$$

$$
\begin{aligned}
100 * \Delta RA(s, d, c) \\
= \frac{T_{sd,c} * QA(s, d, c) * WA(s)}{\Phi A(s, c)} * \left(t_{sd,c} + qa(s, d, c) + wa(s) - \phi a(s) \right) \\
- \frac{QA(s, d, c) * WA(s)}{\Phi A(s, c)} * (qa(s, d, c) + wa(s) - \phi a(s))
\end{aligned}
\tag{6.22}
$$

---

[13]See (5.13) and (5.14) and the discussion that follows.

$$\text{GDPA}(d) * \text{gdpa}(d) = (\text{WA}(d) * \text{LXd}) * (\text{wa}(d) + \text{lx}(d))$$
$$+ 100 * \sum_{c,s} \Delta \text{RA}(s,d,c) \tag{6.23}$$

$$\text{pca}(d,c) + \text{qca}(d,c) = \text{gdpa}(d). \tag{6.24}$$

The only new notation in these equations is SA(s, d, c) and ΔRA(s, d, c). SA(s, d, c) is the share of d's expenditure on c that is devoted to source s. It is given by[14]:

$$\text{SA}(s,d,c) = \frac{\text{PA}(s,d,c) * \text{QA}(s,d,c)}{\sum_j \text{PA}(j,d,c) * \text{QA}(j,d,c)} \tag{6.25}$$

or equivalently by[15]

$$\text{SA}(s,d,c) = \frac{\text{PA}(s,d,c) * \text{QA}(s,d,c)}{\text{PCA}(d,c) * \text{QCA}(d,c)}. \tag{6.26}$$

ΔRA(s, d, c) is the change in RA(s, d, c). Because tariff collection can be zero, we use the change rather than the percentage change in RA(s, d, c).

Our first step in deriving the decomposition equation is to substitute from (6.24) and (6.19) into (6.17). This gives

$$\text{welfare}(d) = \text{gdpa}(d) - \sum_c \sum_s \text{ZA}(d,c) * \text{SA}(s,d,c) * \text{pa}(s,d,c)$$
$$- \frac{\sigma}{1-\sigma} \sum_c \sum_s \text{ZA}(d,c) * \text{SA}(s,d,c) * \widehat{\delta}\text{a}(s,d,c) \tag{6.27}$$

Now we work on gdpa(d). We substitute from (6.22) into (6.23) to obtain

$$\text{GDPA}(d) * \text{gdpa}(d) = \text{WA}(d) * \text{LX}(d) * (\text{wa}(d) + \text{lx}(d))$$
$$+ \sum_{c,s} \frac{T_{sd,c} * \text{QA}(s,d,c) * \text{WA}(s)}{\Phi\text{A}(s,c)}$$
$$* \left(t_{sd,c} + \text{qa}(s,d,c) + \text{wa}(s) - \phi\text{a}(s) \right) \tag{6.28}$$
$$- \sum_{c,s} \frac{\text{QA}(s,d,c) * \text{WA}(s)}{\Phi\text{A}(s,c)}$$
$$* (\text{qa}(s,d,c) + \text{wa}(s) - \phi\text{a}(s))$$

---

[14]In deriving (6.19), we use (T5.3) to obtain $\text{SA}(s,d,c) = \frac{\delta\text{A}(s,d,c)^\sigma * \text{PA}(s,d,c)^{1-\sigma}}{\sum_j \delta\text{A}(j,d,c)^\sigma * \text{PA}(j,d,c)^{1-\sigma}}.$

[15](T5.2) and (T5.3) imply that $\text{PCA}(d,c) * \text{QCA}(d,c) = \sum_j \text{PA}(j,d,c) * \text{QA}(j,d,c).$

Substituting from (6.18) into (6.28) and using (T5.1) gives

$$
\begin{aligned}
GDPA(d) * gdpa(d) = {} & WA(d) * LX(d) * (wa(d) + lx(d)) \\
& + \sum_{c,s} PA(s,d,c) * QA(s,d,c) * (pa(s,d,c) + qa(s,d,c)) \\
& - \sum_{c,s} \frac{QA(s,d,c) * PA(s,d,c)}{T_{sd,c}} * \left(qa(s,d,c) + pa(s,d,c) - t_{sd,c} \right)
\end{aligned}
$$

$$(6.29)$$

The formula in Box 6.2 is for two countries. It is easy to generalize to the r-country case. However, two countries is convenient and we continue the algebra on that basis. We rearrange (6.29) as

$$
\begin{aligned}
GDPA(d) * gdpa(d) = {} & WA(d) * LX(d) * lx(d) + WA(d) * LX(d) * wa(d) \\
& + \sum_{c} \sum_{s} \frac{PA(s,d,c) * QA(s,d,c)}{T_{sd,c}} * (T_{sd,c} - 1) * qa(s,d,c) \\
& - \sum_{c} \frac{PA(F,d,c) * QA(F,d,c)}{T_{Fd,c}} * \left(pa(F,d,c) - t_{Fd,c} \right) \\
& + \sum_{c} \frac{PA(d,F,c) * QA(d,F,c)}{T_{dF,c}} * \left(pa(d,F,c) - t_{dF,c} \right) \\
& + \sum_{c} \frac{PA(d,d,c) * QA(d,d,c)}{T_{dd,c}} * t_{dd,c} + \sum_{c} \frac{PA(d,F,c) * QA(d,F,c)}{T_{dF,c}} * t_{dF,c} \\
& + \sum_{c} \sum_{s} PA(s,d,c) * QA(s,d,c) * pa(s,d,c) \\
& - \sum_{c} \frac{PA(d,d,c) * QA(d,d,c)}{T_{dd,c}} * pa(d,d,c) \\
& - \sum_{c} \frac{PA(d,F,c) * QA(d,F,c)}{T_{dF,c}} * pa(d,F,c)
\end{aligned}
$$

$$(6.30)$$

In (6.30), as in Box 6.2, we use the argument F to denote foreign country. From here, we: use (6.18) to substitute out pa in the last two terms on the RHS of (6.30); cancel out some t terms; separate newly introduced wa and ϕa terms; and use (T5.4) and (T5.1) to eliminate wa terms. These operations give

$$
\text{GDPA}(d) * \text{gdpa}(d) = \text{WA}(d) * \text{LX}(d) * \text{lx}(d)
$$

$$
+ \sum_c \sum_s \frac{\text{PA}(s, d, c) * \text{QA}(s, d, c)}{T_{sd,c}} * \left(T_{sd,c} - 1\right) * \text{qa}(s, d, c)
$$

$$
- \sum_c \frac{\text{PA}(F, d, c) * \text{QA}(F, d, c)}{T_{Fd,c}} * \left(\text{pa}(F, d, c) - t_{Fd,c}\right)
$$

$$
+ \sum_c \frac{\text{PA}(d, F, c) * \text{QA}(d, F, c)}{T_{dF,c}} * \left(\text{pa}(d, F, c) - t_{dF,c}\right)
$$

$$
+ \sum_c \sum_s \text{PA}(s, d, c) * \text{QA}(s, d, c) * \text{pa}(s, d, c)
$$

$$
+ \sum_{c,j} \frac{\text{PA}(d, j, c) * \text{QA}(d, j, c)}{T_{dj,c}} * \phi\text{a}(d, c)
$$

$$
\tag{6.31}
$$

Now we return to (6.27). Substituting from (6.31) into (6.27) gives

$$
\text{GDPA}(d) * \text{welfare}(d) = \text{WA}(d) * \text{LX}(d) * \text{lx}(d)
$$

$$
+ \sum_c \sum_s \frac{\text{PA}(s, d, c) * \text{QA}(s, d, c)}{T_{sd,c}} * \left(T_{sd,c} - 1\right) * \text{qa}(s, d, c)
$$

$$
- \sum_c \frac{\text{PA}(F, d, c) * \text{QA}(F, d, c)}{T_{Fd,c}} * \left(\text{pa}(F, d, c) - t_{Fd,c}\right)
$$

$$
+ \sum_c \frac{\text{PA}(d, F, c) * \text{QA}(d, F, c)}{T_{dF,c}} * \left(\text{pa}(d, F, c) - t_{dF,c}\right)
$$

$$
+ \sum_{c,j} \frac{\text{PA}(d, j, c) * \text{QA}(d, j, c)}{T_{dj,c}} * \phi\text{a}(d, c)
$$

$$
+ \sum_c \sum_s \text{PA}(s, d, c) * \text{QA}(s, d, c) * \text{pa}(s, d, c)
$$

$$
- \text{GDPA}(d) * \sum_{c,s} \text{ZA}(d, c) * \text{SA}(s, d, c) * \text{pa}(s, d, c)
$$

$$
- \text{GDPA}(d) * \frac{\sigma}{1 - \sigma} \sum_{c,s} \text{ZA}(d, c) * \text{SA}(s, d, c) * \widehat{\delta}\text{a}(s, d, c)
$$

$$
\tag{6.32}
$$

Recalling that $\text{ZA}(d, c)$ is the same as $\mu_{d,c}$ and using (T5.7) and (6.26) we see that

$$
\text{GDPA}(d) * \text{ZA}(d, c) * \text{SA}(s, d, c) = \text{PA}(s, d, c) * \text{QA}(s, d, c). \tag{6.33}
$$

This allows us to cancel the second-last and third-last terms in (6.32). Because $\sum_c \mu_{d,c} = 1$, (T5.7) implies that

$$\text{GDPA}(d) = \sum_{c,s} \text{PA}(s,d,c) * \text{QA}(s,d,c) \tag{6.34}$$

Using (6.33) and (6.34) in (6.32) then gives us the decomposition equation in Box 6.2.

References

Abayasiri-Silva, K., & Horridge, J. M. (1998). Economies of scale and imperfect competition in an applied general equilibrium model of the Australian economy (Chap. 14). In: K. J. Arrow, Y.-K. Ng & X. Yang (Eds.), *Increasing returns and economic analysis* (pp. 307–334). Great Britain: Macmillan Press Ltd; New York:St. Martin's Press, Inc.

Akgul, Z., Villoria, N. B., & Hertel, T. W. (2016). GTAP-HET: Introducing firm heterogeneity into the GTAP model. *Journal of Global Economic Analysis, 1*(1), 111–180.

Arkolakis, C., Demidova, S., Klenow, P. and Rodriguez-Clare, A. (2008). "Endogenous variety and the gains from trade?" *American Economic Review, 98*(2), 444–450.

Arkolakis, C., Costinot, A., & Rodriguez-Clare, A. (2012). New trade models, same old gains? *American Economic Review, 102*(1), 94–130.

Balistreri, E., & Rutherford T. (2013). Computing general equilibrium theories of monopolistic competition and heterogeneous firms (Chap. 23). In: P. B. Dixon & D. W. Jorgenson (Eds.), *Handbook of computable general equilibrium modeling* (pp. 1513–1570.). Amsterdam: Elsevier.

Balistreri, E. J., Hillberry, R. H., & Rutherford, T. F. (2010). Trade and welfare: Does industrial organization matter? *Economic Letters, 109,* 85–87.

Balistreri, E. J., Hillberry, R. H., & Rutherford, T. F. (2011). Structural estimation and solution of international trade models with heterogeneous firms. *Journal of International Economics, 83,* 95–108.

Corden, W. M. (1957). The calculation of the cost of protection. *Economic Record, 33,* 29–51.

Dixon, P. B., Parmenter, B. R., Sutton J., Vincent, D. P. (1982). *ORANI: A multisectoral model of the Australian economy.* Contributions to economic analysis 142 (pp. xviii + 372). North-Holland Publishing Company.

Dixon, P. B., Koopman R. B., and Rimmer, M.T. (2013). The MONASH style of CGE modeling: a framework for practical policy analysis (Chap. 2). In: P. B. Dixon & D. W. Jorgenson (Eds.), *Handbook of computable general equilibrium modeling* (pp. 23–102). Amsterdam: Elsevier.

Dixon, P. B., & Rimmer, M. T. (2010). Optimal tariffs: Should Australia cut automotive tariffs unilaterally? *Economic Record, 86*(273), 143–161.

Dixon, P. B., Jerie, M., & Rimmer, M. T. (2016). Modern trade theory for CGE modelling: The Armington, Krugman and Melitz Models. *Journal of Global Economic Analysis, 1*(1), 1–110.

Harrison, W. J., Horridge, J. M., & Pearson, K. R. (2000). Decomposing simulation results with respect to exogenous shocks. *Computational Economics, 15,* 227–249.

Horridge, J. M. (1987). *The long-term costs of protection: Experimental analysis with different closures of an Australian computable general equilibrium model.* Ph. D. thesis (pp. xii+315+-appendices). University of Melbourne.

Horridge, J. M., Meeraus, A., Pearson, K., & Rutherford, T. (2013). Software platforms: GAMS and GEMPACK (Chap. 20). In P. B. Dixon & D. W. Jorgenson (Eds.), *Handbook of computable general equilibrium modeling* (pp. 1331–1382). Amsterdam: Elsevier.

Johansen, L. (1960), *A multisectoral study of economic growth*. Contributions to economic analysis 21 (pp. vii +177). North-Holland Publishing Company.

Johnson, H. G. (1960). Cost of protection and the scientific tariff. *Journal of Political Economy, 68*(4), 327–345.

Melitz, M. J., & Trefler, D. (2012). Gains from trade when firms matter. *Journal of Economic Perspectives, 26*(2), 91–118.

Pearson, K. R. (1988). Automating the computation of solutions of large economic models. *Economic Modelling, 5*(4), 385–395.

Swaminathan, P., & Hertel, T. (1996), *Introducing monopolistic competition into the GTAP model*. GTAP Technical Paper No. 6, available at https://www.gtap.agecon.purdue.edu/resources/download/1565.pdf.

Zhai, F. (2008). Armington meets Melitz: introducing firm heterogeneity in a global CGE model of trade. *Journal of Economic Integration, 23*(3), 575–604.

Chapter 7
Converting an Armington Model into a Melitz Model: Giving Melitz Sectors to GTAP

Abstract This chapter describes how to convert an existing Armington CGE model into a Melitz CGE model with minimal changes to the original Armington model. The main task is to add equations to the bottom of the Armington model to form what we call an Armington-to-Melitz or A2M system. With an A2M system, industries can be switched between Armington and Melitz treatments by closure swaps. We use BasicArmington (a simple Armington model) to explain how to create an A2M system. Then we apply the method to a 10-region, 57-commodity version of the frequently applied policy-oriented GTAP model to create a GTAP-A2M system. Using this system, we compare the effects under Armington and Melitz assumptions of a tariff imposed by North America on imports of wearing apparel (Wap). To facilitate the comparison, we decompose the welfare effects for each region into parts attributable to changes in employment, terms of trade and scale-related efficiency. This helps us to understand how each of these factors operates under Armington and Melitz, but it does not give us an intuitive explanation of their net outcome. To explain net outcomes for welfare effects by region we set out an intuitive overarching theory. We check its validity by back-of-the-envelope (BOTE) calculations using GTAP data items and selected simulation results. BOTE calculations enable us to cut through the maze of complications in CGE models to locate, for any specific result, the essential underlying ingredients.

Keywords Converting Armington to Melitz · BasicArmington-A2M system GTAP-A2M system · BOTE calculations · Welfare decomposition

In Chaps. 5 and 6 we moved from a Melitz CGE model to an Armington CGE model. This chapter is about how to adapt an existing Armington model so that it becomes a Melitz model. That is, we are concerned with moving in the other direction: from Armington to Melitz.

Electronic supplementary material Readers can access the GEMPACK programs for running the simulations reported in this chapter at https://doi.org/10.1007/978-981-10-8325-9_7.

Our approach in Chaps. 5 and 6 was motivated by Balistreri and Rutherford (2013), hereafter BR. Starting from a Melitz model, BR developed an auxiliary Armington model as a computational device for solving the Melitz model by an iterative method, using GAMS. Using GEMPACK, we can solve Melitz models directly. However, we found BR's Armington auxiliary model to be a valuable interpretive device, enabling us to describe a Melitz model as an Armington model with extra equations to endogenize productivity variables on the supply side and preference variables on the demand side.

It would be possible to reverse the Melitz-to-Armington method described in Chaps. 5 and 6 to develop an approach for converting an Armington model into a Melitz model. Nevertheless, that is not the route we have chosen. The method in Chaps. 5 and 6 depends on specifying in the Armington model movements in CES distribution "parameters" [δ's, see Eq. (5.7)]. These are not conveniently available in Armington models such as GTAP specified in percentage-change form suitable for solution by GEMPACK. Instead, these models include input-saving technical change variables associated with every commodity flow. Consequently, faced with the task of converting the Armington-based GTAP model into a Melitz model, we have adopted a method in which input-saving technical changes are endogenized, rather than CES distribution parameters.

A key property of our Armington-to-Melitz conversion method is that it requires minimal alteration to the Armington model. Given an Armington model, the conversion can be made by adding equations to the bottom of the existing code to form what we refer to as an A2M system. With closure switches the A2M system can be run as pure Armington, pure Melitz or mixed Armington-Melitz.

The principal aim of this chapter is to demonstrate the practicality of our A2M conversion method by applying it to GTAP.[1] This is the world's most widely used global CGE model, see Hertel (1997). The standard version relies on Armington assumptions and is solved in percentage-change form using GEMPACK. Because GTAP is designed to facilitate practical policy analysis it contains details that can inhibit understanding of what is involved in converting Armington to Melitz. Consequently we will explain our conversion method in the context of a simple Armington model. After that, it will be straightforward to describe the Armington-to-Melitz conversion for GTAP.

The rest of this chapter is organized as follows. Section 7.1 sets out what we call the BasicArmington model. This is the vehicle through which we explain our A2M method. Section 7.2 explains the additions that are made to BasicArmington to form the related A2M system, that is the BasicArmington-A2M system. Section 7.3 explains the database for the BasicArmington model and the BasicArmington-A2M system. Section 7.4 presents illustrative Armington and Melitz results from the BasicArmington-A2M system. Section 7.5 describes the additions and alterations to the Armington-based GTAP model required to produce a GTAP-A2M system. Illustrative Armington and Melitz results from the GTAP-A2M system are presented

---

[1]The GTAP website is at https://www.gtap.agecon.purdue.edu/.

in Sect. 7.6. Concluding remarks are in Sect. 7.7. Annotated GEMPACK code for the BasicArmington-A2M system is in Appendix 7.1, together with closures and download instructions. Appendix 7.2 derives a decomposition equation for explaining welfare results from the BasicArmington-A2M system. In Appendix 7.3 we show that the A2M method proposed by Akgul et al. (2016) for the GTAP model falls short of achieving a valid Armington-to-Melitz conversion.

7.1 Equations for the BasicArmington Model

The BasicArmington model on which we will focus is the same as the Armington auxiliary model (Table 5.1) except for the inclusion of some additional tax, technology and price variables. BasicArmington has two identical countries each producing two commodities using labor and no intermediate inputs. Each country has one final user (households) with a Cobb-Douglas utility function. Both commodities are traded and, in the Armington style, the countries treat imported commodities as imperfect substitutes for domestic commodities.

The first part of Table 7.1 lists percentage-change equations for the BasicArmington model. The second part lists the extra equations necessary for transforming Armington to Melitz. Notation is given in Table 7.2, also see the foot of Table 7.1.

Equations for the BasicArmington model: (T7.1)–(T7.16) in Table 7.1

Equation (T7.1) defines movements in factory prices. The factory price of a widget (commodity c) from country s is the price at the factory door. In an Armington model this is the same for all widgets produced in country s.[2] The percentage movement in the factory price is determined by the percentage movements in input prices (the wage rate in the BasicArmington model because labor is the only input) and in input per unit of output denoted by the technology variable, aoMel$_{s,c}$. Our reason for including "Mel" in the name of this variable is to indicate that it has a special role in the conversion from Armington to Melitz. While this variable is normally exogenous in an Armington model, as we will see, it becomes endogenous in the A2M system to generate Melitz solutions.

Equation (T7.2) determines market prices. Consistent with GTAP terminology, these are prices of widgets just beyond the factory door. In BasicArmington, market prices are factory prices after the application of a destination-specific tax. The percentage change in the power of this tax is txMel$_{sd,c}$. Again, the 'Mel' suffix is

---

[2]We include the dot subscript on factory, market, fob, cif, and purchasers prices. The dot signifies the typical firm. All firms are "typical" in Armington. Consequently for Armington the dots are not required. However, their inclusion does no harm and is convenient for linking Armington to Melitz where the dots do have a role.

Table 7.1 An A2M system: percentage-change versions of equations for the BasicArmington model and additional equations for conversion to Melitz

	BasicArmington model
(T7.1)	$\text{pfactory}_{\bullet s,c} = w_s - \text{aoMel}_{s,c}$
(T7.2)	$\text{pmarket}_{\bullet sd,c} = \text{pfactory}_{\bullet s,c} + \text{txMel}_{sd,c}$
(T7.3)	$\text{pfob}_{\bullet sd,c} = \text{pmarket}_{\bullet sd,c}$
(T7.4)	$\text{pcif}_{\bullet sd,c} = \text{pfob}_{\bullet sd,c}$
(T7.5)	$\text{p}_{\bullet sd,c} = \text{pcif}_{\bullet sd,c} + \text{tm}_{sd,c}$
(T7.6)	$\text{qcount}_{sd,c} + \text{aaMel}_{sd,c} = q_{d,c} - \sigma * \left(\left[\text{p}_{\bullet sd,c} - \text{aaMel}_{sd,c} \right] - p_{d,c} \right)$
(T7.7)	$p_{d,c} = \sum_s \text{SHA}(s,d,c) * \left[\text{p}_{\bullet sd,c} - \text{aaMel}_{sd,c} \right]$
(T7.8)	$q_{sd,c} = \text{qcount}_{sd,c} + \text{aaMel}_{sd,c}$
(T7.9)	$q_{d,c} = -p_{d,c} + \text{fmu}_d + \text{gdp}_d$
(T7.10)	$\ell_{s,c} = \text{qotot}_{s,c} - \text{aoMel}_{s,c}$
(T7.11)	$\text{LTOT}_s * \ell\text{tot}_s = \sum_c L_{s,c} * \ell_{s,c}$
(T7.12)	$\left[\sum_d \text{FACTORYV}(s,d,c) \right] * \text{qotot}_{s,c} = \sum_d \text{FACTORYV}(s,d,c) * \text{qcount}_{sd,c}$
(T7.13)	$\text{GDP}_d * \text{gdp}_d = W_d * \text{LTOT}_d * \left[w_d + \ell\text{tot}_d \right]$ $+ 100 * \sum_c \sum_s \text{drevm}_{sd,c} + 100 * \sum_c \sum_s \text{drevx}_{ds,c}$
(T7.14)	$100 * \text{drevm}_{sd,c} = \text{TM}_{sd,c} * \text{VCIF}(s,d,c) * \left[\text{qcount}_{sd,c} + \text{pcif}_{\bullet sd,c} + \text{tm}_{sd,c} \right]$ $- \text{VCIF}(s,d,c) * \left[\text{qcount}_{sd,c} + \text{pcif}_{\bullet sd,c} \right]$
(T7.15)	$100 * \text{drevx}_{sd,c} = \text{TX}_{sd,c} * \text{FACTORYV}(s,d,c) * \left[\text{qcount}_{sd,c} + \text{pfactory}_{\bullet s,c} + \text{txMel}_{sd,c} \right]$ $- \text{FACTORYV}(s,d,c) * \left[\text{qcount}_{sd,c} + \text{pfactory}_{\bullet s,c} \right]$

(continued)

Table 7.1 (continued)

(T7.16) $\left[\sum_s \text{LTOT}_s\right] * \text{avewage} = \sum_s \text{LTOT}_s * w_s$

Additional equations for converting Armington to Melitz

(T7.17) $\text{qcount}_{sd,c} = n_{sd,c} + q_{\bullet sd,c}$

(T7.18) $\text{txMel}_{sd,c} = \text{aoMel}_{s,c} - \phi_{\bullet sd,c} + \text{ftxMel}_{sd,c}$

(T7.19) $\text{aaMel}_{sd,c} = (1/(\sigma-1)) * n_{sd,c} + \text{faaMel}_{sd,c}$

(T7.20)
$$W_s * L_{s,c} * [w_s + \ell_{s,c}]$$
$$= [(\sigma-1)/\sigma] * \sum_d \text{MARKETV}(s,d,c) * [n_{sd,c} + q_{\bullet sd,c} - \phi_{\bullet sd,c} + w_s]$$
$$+ [(\sigma-1)/(\alpha\sigma)] * \sum_d \text{MARKETV}(s,d,c) * [n_{s,c} + h_{s,c} + w_s]$$
$$+ [(\alpha - (\sigma-1))/(\alpha\sigma)] * \sum_d \text{MARKETV}(s,d,c) * [n_{sd,c} + f_{sd,c} + w_s]$$
$$+ 100 * \text{df}\ell_{s,c}$$

(T7.21) $n_{sd,c} - n_{s,c} = -\alpha * \phi_{\min(s,d,c)}$

(T7.22) $q_{\min(s,d,c)} = \phi_{\min(s,d,c)} + f_{sd,c}$

(T7.23) $\phi_{\bullet sd,c} = \phi_{\min(s,d,c)}$

(T7.24) $q_{\bullet sd,c} = q_{\min(s,d,c)}$

(T7.25) $\text{dcolrevx}_{s,c} = \sum_d \text{drevx}_{sd,c}$

Notation See Table 7.2. Also note that we use lowercase symbols for percentage changes in the variables denoted by the corresponding uppercase symbols. For example, $p_{\bullet sd,c} = 100 * \Delta P_{\bullet sd,c}/P_{\bullet sd,c}$. Tax collections which can be zero or negative (subsidies) are presented as change variables rather than percentage change. This is indicated by a "d" at the start of a variable name. For example, drevx$_{sd,c}$ is the change in the revenue derived by country s from the factory-door tax imposed on c flowing from s to d. Coefficients are presented in uppercase symbols often ending with "V" for value

Table 7.2 Notation for A2M system and closure status of variables in BasicArmington and MelitzGE models: exogenous (X) or endogenous (N) with closure switches highlighted

		Armington	Melitz
Variables in the basicArmington model			
$\text{pfactory}_{\bullet s,c}$	Factory price of c-producing firm in s	N	N
$\text{txMel}_{sd,c}$	Destination-specific power of tax charged by s on factory value c to d	X	N
$\text{pmarket}_{\bullet sd,c}$	Price just beyond the factory door of c,s to d	N	N
$\text{pfob}_{\bullet sd,c}$	Fob price of flow c,s to d	N	N
$\text{pcif}_{\bullet sd,c}$	Cif price of flow c,s to d	N	N
$\text{P}_{\bullet sd,c}$	Purchasers price of c,s,d	N	N
$\text{tm}_{sd,c}$	Power of tariff on flow c,s to d, applied to cif value	X	X
$\text{qcount}_{sd,c}$	Quantity of c (number of widgets) sent from s to d	N	N
$\text{q}_{sd,c}$	Effective qty of c sent from s to d, see (7.1)–(7.3)	N	N
w_s	Wage rate in region s	N	N
$\text{aoMel}_{s,c}$	All input tech variable: output per unit of input in industry c,s	X	N
$\text{q}_{d,c}$	Qty of composite c consumed in d, not differentiated by source	N	N
$\text{aaMel}_{sd,c}$	Pref variable for c,s to satisfy d's demands for c	X	N
$\text{fmu}_d(\text{"CNT1"})$	Country 1's average propensity to consume out of GDP	X	X
$\text{fmu}_d(\text{"CNT2"})$	Country 2's average propensity to consume out of GDP	N	N
gdp_d	GDP in d	N	N
$\text{P}_{d,c}$	Price of the c-composite in d	N	N
$\ell_{s,c}$	Quantity of labor used in industry c,s	N	N
$\text{qotot}_{s,c}$	Total qty (no. of widgets) produced by industry c in region s	N	N
ℓtot_s	Employment in country s	X	X
$\text{drevm}_{sd,c}$	d's tariff revenue on flow c from s to d	N	N
$\text{drevx}_{sd,c}$	s's tax revenue on flow c from s to d	N	N
avewage	World-wide average wage rate	X	X
Additional variables for the Melitz model			
$\text{ftxMel}_{sd,c}$	Exogenous to turn on Melitz factory-door tax rates	N	X
$\text{faaMel}_{sd,c}$	Exogenous to turn on Melitz love of variety	N	X
$\text{df}\ell_{s,c}$	Exogenous to turn on Melitz total inputs to c-firms in s	N	X
$\phi_{\bullet sd,c}$	Productivity of a typical c firm on sd-link	N	N
$\text{n}_{sd,c}$	No. of c-producing firms (varieties) on the sd-link	N	N

		Armington	Melitz
$f_{sd,c}$	Qty of inputs required to set up on the sd,c-link	X	X
$n_{s,c}$	Number of c-firms in country s	X	N
Variables in the BasicArmington model			
$h_{s,c}$	Qty of inputs for a c-firm to set up the opportunity to produce	X	X
$\phi_{min(s,d,c)}$	Productivity of minimum productivity c-firm on sd-link	N	N
$q_{min(s,d,c)}$	Sales to d of c-firm with min. productivity on sd-link	N	N
$q_{\bullet sd,c}$	Sales to d of c-firm with typical productivity on sd-link	N	N
$\phi_{\bullet sd,c}$	Productivity of typical productivity c-firm on sd-link	N	N
$dcolrevx_{s,c}$	Rev from dest-specific factory-door tax on c-firms in s	N	X
Other notation: parameters and coefficient in levels			
σ	Substitution elasticity		
α	Parameter in Pareto distribution of firm productivities		
SHA(s,d,c)	Share of d's purchases of c that is sourced from s		
$LTOT_s$	Aggregate employment in region s		
$L_{s,c}$	Quantity of labor used in industry c, country s		
FACTORYV (s,d,c)	Factory value of commodity c sent from s to d		
GDP(d)	Nominal GDP in region d		
$TM_{sd,c}$	Power of tariff imposed by d on cif flow of c from s		
VCIF(s,d,c)	Cif value of c sent from s to d		
$TX_{sd,c}$	Power of factory-door tax imposed by s on flow of c to d		
MARKETV(s,d,c)	Market value of c flowing from s to d		
W_s	Wage rate in country s		

included to denote a special role in the A2M conversion, with the variable normally being exogenous in Armington but becoming endogenous in Melitz. The destination-specific nature of the tax becomes important when we introduce the Melitz specification of productivity differences in country s between the firms that supply widgets to different destinations.

Equation (T7.3) defines fob prices. In BasicArmington these are the same as market prices. In a more detailed model, margin costs (e.g. transport to ports of exit) and taxes and subsidies cause a wedge between market prices and fob prices.

Equation (T7.4) defines cif prices. In BasicArmington these are the same as fob prices. In GTAP, transport costs from port of exit to port of entry provide a wedge between the two sets of prices. By making transport costs ad valorem with respect to fob prices we can maintain the percentage-change equation (T7.4), with an additional exogenous variable to represent percentage changes in the power of transport costs.

Equation (T7.5) defines purchasers prices as cif prices plus tariffs. In a detailed model such as GTAP, purchasers prices carry a user subscript. In BasicArmington this is not necessary because there is only one user of commodity c flowing from s to d, namely households in country d. Also, we have assumed in BasicArmington that there are no margins and sales taxes that separate cif prices from purchasers prices. In GTAP there are sales taxes but no margins. By treating the sales taxes as ad valorem on cif values, we can use (T7.5) in GTAP with additional exogenous variables to represent the powers of sales taxes.

Equation (T7.6), (T7.7) and (T7.8) determine the demand in country d for units of c from country s. Underlying these equations is an optimization problem of the form:

$$\text{choose } QCOUNT_{sd,c} \text{ and } Q_{sd,c} \text{ for all } d$$
$$\text{to minimize } \sum_{v} P_{vd,c} * QCOUNT_{vd,c} \tag{7.1}$$

$$\text{subject to } Q_{d,c} = CES_{d,c}\left(Q_{sd,c}, \text{ for all } s \in CNT\right) \tag{7.2}$$

$$\text{and } Q_{sd,c} = AAMel_{sd,c} * QCOUNT_{sd,c} \tag{7.3}$$

Via (7.1)–(7.3), households in country d are assumed to choose the number of units ($QCOUNT_{sd,c}$) and utility-generating or effective quantities ($Q_{sd,c}$) of commodity c that they buy from each country s (including their own) to minimize their total expenditure on c subject to meeting their overall requirements for c. In calculating expenditure, households use purchasers prices ($P_{vd,c}$). Overall requirements ($Q_{d,c}$) are specified as a CES aggregate of effective quantities purchased from each source (supplying country in the set CNT). Via this specification, we introduce the Armington assumption that units of commodity c from different sources are imperfect substitutes in satisfying household d's requirements. The two quantity concepts, $QCOUNT_{sd,c}$ and $Q_{sd,c}$, are related in (7.3) by $AAMel_{sd,c}$. This is a taste change variable. An increase in $AAMEL_{sd,c}$ means that household d is able to meet a given requirement for c ($Q_{d,c}$) with less purchases of c from s (a lower value for $QCOUNT_{sd,c}$ but the original value for $Q_{sd,c}$) while holding constant purchases of c from all other sources. That is, an increase $AAMEL_{sd,c}$ simulates a (s,c)-saving preference shift for household d. In Armington models, preference shift variables and more generally input-saving technology variables are normally exogenous. In moving from Armington to Melitz we will add equations that endogenize these variables to reflect the Meltiz specification of love of variety. To indicate this we have included the "Mel" designation in the taste-change variables.

Equation (T7.9) determines household d's requirement for commodity c. Underlying this equation is a Cobb-Douglas utility maximization problem of the form:

$$\text{choose } Q_{d,c} \text{ for all } c \text{ to maximize } \prod_{c} Q_{d,c}^{MU(d,c)} \tag{7.4}$$

$$\text{subject to } \sum_c P_{d,c} * Q_{d,c} = FMU_d * GDP_d, \tag{7.5}$$

where the MU(d,c)s are positive parameters satisfying $\sum_c MU(d,c) = 1.$[3] MU(d,c) is the share of household expenditure in country d devoted commodity c.

Normally, FMU_d is set on one. In this case, household d spends the country's entire GDP, a reasonable assumption for a model in which households are the only final demanders. The inclusion of the variable FMU_d is convenient for handling Walras' law: if we set FMU("CNT1") exogenously at unity thereby assuming that the first country consumes all its income, then the second country must also consume all its income meaning that FMU("CNT2") must be determined endogenously at unity.

Equation (T7.10) specifies the percentage change in the demand for inputs (labor) to be used in the production of c in country s. This is the percentage change in output less the percentage change in output per unit of input (productivity).

Equation (T7.11) adds up demands for labor in country s across industries (commodities) to determine total demand for labor in country s. Total demand for labor in s is usually set exogenously in line with exogenous specification of labor supply.

Equation (T7.12) adds up demands across destination countries d for commodity c produced in country s. Notice that the coefficients used in this equation are factory values, FACTORYV(s,d,c). These values are quantities times factory prices. Because factory prices are independent of destination d, factory values are proportional to quantities. That is, if FACTORYV(s,d,c) is twice FACTORYV(s,v,c), then we know that twice as many widgets (commodity c) are sent from s to d as are sent from s to v.

Equation (T7.13) determines GDP for country d as factor income (labor) in country d plus indirect taxes collected by country d.

Equation (T7.14) defines the change in the collection of tariff revenue by country d on the flow from s to d of commodity c. This change version is derived from the levels equation:

$$REVM_{sd,c} = \left[TM_{sd,c} - 1 \right] * VCIF(s,d,c) \tag{7.6}$$

where

$$VCIF(s,d,c) = QCOUNT_{sd,c} * PCIF_{sd,c} \tag{7.7}$$

Equation (T7.15) defines the change in the collection of tax revenue by country s on the flow from s to d of commodity c, derived from the levels equation:

$$REVX_{sd,c} = \left[TX_{sd,c} - 1 \right] * FACTORYV(s,d,c) \tag{7.8}$$

---

[3]In Chap. 6 we treated the MU's as variables. This was necessary for illustrating how the BR algorithm works.

where

$$\text{FACTORYV}(s, d, c) = \text{QCOUNT}_{sd,c} * \text{PFACTORY}_{sd,c}. \qquad (7.9)$$

Equation (T7.16) defines the average world-wide wage rate, avewage. This variable is a convenient numeraire. We set avewage exogenously to tie down absolute prices.

Equations (T7.1)–(T7.16) form the BasicArmington model. As indicated in Table 7.2, in the standard closure for this model, tax rates, tariff rates, technology variables, preference variables and the average propensity to consume in all except one country are exogenous.

7.2 Forming the BasicArmington-A2M System

This section presents the equations that, when added to those of the BasicArmington model, complete the A2M system. In describing these equations we show how the A2M system can be used to bring the BasicArmington model into line with the Melitz model set out in equations (T2.1)–(T2.12) in Table 2.2 plus (5.1)–(5.4) in Chap. 5.

Equations added to Armington to form the A2M system: (T7.17)–(T7.25) in Table 7.1

Equation (T7.17) links the Armington concept of quantity ($\text{QCOUNT}_{sd,c}$) to Melitz variables: sales by the typical c-producing firm on the sd-link ($Q_{\bullet sd,c}$) and the number of c-firms on the sd-link ($N_{sd,c}$).

Equation (T7.18) allows us to endogenize the factory-door tax rates. With the shift variable, $\text{ftxMel}_{sd,c}$ set exogenously on zero, (T7.18) together with (T7.1) and (T7.2) implies

$$\text{pmarket}_{\bullet sd,c} = w_s - \phi_{\bullet sd,c}. \qquad (7.10)$$

In combination with (T7.3), (T7.4) and (T7.5), Eq. (7.10) implies, as required in Melitz [see (T2.1) in Table 2.2], that

$$P_{\bullet sd,c} = w_s - \phi_{\bullet sd,c} + tm_{sd,c}. \qquad (7.11)$$

Equation (T7.19) allows us to endogenize preference variables. With the shift variable $\text{faaMel}_{sd,c}$ set exogenously on zero, (T7.19) and (T7.17) bring the Armington demand system for commodities distinguished by source, (T7.6)–(T7.8), into line with the Melitz specification in (T2.2)–(T2.4). To demonstrate this we start by substituting from (T7.19) and (T7.17) into (T7.6) to obtain

$$n_{sd,c} + q_{\bullet sd,c} + \frac{1}{(\sigma - 1)} * n_{sd,c} = q_{d,c} - \sigma * \left(\left[p_{\bullet sd,c} - \frac{1}{(\sigma - 1)} * n_{sd,c} \right] - p_{d,c} \right)$$

$$(7.12)$$

The n's drop out of (7.12) giving a percentage change version of (T2.3).[4] By substituting from (T7.19) into (T7.7) we obtain

$$P_{d,c} = \sum_s SHA(s, d, c) * \left[p_{\bullet sd,c} - \frac{1}{(\sigma - 1)} * n_{sd,c} \right] \tag{7.13}$$

which is a percentage change version of (T2.2).[5] By substituting from (T7.19) and (T7.17) into (T7.8) we obtain

$$q_{sd,c} = q_{\bullet sd,c} + n_{sd,c} + \frac{1}{(\sigma - 1)} * n_{sd,c} = q_{\bullet sd,c} + \frac{\sigma}{(\sigma - 1)} * n_{sd,c} \tag{7.14}$$

This is a percentage change version of (T2.4).

Equation (T7.20) is a percentage change version of the Melitz equation (T2.7). The derivation of (T7.20) from (T2.7) can be found in Appendix 4.3 [see the derivation of (T4.6P)].[6] When (T7.20) is imposed by exogenizing its shift variable [df$\ell_{s,c}$], we endogenize aoMel$_{s,c}$ appearing in equations (T7.1) and (T7.10). Thus, (T7.20) introduces the Melitz determination of movements in the overall productivity of industry s,c. With labor being the only input cost:

$$\sum_d FACTORYV(s, d, c) = W_s L_{s,c} \tag{7.15}$$

Using (T7.10), (T7.12), (T7.17) and (T7.20) together with (7.15), we find that if df$\ell_{s,c}$ is exogenous on zero, then aoMel is endogenously determined according to

---

[4] $\delta_{sd,c}$ is treated as a parameter throughout this chapter.

[5] In deriving (7.13) from the Melitz version of (T2.2) it is useful to note that $SHA(s, d, c) = N_{sd,c} \delta_{sd,c}^{\sigma} P_{\bullet sd,c}^{1-\sigma} \Big/ \sum_v N_{vd,c} \delta_{vd,c}^{\sigma} P_{\bullet vd,c}^{1-\sigma}$, see (4.66).

[6] In using Appendix 4.3 to follow the derivation of (T7.20), it is helpful to note that in the Appendix: the c subscript is dropped; T_{sd} represents the power of a tariff, now denoted by $TM_{sd,c}$; and $V(s,d)/T_{sd}$ is now denoted by MARKETV(s,d,c). Also recall from (2.27) that $\beta^{\sigma-1} = \alpha/(\alpha - (\sigma - 1))$.

$$\sum_d FACTORYV(s,d,c) * aoMel_{s,c} = \sum_d FACTORYV(s,d,c) * (n_{sd,c} + q_{\bullet sd,c} + w_s)$$

$$- [(\sigma - 1)/\sigma] * \sum_d MARKETV(s,d,c) * \left[n_{sd,c} + q_{\bullet sd,c} - \phi_{\bullet sd,c} + w_s\right]$$

$$- [(\sigma - 1)/(\alpha\sigma)] * \sum_d MARKETV(s,d,c) * \left[n_{s,c} + h_{s,c} + w_s\right]$$

$$- [(\alpha - (\sigma - 1))/(\alpha\sigma)] * \sum_d MARKETV(s,d,c) * \left[n_{sd,c} + f_{sd,c} + w_s\right]$$

$$(7.16)$$

Equation (T7.21)–(T7.24) are the percentage change versions of the Melitz equations (T2.8), (T2.10), (T2.11) and (T2.12).

Equation (T7.25) specifies the total collection of factory-door taxes from firms in industry s,c [dcolrevx$_{s,c}$]. Factory-door taxes (which can be positive or negative) are an artificial device introduced as part of the preparation of an Armington model for transition to Melitz. The role of these taxes is to introduce the Melitz specification of destination prices in an Armington framework. Totaled across destinations, we require the collection of these taxes for each industry s,c to be zero in the initial database, ensuring that:

$$\sum_d FACTORYV(s,d,c) = \sum_d MARKETV(s,d,c) \text{ for all s,c.} \qquad (7.17)$$

We also require the ability to keep tax collections on zero. This can be done by exogenizing dcolrevx$_{s,c}$ on zero change.

With dcolrevx$_{s,c}$, ftxMel$_{sd,c}$ and df$\ell_{s,c}$ set exogenously on zero, (T7.25) imposes the zero-profit condition for industry s,c in accordance with the Melitz equations (T2.5), (T2.6) and (T2.9). Corresponding to the exogenization of dcolrevx$_{s,c}$ is endogenization of n$_{s,c}$: under Melitz assumptions the number of firms in industry s,c adjusts to maintain zero profits in response to shocks to tariffs or other exogenous variables.

To demonstrate that setting dcolrevx$_{s,c}$, ftxMel$_{sd,c}$ and df$\ell_{s,c}$ exogenously on zero imposes Melitz specification of zero-profits, we substitute from (T7.17), (T7.18) and (T7.1) into (T7.15). This gives

$$100 * drevx_{sd,c} = TX_{sd,c} * FACTORYV(s,d,c) * \left[n_{sd,c} + q_{\bullet sd,c} + w_s - \phi_{\bullet sd,c}\right]$$

$$- FACTORYV(s,d,c) * \left[n_{sd,c} + q_{\bullet sd,c} + w_s - aoMel_{s,c}\right]$$

$$(7.18)$$

Next, we add over d on both sides of (7.18). The resulting left hand side is zero. This follows from (7.25) and the assumption that dcolrevx$_{s,c}$ is zero. On the right hand side we replace TX$_{sd,c}$ * FACTORYV(s, d, c) by MARKETV(s, d, c) and use (7.16) to eliminate aoMel$_{s,c}$. After making simplifications we reach:

$$0 = \frac{1}{\sigma} * \sum_{d} \text{MARKETV}(s, d, c) * [w_s - \phi_{\bullet sd,c} + q_{\bullet sd,c} + n_{sd,c}]$$

$$- \frac{\alpha - (\sigma - 1)}{\alpha\sigma} \sum_{d} \text{MARKETV}(s, d, c) * [n_{sd,c} + f_{sd,c} + w_s]. \qquad (7.19)$$

$$- \frac{(\sigma - 1)}{\alpha\sigma} \sum_{d} \text{MARKETV}(s, d, c) * [n_{s,c} + h_{s,c} + w_s]$$

Equation (7.19) is a percentage change version of the Melitz zero-profit condition for industry s,c. This was demonstrated in Appendix 4.3 where we derived (T4.5P) as the percentage change version of the zero-profit condition. All that is required to see that (7.19) is the same as (T4.5P) is an adjustment of notation. In (7.19) we denote the market value of the sd,c flow as MARKETV(s,d,c), whereas in (T4.5P) it was $V(s,d)/T_{sd}$. In (T4.5P) we eliminated α in favor of β by using (2.27). In (7.19), we retain α. Finally, in the first term on the RHS of (7.19) we use $[w_s - \phi_{\bullet sd,c}]$ instead of $[p_{\bullet sd,c} - t_{sd,c}]$. The equivalence of these two terms follows from (T7.1) to (T7.5) and (T7.18) with $ftxMel_{sd,c}$ set exogenously on zero.

The beginning of this section set the task of describing how Eqs. (T7.17)–(T7.25) which complete the A2M system can be used to convert the BasicArmington model into the Melitz model set out in equations (T2.1)–(T2.12) plus (5.1)–(5.4). We have now completed the task with respect to (T2.1)–(T2.12). What about (5.1)–(5.4)? In combination with other equations in Table 7.1, Eq. (T7.14) is a percentage change version of (5.1). With $dcolrevx_{s,c}$ set exogenously on zero for all s and c, Eq. (T7.13) is a percentage change version of (5.3). Equations (T7.11) and (T7.9) are percentage change versions of (5.2) and (5.4).

Table 7.2 shows the Melitz closure of the A2M system. As can be seen from the table, in moving from the Armington closure to the Melitz closure, we exogenize $dcolrevx_{s,c}$ together with the shift variables in (T7.18), (T7.19) and (T7.20). Correspondingly, we endogenize movements in the number of firms in each industry ($n_{s,c}$), productivity in each industry ($aoMel_{s,c}$), household preferences over sources ($aaMel_{sd,c}$) and factory-door tax rates ($txMel_{sd,c}$). This last endogenization allows movements in destination-specific productivity variables ($\phi_{\bullet sd,c}$) to affect market prices in accordance with Melitz theory.

7.3   Data for the BasicArmington-A2M System

In Sect. 7.4 we report simulation results from the A2M system. In this section we describe the database underlying those simulations. The input-output data and parameter values are identical to those for nearly all the simulations in Chap. 6.[7]

---

[7]The only exceptions are the Armington simulations in Table 6.5 with σ not equal to 3.8.

Consequently, we can check the legitimacy of the A2M system by comparing Armington and Melitz results reported in Sect. 7.4 with corresponding results in Chap. 6.

The input-output data for the A2M system (and the Chap. 6 models) are in Table 7.3. As is the case for detailed models, these data are in market values. It is market values that are observed and collated by statistical agencies. The data in Table 7.3 show a world of two identical countries, each producing two commodities using labor and no intermediate inputs and each having a single final user (households). GDP in both countries is $1.8588 split equally between wages in the production of commodities 1 and 2. There are no tariffs in the initial situation. Households in each country consume an amount of commodity 1 produced in their own country with a market value of $0.69311 and an amount of commodity 1 imported from the other country with a market value of $0.23629. Similarly with commodity 2.

As can be seen from Table 7.1, in addition to input-output data in market values, implementation of the A2M system requires values for the substitution elasticity (σ), the Pareto parameter (α) and factory-door tax powers, $TX_{sd,c}$. Initial values for theses tax powers are required not only in (T7.15) but also in setting initial values for FACTORYV(s,d,c) using the identity:

$$FACTORYV(s, d, c) = MARKETV(s, d, c)/TX_{sd.c} \qquad (7.20)$$

For σ, we use the value 3.8. This was the value that we used in all simulations in Chap. 6 except for some of the Armington simulations reported in Table 6.5. In an Armington model σ is the elasticity of substitution from the point of view of users between imported and domestic products. For Melitz, it is the elasticity of substitution between varieties of widgets produced by different firms. As discussed in Chapt. 6, in comparing Armington and Melitz models it is not appropriate to use the same σ values: they refer to different things in the two models. However, in the A2M system, there is only one σ parameter. In using the system to produce Armington results, care should be taken to adopt a σ value appropriate for Armington. In using the system to produce Melitz results we should use a value appropriate for Melitz. Our focus in the next section is on checking whether the A2M system correctly produces MelitzGE results. Consequently, we set σ at a value appropriate for Melitz [3.8, see Balistreri and Rutherford (2013)].

For α we use the value 4.6, as in Chap. 6. This parameter plays a role only in Melitz simulations.

Setting the initial values for the factory-door tax powers, $TX_{sd,c}^{Init}$

The appropriate initial values for TX differ depending on whether we wish to adopt Armington or Melitz assumptions. If we are treating sector c as Armington, then usually we will set

Table 7.3 Data for BasicArmington: input-output flows valued at market prices

	Ind1, Cnt 1	Ind2, Cnt1	Ind1, Cnt 2	Ind2, Cnt2	Hhlds, Cnt1	Hhlds, Cnt2	Total
Com and factor flows							
Com1, Country1					0.69311	0.23629	*0.9294*
Com2, Country1					0.69311	0.23629	*0.9294*
Com1, Country2					0.23629	0.69311	*0.9294*
Com2, Country2					0.23629	0.69311	*0.9294*
Labor	0.9294	0.9294	0.9294	0.9294			
Tariff revenue							
Com1, Country1						0	
Com2, Country1						0	
Com1, Country2					0		
Com2, Country2					0		
Total	0.9294	0.9294	0.9294	0.9294	1.8588	1.8588	

$$TX_{sd,c}^{Init} = 1 \text{ for all } s, d \tag{7.21}$$

It is possible in an Armington model to have destination-specific taxes in the database but this is not usually the case, and it is not the case for the BasicArmington model. By adopting (7.21) for all c we effectively rule out destination-specific taxes in the database for Armington.

If we are treating sector c as Melitz, then we decided to set the initial values for the $TX_{sd,c}$ for each s,d to reflect the reciprocal of the initial values assumed for link-specific productivities $(1 \big/ \Phi_{\bullet sd,c}^{Init})$. Why did we do this?

In answering this question we start by noting that the data for MARKETV(s,d,c) is interpreted in the A2M system as the product of the initial market price of c on the s,d-link and the initial number of units of c sent on the s,d-link, that is,

$$MARKETV^{Init}(s, d, c) = PMARKET_{sd,c}^{Init} * COUNT_{sd,c}^{Init} \tag{7.22}$$

Under Melitz specifications, market prices are proportional to wage rates (which don't depend on destination, d) divided by link-specific productivity levels (which do depend on d). Thus for Melitz we interpret the observed values for MARKETV(s,d,c) for all d as satisfying

$$MARKETV^{Init}(s, d, c) = \kappa(s, c) * \frac{1}{\Phi_{\bullet sd.c}^{Init}} * COUNT_{sd,c}^{Init} \tag{7.23}$$

where

$\kappa(s, c)$ is the factor of proportionality and

$\Phi_{\bullet sd.c}^{Init}$ is the initial productivity level for the typical c-producing firm on the s, d-link.

FACTORYV(s,d,c) in the A2M system is interpreted as the product of the initial factory price of c in s (which doesn't depend on d) and the initial number of units of c sent on the s,d-link. Thus,

$$\text{FACTORYV}^{\text{Init}}(s, d, c) = \zeta(s, c) * \text{COUNT}^{\text{Init}}_{sd,c} \tag{7.24}$$

where $\zeta(s, c)$ is the factor of proportionality.

Combining (7.20), (7.23) and (7.24) suggests, for Melitz sectors, that the settings for the initial values of $\text{TX}_{sd,c}$ across all d should be proportional to $1/\Phi^{\text{Init}}_{\bullet sd,c}$. That is,

$$\text{TX}_{sd,c} = \psi(s, c) * \frac{1}{\Phi^{\text{Init}}_{\bullet sd,c}} \tag{7.25}$$

where $\psi(s, c)$ is the factor of proportionality.

To tie down the value of $\psi(s, c)$ we use (7.17) and (7.20) which lead via (7.25) to

$$\text{TX}^{\text{Initial}}_{sd,c} = \frac{\sum_j \left[\dfrac{\text{MARKETV}(s,j,c)}{\sum_{dd} \text{MARKETV}(s,dd,c)} \right] * \Phi^{\text{Initial}}_{sj,c}}{\Phi^{\text{Initial}}_{sd,c}}. \tag{7.26}$$

In generating the results reported in the next section, we use the same initial values of Φ as those for the MelitzGE computations in Chap. 6. For the two countries (s and d equal to 1 and 2),

$$\Phi^{\text{Init}}_{sd,c} = \begin{cases} 1.1 & \text{for } s = d \text{ and all } c \\ 2.0 & \text{for } s \neq d \text{ and all } c \end{cases} \tag{7.27}$$

Applying (7.26) with the data in Table 7.3 we obtain

$$\text{TX}^{\text{Init}}_{sd,c} = \begin{cases} 1.208 & \text{for } s = d \text{ and all } c \\ 0.664 & \text{for } s \neq d \text{ and all } c \end{cases} \tag{7.28}$$

The validity of the GEMPACK solution method depends on computing deviations away from an initial solution. An initial solution is a list of values for prices, quantities, tax and tariff rates, preference and technology variables, and macro variables that satisfy the model's equations. Equation (7.26) is required so that the initial value of $\text{TX}_{sd,c}$ forms part of a legitimate initial solution for the Melitz model. However, provided that the setting of the $\text{TX}^{\text{Initial}}_{sd,c}$'s is consistent with (7.17) [initial tax collection is zero], we found by experimentation that the setting of the TX's for Melitz sectors does not affect Melitz simulation results for percentage changes in variables representing welfare, employment by industry, wage rates and values for imports, exports and consumption. Nevertheless, we recommend using (7.26).

Being meticulous about setting a legitimate initial solution is good practice. While from the point of view of percentage change results, (7.26) is not strictly required for Melitz sectors, (7.21) is strictly required for Armington sectors.[8]

7.4   Illustrative Simulations with the BasicArmington-A2M System

Table 7.4 contains two sets of results computed with the A2M system for the BasicArmington model and the database described in Sect. 7.3. Both sets give the effects of a 10% tariff imposed by country 2 on all imports ($tm_{12,c} = 10$ for all c). The first set was generated with the Armington closure from Table 7.2 and the second was generated with the Melitz closure.

The main purpose of Table 7.4 is to check the validity of the conversion from the BasicArmington model to Melitz. We have done this by comparing the Armington and Melitz results in Table 7.4 with those for equivalent variables[9] in the first panel

Table 7.4 BasicArmington-A2M simulations: Armington and Melitz results for the effects of a 10% tariff imposed by country 2 on all imports from country 1 (percentage changes)

	Armington with Armington data[a]		Melitz with Melitz data[b]	
	Country d = 1	Country d = 2	Country d = 1	Country d = 2
Real consumption (welfare)	*−1.258*	*1.102*	*−1.321*	*1.044*
Welfare decomposition				
Armington effects	−1.258	1.102	−1.159	0.886
Employment	0.000	0.000	0.000	0.000
Genuine tax-carrying flows (tariffs)	0.000	−0.126	0.000	−0.248
Traditional terms of trade	−1.258	1.227	−1.159	1.134
Additional Melitz effects	*0.000*	*0.000*	*−0.162*	*0.158*
Extra Melitz terms of trade	0.000	0.000	−0.162	0.158
Efficiency in producing effective units	0.000	0.000	0.000	0.000

[a]$TX_{sd,c}^{Init} = 1$ for all sd,c
[b]$TX_{sd,c}^{Init}$ determined by (7.26)–(7.28)

---

[8]As mentioned earlier we assume that there are no real-world destination-specific taxes.
[9]This is all the variables for Armington and the welfare variables for Melitz, but not the decomposition variables for Melitz. Melitz welfare is decomposed in a different way in the two tables.

of Table 6.4. Reassuringly these are close to identical for all equivalent variables, not just those shown in the tables.

The welfare decomposition results shown in Table 7.4 are based on the equation:

$$\left(\sum_c \sum_s VPUR(s, d, c)\right) * welfare_d$$

$$= \{W_d * LTOT_d * \ell tot_d$$

[*changes in employment*]

$$+ \sum_c \sum_s \left(TM_{sd,c} - 1\right) * VCIF(s, d, c) * q_{sd,c}$$

[*changes in tax-carrying flows*]

$$+ \sum_c \sum_{s \neq d} \{TX_{ds,c} * FACTORYV(d, s, c) * peffobave_{d,c} - VCIF(s, d, c) * peffobave_{s,c}\}$$

[*Traditional changes in terms of trade*]

$$+ \sum_c \sum_{s \neq d} \{TX_{ds,c} * FACTORYV(d, s, c) * \left[peffob_{ds,c} - peffobave_{d,c}\right]$$

$$- VCIF(s, d, c) * \left[peffob_{sd,c} - peffobave_{s,c}\right]\}$$

[*Additional Melitz changes in terms of trade*]

$$+ \sum_c \sum_s TX_{ds,c} * FACTORYV(d, s, c) * [q_{ds,c} - \ell_{d,c}]$$

$$+ \sum_c \{\sum_s [TX_{ds,c} - 1] * FACTORYV(d,s,c)\} * \ell_{d,c}$$

[*Changes in efficiency in producing effective units*]

$$(7.29)$$

where

$$peffob_{sd,c} = pfob_{\bullet sd,c} - aaMel_{sd,c}. \tag{7.30}$$

and

$$[\sum_d TX_{sd,c} * FACTORYV(s, d, c)] * peffobave_{s,c}$$

$$= \sum_d TX_{sd,c} * FACTORYV(s, d, c) * peffob_{sd,c}. \tag{7.31}$$

In (7.29)–(7.31), $peffob_{sd,c}$ is the percentage change in the fob price of an effective unit of commodity c sent from s to d and $peffobave_{s,c}$ is an average over d of the $peffob_{sd,c}$'s. The percentage change in the quantity of effective units of c sent on the sd-link ($q_{sd,c}$), is the percentage change in count units ($qcount_{sd,c}$) modified for changes in quality ($aaMel_{sd,c}$). By the quality of the sd,c flow, we mean the suitability of this flow for satisfying demands for c in d, or in Melitz terms the variety embedded in the flow. Our definition of the price of effective units is consistent with this definition of effective quantity units.

Equation (7.29) is a decomposition of the percentage change in welfare for country d, measured by the percentage change in real consumption:

$$\left(\sum_c \sum_s \text{VPUR}(s, d, c)\right) * \text{welfare}_d = \sum_c \sum_s \text{VPUR}(s, d, c) * q_{sd,c}. \quad (7.32)$$

Equation (7.32) defines welfare in the same way as in Chap. 6. However, the decomposition in (7.29) is different from that set out in Box 6.2 and derived in Appendix 6.4. We provide a derivation of (7.29) in Appendix 7.2, using only equations for BasicArmington, that is Eqs. (T7.1)–(T7.16). Consequently (7.29) is a decomposition that could appear in an Armington model before the addition of equations to convert the model to Melitz.

The first term in (7.29) takes account of extra consumption (welfare) made possible by extra employment. The second term captures welfare gains or losses associated with increased or reduced quantities of tariff-bearing imports, with quantities measured in effective units ($q_{sd,c}$). The terms-of-trade contribution in (7.29) involves a comparison of the prices that country d receives for exports of effective units with the prices that it pays for imports of effective units, that is a comparison of peffob$_{ds,c}$ with peffob$_{sd,c}$. In using fob prices for effective units of imports (as well as exports), we take advantage of the assumption built into BasicArmington that percentage movements in cif prices of imports are the same as those in the fob prices of the corresponding exports.

As can be seen from (7.29) we break the terms-of-trade contribution into two parts: a Traditional part and an additional Melitz part. The Traditional part compares export and import prices excluding Melitz pricing-to-market effects based on productivity differences between firms on different trade links. The Traditional part reflects the Armington-compatible idea that industry c in country d charges the same price for effective units leaving its factories, irrespective of destination. The Melitz idea that firms price to market is captured by the second part that takes account of differences between destination-specific fob prices and average fob prices at source.

This brings us to the last two terms in (7.29), labeled Changes in efficiency in producing effective units. As explained in Sect. 7.3 [see Eq. (7.17)] the collection of factory-door taxes is set at zero in both Armington and Melitz applications of the A2M system. We limit our explanation of the last two terms in (7.29) to this case. With zero collection, the last term is zero. Thus, Changes in efficiency in producing effective units reduces to:

$$\Delta\text{Efficiency}_d = \sum_c \sum_s \text{TX}_{ds,c} * \text{FACTORYV}(d, s, c) * [q_{ds,c} - \ell_{d,c}] \quad (7.33)$$

Under the zero collection assumption and (7.15), (7.33) can be rewritten as:

$$\Delta \text{Efficiency}_d = \sum_c [\{\sum_s TX_{ds,c} * \text{FACTORYV}(d, s, c) * q_{ds,c}\} - W_d L_{d,c} * \ell_{d,c}] \quad (7.34)$$

Written like this, we see that the efficiency term for country d is a sum of industry productivity increases. The productivity increase for industry c is calculated by comparing the change in output of effective units of c in country d with the change in d's employment devoted to c.

If c is produced in an Armington industry and we make standard assumptions (zero changes in aoMel$_{d,c}$, aaMel$_{ds,c}$ and txMel$_{ds,c}$) then, as shown in Appendix 7.2, the productivity change in industry d,c is zero. In these circumstances, (7.34) reduces to

$$\Delta \text{Efficiency}_d = \sum_{c \in M} [\{\sum_s TX_{ds,c} * \text{FACTORYV}(d, s, c) * q_{ds,c}\} - W_d L_{d,c} * \ell_{d,c}]$$

$$(7.35)$$

where M is the set of Melitz industries.

If c is produced in a Melitz industry and we assume no changes in input requirements to set up firms and to set up on links (h$_{d,c}$ and f$_{ds,c}$ equal to zero) then, as shown in Appendix 7.2, the productivity change in industry d,c is given by $1/\sigma$ times the output change. In these circumstances, (7.34) becomes

$$\Delta \text{Efficiency}_d = \frac{1}{\sigma} * \sum_{c \in M} \sum_s TX_{ds,c} * \text{FACTORYV}(d, s, c) * q_{ds,c} \quad (7.36)$$

or equivalently

$$\Delta \text{Efficiency}_d = \frac{1}{\sigma - 1} * \sum_{c \in M} W_d L_{d,c} * \ell_{d,c} \quad (7.37)$$

Equations (7.36) and (7.37) reveal that for Melitz the efficiency gains identified in (7.29) arise from economies of scale. If output of effective units in industry d,c increases or equivalently if industry d,c uses more labor, then the industry experiences a positive efficiency effect, that is an increase in effective units of output per unit of labor input. Economies of scale in Melitz can be either internal to firms or external. Internal economies of scale arise from longer production runs which reduce fixed costs per unit of output. However, in our experience with Melitz-based models, external economies of scale are generally more important. In the absence of changes in the input requirements for d,c firms to setup for business and to setup on links, the average size of these firms is constant [this is demonstrated in Appendix 7.2, see (7.55)]. Thus on average there are no realized internal economies of scale. However, if industry d,c expands then there are external economies of scale: by having more firms and therefore more varieties, the industry is able to satisfy consumer requirements more precisely (increasing effective output) while holding output in count terms per unit of input constant.

In the experiment reported in Table 7.4, there is no change in employment in any industry or country. This follows from the assumed constancy of aggregate employment in each country and the symmetric treatment of the industries in each country (see Appendix 6.2). With no change in employment at the industry level, (7.37) explains why the Melitz panel of Table 7.4 shows zero effects in the efficiency row.

The only other feature of Table 7.4 warranting further comment is the split of the Melitz terms-of-trade effects. In this experiment, the Traditional terms-of-trade effects, based on the assumption that fob prices of effective units are independent of destination, are less extreme than the total terms-of-trade effects. Melitz pricing to market accentuates the terms-of-trade effects. For both countries, the contraction in the scale of exports caused by country 2's tariffs raises costs per unit of effective export: export firms are larger and have increased productivity but in the calculation of the prices of effective units the productivity effect is outweighed by reductions in variety. Both countries increase the prices of effective units destined for export relative to those destined for domestic sales ($\text{peffob}_{sd,c} - \text{peffobave}_{s,c}$ is positive for $d \neq s$). Consequently, a priori it is not clear how Melitz pricing to market will affect the terms of trade. However, because trade is balanced in value terms and country 1 suffers a Traditional terms-of-trade loss, country 1 reduces the effective quantity of its exports by less than country 2.[10] Thus, compared with country 2, country 1 experiences a smaller efficiency loss in creating effective units for export relative to units for its domestic market. This means that the pricing-to-market increase in export prices for country 1 is less than that for country 2, giving a positive additional Melitz terms-of-trade effect for country 2 and a negative effect for country 1.

7.5 Converting the GTAP Model to Melitz: The GTAP-A2M System

This section describes the application of our A2M method to create a GTAP model in which industries can be treated as either Armington or Melitz. The GEMPACK code for this Melitz-enhanced version of GTAP can be downloaded, together with zips of simulations presented in Sect. 7.6 using the Electronic Supplementary Material, see footnote at the opening page of this chapter. Readers can follow the changes and additions we made to the original GTAP code by looking at notes in the downloadable code marked with our initials, PDMJMR. We created the Melitz-enhanced version of GTAP in five steps.

---

[10]This can be seen in the first panel of Table 6.4: country 1's exports fall by 20.648% whereas country 2's exports fall by 25.046%.

Step 1. Downloaded GTAP model

We downloaded from the GTAP website the standard GTAP model, version 7.0 Novemner 2008. This is a large Armington model frequently used in policy analysis. We ran test simulations using the 57-commodity by 10-region database.

Step 2. Preliminary modifications of parameters and flow data

In standard GTAP, user requirements for good i are specified via nested CES functions. In the top nest, substitution between domestic commodity i and a composite imported i is specified with a substitution elasticity of ESUBD(i). In the lower nest, composite imports are formed from imports distinguished by source region. Substitution between imports by source is specified by a CES function with elasticity ESUBM(i). In standard GTAP it is assumed that ESUBM(i) is twice ESUBD(i). For Melitz, requirements for commodity i are specified by unnested CES functions. Unnested functions are equivalent to nested functions if the substitution elasticities have the same value in each nest. In preparation for Melitz, we reset ESUBM(i) to be the same as ESUBD(i). This left us with elasticity values for some commodities that are too low for a Melitz model in which substitution elasticities should be substantially greater than one. Consequently we reset ESUBD(i) at 2.5 for all i for which the standard GTAP value is less than 2.5.

In standard GTAP, diagonal trade flows, VXMD(i,r,r), are not necessarily zero. This gives us the awkward idea that there are exports from region r to itself, separate from domestic flows from r to r denoted in GTAP by VMD(i,r). Non-zero diagonal trade flows are an outcome of regional aggregation, but they add complexity to modelling, especially in the context of Melitz. We formed a new database simply by adding the diagonal trade flows VXMD(i,r,r) to VMD(i,r) and then zeroing out VXMD(i,r,r). This does not upset database balancing conditions.

Step 3. Preliminary modifications of the GTAP theory

Standard GTAP includes the variable ams(i,r,s) that allows for input-saving technical change in region s associated with the use of commodity i imported from region r. Surprisingly, there is no corresponding variable for input-saving technical change in region s associated with the use of commodity i produced in s. We added such a variable. In keeping with GTAP notation this variable is ads(i,s). Without this new variable, it would not be possible to follow the method we have devised for implementing the Melitz love-of-variety specification.

The cost of transporting a unit of commodity i between regions r and s is specified in GTAP as being independent of the price of the commodity. This means that changes in costs in region r can cause differences in the percentage changes in the fob price of i exported from r to s and the cif price of i imported by s from r. Melitz theory requires equal percentage changes in fob and corresponding cif prices. We added equations to GTAP that allow international transport costs to be ad valorem on fob values. Under this specification, fob and cif prices can move together.

In preparation for Melitz, we added new tax and technology variables [txMel(i,r,s) and aoMel(i,r)] to GTAP. The new taxes are charged just beyond the factory door. We include these taxes in market prices. Their special feature is that they are destination specific. Thus, market prices which are now denoted by pmarket(i,r,s) become destination specific. In standard GTAP, market prices are denoted by pm(i,r). We retain this variable but now refer to it as the factory price of i produced in r. The factory price is determined by costs in the factory including production taxes. Factory prices do not vary with destination. If the powers of the newly included factory-door taxes are set at one, then there is no substantive change from standard GTAP, no difference between market prices and factory prices.

The new technology variable, aoMel(i,r), is an additional all-input-saving technical change in industry i and country r.[11] For Armington this is an additional exogenous variable. For Melitz it is endogenously determined according to the Melitz specification of changes in industry productivity. We define a new cost variable for industry i,r, pbundle(i,r) as the factory price, pm(i,r), excluding the effects of aoMel(i, r). This new variable plays the role in the GTAP-A2M system of w_r in the BasicArmington-A2M system. The variable pbundle(i,r) is the percentage change in the cost of a bundle of inputs used in industry i,r. The variable aoMel(i,r) affects the number of such bundles required by industry i,r per unit of output. As in BasicArmington-A2M, we assume in GTAP-A2M that current production and setup costs for industry i,r, have the same input mix.[12] This contrasts with GTAP-Het created by Akgul et al. (2016) in which setup costs use only primary factors whereas current production uses both primary factors and intermediate inputs.

The final preliminary modification is the addition to the standard GTAP code of equations that we find helpful in interpreting results and setting closures. These equations define: expenditure-side aggregates for each region in real terms (C, I, G, X and M); real GDP by region from the income side including our factory-door taxes; imports by commodity and importing region but undifferentiated by source region; world GDP; and world consumption. We also set up a decomposition of private consumption for each region. This is a legitimate decomposition of welfare when consumption is a legitimate measure of welfare. Consumption measures welfare when we exogenize the balance of trade, investment and government expenditure. Our private-consumption decomposition is an alternative to GTAP welfare measures and decompositions which are retained in the model. Our reason for including an additional decomposition is that we are more familiar with it than with the GTAP measures of equivalent variation and other welfare variables.

Step 4. Adding the Melitz equations

None of the modifications described in steps 2 and 3 is fundamental. Their implementation still leaves us with an Armington model, only slightly changed from the original model. In this step we add Melitz equations and data which allow

---

[11]The standard version of GTAP includes all-input-saving technical change variables ao(i,r) determined by several shift variables. Our aoMel(i,r) appears as an additional shifter in the determination of ao(i,r).

[12]This is trivial in BasicArmington-A2M: there is only one input, labor.

us to implement a distinctly different model. These additions are given in the GEMPACK code under the heading Melitz additions, found towards the end of our Melitz-enhanced GTAP code.

Apart from the notation, readers who have worked through the A2M system for BasicArmington will be able to follow the Melitz additions without difficulty. Notes in our downloadable GTAP code point to the corresponding parts in the A2M code in Appendix 7.1. Unfortunately, unavoidable notational complexity is caused by the GTAP convention of using separate variables and coefficients to identify flows of commodities between regions and within regions, e.g. VXMD(i,r,s) and VMD(i,r).

Step 5. Closures

As with the BasicArmington model, the conversion of GTAP to Melitz is completed by closure changes that turn on the Melitz specifications of: destination-specific pricing (endogenization of txMel); average productivity in industries (endogenization of aoMel); love of variety (endogenization of aaMel); and number of firms in each industry and country (endogenization of n). An Armington closure for standard GTAP and the swaps necessary to convert a particular industry, "Wap", from Armington to Melitz are shown in our annotated downloadable GTAP files.

7.6   Illustrative Results from the GTAP-A2M System

Tables 7.5 and 7.6 provide illustrative results from our 10-region 57-commodity GTAP-A2M system. The tables show the percentage effects on private consumption in the 10 regions of an increase of 10% in the power of the tariffs on all imports to North America of wearing apparel (Wap), from an average tariff rate of 9.89% to 20.88% [$=100 * (1.0989 * 1.10-1)$]. In Table 7.5, Wap is modeled as a Melitz industry while all other industries are Armington. In Table 7.6, all industries are Armington. In both simulations, private consumption is a legitimate measure of welfare: we hold constant the balance of trade, aggregate investment and public expenditure in all regions.

The tables show a decomposition of the welfare results into five contributing factors. The theoretical structure of the decomposition is similar to that in Table 7.4.[13] However, unlike BasicArmington, GTAP has many genuine indirect taxes besides tariffs. Consequently, an extra factor is required in Tables 7.5 and 7.6 to account for the welfare effects of changes in tax-carrying flows apart from the directly affected

---

[13]Direct tax-carrying flow in Tables 7.5 and 7.6 corresponds to Genuine tax-carrying flows (tariffs) in Table 7.4. Traditional terms of trade and Extra Melitz terms of trade in Tables 7.5 and 7.6 correspond to the two terms-of-trade effects in Table 7.4. Extra Melitz efficiency in Tables 7.5 and 7.6 corresponds to Efficiency in producing effective units in Table 7.4. We omit the "employment factor" from Table 7.5 and 7.6: it would simply be a column of zeros because we hold all primary factor inputs (labor, capital, land and natural resources) constant in each country.

flow of imports of Wap into NAmerica. The details of the decomposition can be seen in the downloadable code referenced at the start of Sect. 7.5.

Comparison of the first columns in Tables 7.5 and 7.6 shows that Melitz and Armington identify the same regions as the main winners and losers. NAmerica, the region that imposes the Wap tariff, gains 0.1037% in welfare in the Melitz simulation and 0.0193% in the Armington simulation. SEAsia loses 0.7892% under Melitz and 0.3414% under Armington while SouthAsia loses 0.3870 and 0.1442%. As can be seen in Table 7.7, these latter two regions have the greatest reliance on Wap exports to NAmerica. SEAsia's exports of Wap to NAmerica expressed as a percentage of SEAsia's total private consumption (welfare) is 2.57. The corresponding percentage for SouthAsia is 1.20. Figure 7.1 shows that Melitz assumptions generally accentuate Armington results. The main welfare losing regions lose more under Melitz than under Armington and the winning regions win more.

To help us understand these and other features of Tables 7.5 and 7.6 we start by explaining the decomposition results column by column. This enables us to locate the mechanisms that underlie the results and differences in their operation under Armington and Melitz. But understanding why under Melitz and Armington the various mechanisms operate differently and are more or less favourable for some regions than for others does not give us a complete description of the results. After describing the columns individually, we provide a framework for understanding the difference between Melitz and Armington in the net welfare outcome (the addition across the columns) for each region. We focus on SEAsia, SouthAsia and NAmerica.

Decomposition results in Tables 7.5 and 7.6, *column by column*

The first decomposition column in Tables 7.5 and 7.6 gives the welfare contributions of changes in Direct tax-carrying flows. The contraction of NAmerian Wap imports causes a loss of 0.0429% in NAmerican welfare under Melitz and 0.0416% under Armington. Looking at detailed results (not presented here) from the two simulations, we find that the tariff increase by NAmerica reduces their Wap imports by 44%. That these decreases are the same in the two simulations is not an accident. As explained in Sect. 6.5, to improve comparability of Armington and Melitz simulations we should set substitution elasticities in the two models so that the elasticity of demand for imports with respect to tariff changes is approximately the same. In the current application, we achieved comparability by setting the import/domestic substitution elasticity in Armington at 9.5, whereas the corresponding parameter for Melitz (the variety substitution elasticity) was set at 2.5. The NAmerican column of Table 7.8 implies that Wap imports are about 0.6% of NAmerican private consumption (=1.67 − 1.08). As illustrated in Fig. 7.2, with the NAmerican Wap tariff rate moving from 9.89 to 20.88% and with imports falling by 44%, the Direct tax-carrying flow effect must be about −0.042% under either Melitz or Armington assumptions.

In the second decomposition column of Tables 7.5 and 7.6 we see that contributions of Other tax-carrying flows are larger negatives for SEAsia and SouthAsia under Melitz than under Armington, (−0.0760 compared with −0.0524 for SEAsia and −0.0764 compared with −0.0482 for SouthAsia). Other tax-carrying flows tend

Table 7.5 A decomposition of the effects on private consumption (welfare) of a 10% increase in the power of the tariff on Wearing apparel (Wap) into North America: Melitz assumptions

	Percentage effect on:	Percentage point contributions from:					
Region	Private consumption, welfare	Direct tax-carrying flow	Other tax-carrying flows	Traditional terms of trade	Extra Melitz terms of trade	Extra Melitz efficiency	Scale effect
1 Oceania	-0.0065	0.0000	-0.0044	-0.0131	0.0020	0.0091	0.0084
2 EastAsia	-0.1073	0.0000	-0.0301	-0.0157	0.0203	-0.0818	-0.0528
3 SEAsia	-0.7892	0.0000	-0.0760	0.0565	0.1165	-0.8861	-0.8818
4 SouthAsia	-0.3870	0.0000	-0.0764	0.2178	0.0426	-0.5711	-0.5514
5 NAmerica	0.1037	-0.0429	-0.0014	0.0089	-0.0262	0.1653	0.1525
6 LatinAmer	-0.1669	0.0000	-0.0145	-0.0256	0.0347	-0.1615	-0.1613
7 EU_25	0.0186	0.0000	-0.0030	-0.0172	0.0022	0.0367	0.0332
8 MidEastNAfr	-0.1635	0.0000	-0.0078	-0.0679	0.0343	-0.1220	-0.1228
9 SubSahAfr	-0.0842	0.0000	-0.0152	-0.0392	0.0227	-0.0523	-0.0529
10 RestofWorld	-0.0760	0.0000	-0.0060	-0.0151	0.0115	-0.0663	-0.0611

Table 7.6 A decomposition of the effects on private consumption (welfare) of a 10% increase in the power of the tariff on Wearing apparel (Wap) into North America: Armington assumptions

	Percentage effect on:		*Percentage point contributions from:*				
Region	Private consumption, welfare	Direct tax-carrying flow	Other tax-carrying flows	Traditional terms of trade	Extra Melitz terms of trade	Extra Melitz efficiency	Scale effect
1 Oceania	0.0006	0.0000	0.0015	−0.0009	0.0000	0.0000	0.0000
2 EastAsia	−0.1210	0.0000	−0.0709	−0.0501	0.0000	0.0000	0.0000
3 SEAsia	−0.3414	0.0000	−0.0524	−0.2891	0.0000	0.0000	0.0000
4 SouthAsia	−0.1442	0.0000	−0.0482	−0.0960	0.0000	0.0000	0.0000
5 NAmerica	0.0193	−0.0416	0.0057	0.0551	0.0000	0.0000	0.0000
6 LatinAmer	−0.0903	0.0000	−0.0188	−0.0715	0.0000	0.0000	0.0000
7 EU_25	0.0036	0.0000	0.0028	0.0009	0.0000	0.0000	0.0000
8 MidEastNAfr	−0.0702	0.0000	−0.0089	−0.0613	0.0000	0.0000	0.0000
9 SubSahAfr	−0.0452	0.0000	−0.0093	−0.0359	0.0000	0.0000	0.0000
10 RestofWorld	−0.0326	0.0000	−0.0094	−0.0232	0.0000	0.0000	0.0000

Table 7.7 Fob values of Wap flows expressed as percentage of producing region's aggregate consumption: derived from GTAP data for 2004

	Oceania	EastAsia	SEAsia	SouAsia	NAm	LatinAm	EU_25	MENA	SSA	RoW	Total
Oceania	1.30	0.03	0.01	0.00	0.05	0.00	0.03	0.00	0.00	0.00	1.43
EastAsia	0.06	2.57	0.06	0.01	0.43	0.05	0.39	0.07	0.02	0.16	3.82
SEAsia	0.03	0.34	1.98	0.01	2.57	0.05	1.03	0.07	0.05	0.07	6.20
SouthAsia	0.02	0.03	0.03	0.53	1.20	0.02	1.31	0.14	0.02	0.06	3.37
NAmerica	0.00	0.01	0.00	0.00	1.08	0.02	0.01	0.00	0.00	0.00	1.12
LatinAmer	0.00	0.01	0.00	0.00	0.86	2.34	0.06	0.00	0.00	0.01	3.30
EU_25	0.00	0.05	0.01	0.00	0.06	0.01	3.06	0.03	0.00	0.12	3.35
MidEastNAfr	0.01	0.03	0.01	0.01	0.60	0.01	1.53	2.20	0.03	0.07	4.49
SubSahAfr	0.00	0.02	0.01	0.00	0.53	0.01	0.22	0.01	2.81	0.01	3.62
RestofWorld	0.00	0.02	0.00	0.00	0.14	0.00	1.31	0.04	0.00	0.84	2.37

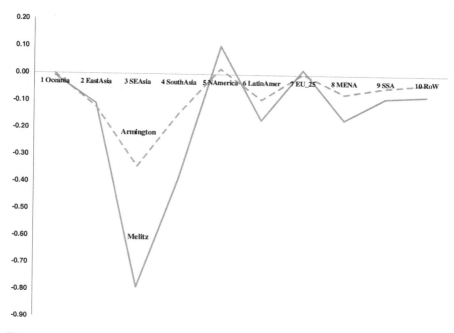

Fig. 7.1 A 10% increase the power of the Wap tariff on North American imports: welfare effects in Armington and Melitz

to make a negative contribution when there is a general contraction in consumption. For SEAsia and SouthAsia, the larger negative contributions under Melitz than under Armington are a reflection of the larger general contractions in consumption in these two regions under Melitz than under Armington. However, differences between the Other tax-carrying-flow contributions explain only 0.0236 percentage points (=0.0760 − 0.0524) of the total welfare difference for SEAsia of 0.4478% (=0.7892 − 0.3414) and only 0.0282 percentage points (=0.0764 − 0.0482) of the total welfare difference for SouthAsia of 0.2428% (=0.3870 − 0.1442).

The contributions of the Traditional terms-of-trade effects (calculated with fob prices of effective units independent of destination) under Melitz and Armington are sharply contrasting. Whereas under Armington assumptions the contributions from this source for SEAsia and SouthAsia are negative (−0.2891 and −0.0960), under Melitz assumptions these contributions are positive (0.0565 and 0.2178). These contrasting results reflect contrasting slopes of the supply curves for effective units of Wap. Under Armington assumptions, these supply curves are close to flat. The terms-of-trade deteriorations under Armington are a reflection of the real factor-price reductions required in the SEAsia and SouthAsia economies to stimulate exports of products outside the Wap sector sufficiently to replace lost Wap exports and rebalance trade. As explained in Sect. 7.4 and demonstrated in Eqs. (7.36) and (7.37), sectors modeled under Melitz assumptions exhibit economies of scale. Thus, in our Melitz simulation, Wap supply curves for effective units are downward sloping. Contraction of Wap output in SEAsia and SouthAsia increases costs in these regions per effective unit of output of Wap. These cost increases are passed on in SEAsia and SouthAsia's export prices per effective unit of Wap, generating terms-of-trade gains for these regions.

Why didn't this happen in the MelitzGE simulation in Table 7.4? There, the movement in the Traditional terms of trade for country 1 in response to country 2's tariffs was negative under Melitz. The salient difference now is the contraction in Wap output in countries that export to NAmerica. In MelitzGE, none of the sectors in country 1 contracted: as explained in Appendix 6.2, this reflected symmetry in the setup of the MelitzGE experiment whereby employment and output in all of country 1's industries was unaffected by country 2's tariffs. Thus, there was no tendency in the MelitzGE simulation reported in Table 7.4 for any of country 1's industries to move up their downward sloping supply curves.

For NAmerica the Traditional terms-of-trade contribution to welfare is positive under Armington. It is still positive under Melitz but much smaller (0.0089 compared with 0.0551). Under both Armington and Melitz, NAmerica reduces its imports of Wap (by 44%), allowing it to reduce its aggregate exports. This pushes its trade partners up their demand curves for NAmerican products, generating terms-of-trade gains for NAmerica. So what is the difference here between Melitz and Armington? Under Melitz, but not under Armington, NAmerica pays higher cif prices for its imports of effective units of Wap reflecting lost scale economies and resulting higher costs in supplying Wap to NAmerica from SEAsia, SouthAsia and other Wap exporting regions. Higher prices for Wap imports under Melitz erode NAmerica's terms-of-trade gain. Another minor contribution to this erosion comes from NAmerica's exports of Wap. With the imposition of the tariff, Wap production expands in NAmerica, with consequent scale economies and reductions in the prices of effective units. However, the negative effect on NAmerica's terms of trade from lower export prices for Wap is small because Wap is a negligible fraction of NAmerica's total exports.

Factoring in the Extra Melitz terms-of-trade effects turns the total terms-of-trade contribution under Melitz for NAmerica negative (0.0089 − 0.0262). While cif count prices charged by typical exporting firms to NAmerica fall, in the calculation of the prices of effective units, the reduction in variety in NAmerican Wap imports is decisive, leading to increases in cif prices of effective units to NAmerica. The mirror image of the Extra Melitz terms-of-trade loss for NAmerica is Extra Melitz terms of trade gains for other regions. The imposition of the tariff by NAmerica, and the contraction in the scale of the NAmerican Wap market for imports, causes prices per effective unit from Wap exporting regions to increase by considerably larger percentages in the NAmerican market than in the domestic markets of these exporting regions. It is these destination-specific differences in price movements that is captured in the Extra Melitz terms-of-trade column of Table 7.5.[14]

---

[14]In Table 7.4, the additional Melitz terms-of-trade effect for the tariff-imposing country (country 2) is positive whereas in Table 7.5 it is negative. In Table 7.5, NAmerica's tariffs inflate the fob cost of its

Table 7.8 Fob values of Wap flows expressed as percentage of consuming region's aggregate consumption: derived from GTAP data for 2004

	Oceania	EastAsia	SEAsia	SouAsia	NAm	LatinAm	EU_25	MENA	SSA	RoW
Oceania	1.30	0.00	0.01	0.00	0.00	0.00	0.00	0.00	0.00	0.00
EastAsia	0.51	2.57	0.50	0.04	0.18	0.22	0.20	0.60	0.30	0.55
SEAsia	0.03	0.04	1.98	0.01	0.13	0.02	0.06	0.06	0.07	0.03
SouthAsia	0.02	0.01	0.03	0.53	0.08	0.01	0.10	0.17	0.04	0.03
NAmerica	0.02	0.02	0.02	0.01	1.08	0.17	0.01	0.03	0.01	0.01
LatinAmer	0.01	0.00	0.01	0.00	0.08	2.34	0.01	0.01	0.01	0.01
EU_25	0.07	0.09	0.13	0.02	0.05	0.06	3.06	0.51	0.10	0.77
MidEastNAfr	0.01	0.00	0.01	0.00	0.03	0.01	0.10	2.20	0.04	0.03
SubSahAfr	0.00	0.00	0.00	0.00	0.02	0.00	0.01	0.01	2.81	0.00
RestofWorld	0.01	0.01	0.01	0.01	0.02	0.00	0.20	0.10	0.01	0.84
	1.98	2.74	2.71	0.61	1.67	2.85	3.75	3.71	3.39	2.27

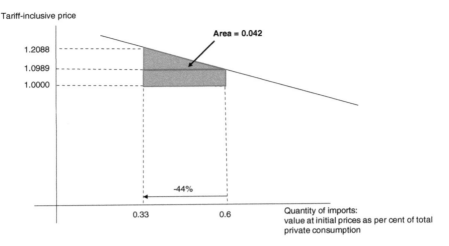

Fig. 7.2 North American imports of Wap

The final column in the welfare decomposition block of Tables 7.5 and 7.6 shows the contributions of Extra Melitz efficiency gains. In the Melitz model derived from BasicArmington, we demonstrated in (7.36) and (7.37) that these gains arise entirely from changes in the scale of production in Melitz industries, measured either by output of effective units or primary factor input. For the GTAP-A2M system, this result is not exact. There are too many other complications in GTAP such as international transport costs. Nevertheless, scale economies in Melitz industries remain the overwhelming component of Extra Melitz efficiency gains. This is demonstrated in Table 7.5 by the close correspondence between the columns for Extra Melitz efficiency and Scale effect. The Scale effect column was calculated according to (7.36) using results from our GTAP-A2M simulations for movements in sales of effective units ($q_{ds,c}$).

NAmerica's tariff on Wap imports causes increases in Wap output in NAmerica, and to a lesser extent in Oceania and EU_25. Consequently, in Table 7.5, these regions have positive entries in the Extra Melitz efficiency column. The tariff directly causes a switch by NAmerican consumers to their domestic product. The Wap industries in Oceania and EU_25 have little dependence on the NAmerican market and are not impacted to a significant extent by the NAmerican tariff. At the same time, the Wap industries in these two regions gain from reduced competition from imports, reflecting higher costs of supplying effective units from the contacting Wap industries in major exporting regions, EastAsia, SEAsia and SouthAsia.

---

imports by reducing the efficiency in exporting of its foreign suppliers of Wap. There is no compensating increase in the fob prices of NAmerica's exports. In Table 7.4, country 2's tariffs inflate the costs of both its exports and imports.

Understanding the net welfare outcomes for Melitz relative to Armington

SEAsia and SouthAsia are the two regions with the largest welfare losses under both Melitz and Armington, and the largest welfares losses in Melitz relative to Armington. That these two regions have the largest welfare losses is readily understandable: as mentioned earlier they have the greatest reliance on Wap exports to NAmerica. Here we provide back-of-the-envelope (BOTE) calculations to explain why Melitz relative to Armington shows an extra welfare loss of 0.4478% (=0.7892 − 0.3414) for SEAsia and an extra welfare loss of 0.2428% (=0.3870 − 0.1442) for SouthAsia. Then we do a BOTE calculation to explain NAmerica's extra welfare gain under Melitz of 0.0844% (=0.1037 − 0.0193).

We start with SEAsia. The Extra Melitz efficiency column in Table 7.5 shows a welfare contribution for SEAsia of −0.8861. In Table 7.6 this contribution is zero. However not all of the −0.8861 in Table 7.5 is an extra negative effect for Melitz relative to Armington. A lot of the loss of efficiency in SEAsia's Wap industry identified by Melitz is passed on to other regions in the form of higher prices for SEAsia's exports of effective units of Wap. What this illustrates is dependence between the decomposition columns of Table 7.5: a negative efficiency effect produces a partially offsetting positive terms-of-trade effect. How can we explain the net effect in an intuitive way?

The net welfare effect for SEAsia of the deterioration in efficiency of its Wap industry and the associated terms-of-trade improvement depends on what happens to the price of domestically produced effective units of Wap in SEAsia's domestic market. Why? What about profits and losses in export and domestic markets? Under Melitz assumptions, SEAsia's Wap industry makes zero total profits. If the shock to the international economy (NAmerica's tariffs) causes SEAsia's Wap exports to generate extra profits in exporting, then the welfare benefit to SEAsia shows up as lower prices for Wap effective units on the domestic market. Similarly, if the shock reduces SEAsia's export profits in the Wap industry, then these lost profits show up as higher prices for Wap effective units on the domestic market. In either case, it doesn't matter from a welfare point of view whether SEAsia's export prices rise or fall relative to domestic prices. All that matters is what happens to domestic prices.

Under Melitz, the imposition of NAmerica's tariffs causes the price to consumers in SEAsia of domestically produced effective units of Wap to increase in *real* terms by 13.07%.[15] This is low compared with the price increase of effective units of Wap exported from SEAsia. In line with the loss of efficiency in SEAsia's Wap industry, the increase in the average real price of effective units produced by the industry is 17.49%. But as we have argued already, this is irrelevant for our current purpose. Only the 13.07% matters. From Table 7.7, we see that absorption of domestically

---

[15] By *real* we mean the price increase relative to the general price level in SEAsia measured by movements in the price index for factors (labor, capital, land and natural resources).

produced Wap in SEAsia is 1.98% of aggregate consumption in the pre-simulation situation.[16] In the post-simulation situation this increases slightly, giving an average through the Melitz simulation of 1.99%. A 13.07% increase in the cost of an item worth 1.99% of consumption generates a welfare loss for SEAsia of 0.2601% (=0.0199 * 13.07). Under Armington, with no change in the efficiency of SEAsia's Wap industry, there is close to zero change in the real price in SEAsia of domestically produced Wap. The 0.2601% welfare loss that we have identified for Melitz as the effect of efficiency deterioration and offsetting terms-of-trade improvement is an extra loss in Melitz relative to Armington.

Under both Armington and Melitz, SEAsia must rebalance its trade after the contraction of its Wap exports. In Table 7.6, rebalancing under Armington assumptions generates a negative terms-of-trade contribution for SEAsia of 0.2891%. Rebalancing under Melitz assumptions causes a larger negative terms-of-trade contribution. While in both simulations SEAsia's exports of effective units of Wap to NAmerica decline by 44%, SEAsia's total exports of effective units of Wap decline by 46.58% under Melitz and 25.82% under Armington.[17] In value terms, SEAsia loses 34.94% of its Wap exports under Melitz and 26.11% under Armington. Under Melitz, SEAsia's Wap exports decline not only to NAmerica but also to its other trade partners. This is because SEAsia, with its heavy dependence on exports to NAmerica, suffers an efficiency loss in its Wap industry relative to that in other Wap exporting regions. By contrast, under Armington, SEAsia's Wap exports increase to most of its trade partners apart from NAmerica. Under Armington assumptions, with no scale-related efficiency loss, SEAsia's Wap industry benefits from the general improvement in SEAsia's competitiveness (real depreciation) associated with rebalancing trade. With a larger loss of Wap export revenue, SEAsia needs a larger real devaluation under Melitz than under Armington. Measured by the reduction in the factor price index relative to the world price level, SEAsia's real devaluation under Melitz is 52% larger than under Armington. With a 52% larger real devaluation for Melitz than for Armington, the expected terms-of-trade contribution from trade rebalancing is 52% larger for Melitz than for Armington: 0.4394 percentage points rather than 0.2891. On this basis, we have explained a further 0.1502 percentage points (=0.4394 − 0.2891) of SEAsia's additional 0.4478% welfare loss in Melitz relative to Armington.

As discussed earlier, Melitz generates an additional tax-carrying-flow loss of 0.0236 percentage points for SEAsia relative to Armington. Taking this into account brings the explained welfare loss for SEAsia under Melitz relative to Armington to 0.4338 percentage points (=0.2601 + 0.1502 + 0.0236), close to the simulated difference of 0.4478 percentage points.

---

[16]This is simply 100 times the ratio of domestically produced Wap used is SEAsia to aggregate consumption. It doesn't mean that Wap is necessarily used by households.

[17]Readers can check these results and others mentioned in this and following paragraphs by rerunning our simulations using the downloadable code mentioned at the start of Sect. 7.5.

For SouthAsia, the ingredients for explaining the additional welfare loss of 0.2428% under Melitz relative to Armington are as follows. Under Melitz, the increase in the real price of effective units of domestically produced Wap in the SouthAsia market is 14.62%. Under Armington it is negligible. On average through the Melitz simulation, sales of domestic Wap in SouthAsia are worth 0.54% of total consumption. Thus, the 14.62% increase in the cost of domestic Wap products in SouthAsia imparts a welfare loss of 0.0790% for Melitz relative to Armington. Real devaluation in SouthAsia is 104% larger under Melitz than under Armington. Applying this percentage to the Armington terms-of-trade contribution (−0.0960, Table 7.6) to SouthAsia's welfare loss gives an extra welfare loss for Melitz of 0.0998% (=0.0960 * 1.04). Factoring in the extra contribution for Melitz from Other tax carrying flows (−0.0282) gives the total estimate for SouthAsia's extra welfare loss under Melitz relative to Armington at 0.2070% (=0.0790 + 0.0998 + 0.0282), again acceptably close to the simulated result of 0.2428%.

For NAmerica, the explanation of the Melitz welfare result relative to the Armington result starts the same way as for the other two regions, but with opposite sign. Efficiency improvement in the expanded NAmerican Wap industry reduces the real price of domestically produced effective units in the NAmerican market by 13.57%. On average through the Melitz simulation, the value of purchases of domestic Wap in NAmerica is 1.175% of the total value of consumption. A 13.57% price reduction applied to an item worth 1.175% of consumption gives a welfare gain of 0.1595%. This is a welfare gain for Melitz relative to Armington: under Armington the change in the price of domestically produced effective units of Wap in the NAmerican market is negligible.

NAmerica's tariffs reduce the value of its Wap imports under both Armington and Melitz. On this account, trade rebalancing requires real appreciation with an associated improvement in the terms of trade. This can be seen in Table 7.6 which shows for the Armington simulation a positive terms-of-trade contribution to NAmerica's welfare of 0.0551%. For Melitz, the terms-of-trade contribution to NAmerica's welfare is negative, −0.0172 = (0.0089 − 0.0262). The rebalancing terms-of-trade effect is dominated for NAmerica under Melitz by increases in the prices of effective units of Wap imported from SEAsia, SouthAsia and other suppliers to the U.S. market. These suppliers have suffered cost increases caused by the reduction in the scale of their output. Relative to Armington, Melitz gives a terms-of-trade contribution for NAmerica of −0.0723 (= −0.0172 − 0.0551).

Tax-carrying flows make a slightly larger negative welfare contribution for NAmerica under Melitz than under Armington, −0.0084 [= (−0.0429 − 0.0014) − (−0.0416 + 0.0057)].

In total, our BOTE calculation for NAmerica explains a welfare benefit of 0.0788% (= 0.1595 − 0.0723 − 0.0084), close to the simulated result of 0.0844.

7.7 Summary and Conclusions

We have found a relatively simple method for converting an existing Armington model into a Melitz model. The initial steps in this method may require minor alterations to the Armington model. Then we add a group of Melitz equations onto the bottom of the Armington model to form what we call an A2M system. Users of the A2M system can switch between Melitz and Armington assumptions by closure swaps. It is also necessary to change the setting of a dummy coefficient that identifies which industries are to be treated as Melitz and which are to be treated as Armington. In going from Armington to Melitz, modelers should consider changing the value of parameters that determine import/domestic substitution in Armington and variety substitution in Melitz. If it is intended to compare Armington and Melitz results, then substitution parameters should be calibrated so that both models give similar realistic import responses to changes in tariffs.

To explain our conversion method we applied it to the BasicArmington model. We tested the method by comparing Melitz results from the BasicArmington-A2M system with results from the directly built Melitz model described in Chap. 6. Subsequently we built an A2M system for a standard 10 region by 57 commodity GTAP model.

Previously it has been argued (see Balistreri and Rutherford, 2013) that Melitz specifications produce a difficult computational problem that needs to be tackled by iterative methods using GAMS software. Because of perceived computational difficulties, earlier CGE models with Melitz features have been rather small, and implemented with stylized data. We have shown that Melitz features can be introduced fully into high-dimension CGE models using GEMPACK software.

Our method depends on the simplifying assumption that in Melitz industries the input-mix (primary factors and materials) for creating the infrastructure for setting up a firm and trading on links is the same as that for producing commodities. This assumption is implicitly part of the original theoretical model in Melitz (2003) where there is only one input, labor. GTAP staff (see Akgul et al. 2016) have created a version of the GTAP model, GTAP-HET, that includes Melitz features and allows differences between the composition of inputs for the production of infrastructure and for the production of commodities. However, as demonstrated in Appendix 7.3, GTAP-HET falls short of being a conversion of the Armington version of GTAP to a Melitz version.

A priority in CGE trade modeling is to gain understanding of how new-trade-theory specifications such as Melitz work in a model with policy relevant industry and regional disaggregation. Towards this objective, we formulated an equation that decomposes Armington and Melitz regional welfare results from an A2M system into the parts attributable to changes in:

- employment of primary factors;
- volumes of tax-carrying flows;
- traditional terms of trade (excludes Melitz destination-specific pricing);
- extra Melitz terms of trade (extra effects due to destination-specific pricing); and
- scale-related efficiency in the production of effective units.

This decomposition reveals how various factors operate under Melitz and Armington. But it doesn't give us an intuitive understanding of the net outcome of these factors. For example, via the decomposition we see, under Melitz assumptions, that the imposition of tariffs on wearing apparel (Wap) by NAmerica causes a welfare-reducing efficiency loss for SEAsia in its Wap industry and an associated welfare-enhancing improvement in SEAsia's terms of trade. The decomposition results show that the net outcome is negative but don't tell us why the negative efficiency effect outweighs the positive terms-of-trade effect.

To go beyond simply observing that some effects are negative and some are positive, and that their total is whatever it is, we need an overarching theory of the net outcome checked out by back-of-the-envelope (BOTE) calculations. In the case of our GTAP-A2M simulations of the effects of a Wap tariff imposed by NAmerica, we set out a 3-part overarching theory of why Melitz welfare results for SEAsia and other major Wap exporting regions are more negative under Melitz than under Armington and why the welfare result for NAmerica is more positive under Melitz than under Armington.

The first part of this theory is that the Melitz-related phenomenon of scale efficiency losses for major Wap-exporting regions is relevant for their welfare only to the extent of the associated increase in the price of domestically produced and consumed effective units of Wap and the importance of domestic Wap in their total consumption. Similarly, Melitz-related efficiency gains in NAmeica's Wap industry are relevant for NAmerica's welfare only to the extent of the associated reduction in the price of domestically produced and consumed effective units of Wap and the importance of domestic Wap in NAmerica's total consumption.

The second part of the theory is that the Wap industry in major Wap-exporting regions is more negatively impacted under Melitz than under Armington. This is despite calibrating substitution elasticities so that the reduction in NAmerica's Wap imports is the same in both the Armington and Melitz simulations. Under Melitz, major Wap-exporting regions lose sales outside NAmerica because of efficiency deterioration. This doesn't happen under Armington. With greater loss of Wap sales, the real devaluations required by major Wap exporters to rebalance trade is greater under Melitz than under Armington. This produces a larger terms-of-trade welfare loss under Melitz than under Armington associated with greater expansion of exports outside Wap.

The third part of the theory is that the welfare effects associated with tax-carrying flows magnify those produced in the first two parts. Contraction of consumption in major Wap-exporting countries reduces their tax-carrying flows while expansion of consumption in NAmerica increases its tax-carrying flows.

By combining elements from the GTAP database with GTAP-A2M results, we were able to confirm numerically that in combination the three parts of the overarching theory explain quite accurately the differences in the Melitz and Armington welfare results. BOTE calculations are an important technique for cutting through the maze of complications in CGE models to locate for any specific result the essential underlying ingredients.

Appendix 7.1: GEMPACK Program for an A2M System: Solving BasicArmington and MelitzGE

This appendix contains GEMPACK code for the A2M system that can generate solutions for the BasicArmington model and the MelitzGE model. The code, together with zipped simulations from Sect. 7.4 can be downloaded using the Electronic Supplementary Material, see footnote at the opening page of this chapter. A2M closures for the BasicArmington and MelitzGE models are at the end of the appendix.

Sections A7.1.1–A7.1.6 is the code for the BasicArmington model, including a welfare decomposition. These sections can be thought of as representing a typical stand-alone Armington model. Sections A7.1.7–A7.1.11 are the additional material required for the conversion from Armington to Melitz. In the case of the BasicArmington model, the inclusion of the additional material requires no alteration to the code of the Armington model.

Being able to convert from Armington to Melitz without altering the Armington model has important practical advantages. When this is possible, it means that we can perform Melitz computations starting from an Armington model, which may be large and complex, without having to undertake time-consuming work in understanding all of the details of the original model or having to reconfigure it. However, in practical applications, alterations of the Armington code may be required. For example, if the original Armington model does not include suitable factory-door taxes [$txMel_{sd,c}$], these need to be added. Fortunately, our experience reported in Sect. 7.5 in creating an A2M system for GTAP suggests that the alterations to the original Armington model will usually be minimal.

GEMPACK code

```
! ****************************************************************** !
! BasicArmington model                        !
! ****************************************************************** !
```

File SETS *# Commodities and countries #* ;
File IODATA *# Input-output data #*;
File OTHDATA *# Other data e.g. parameter values #*;

Set CNT *# Set of regions #* **read elements from file** SETS **header** *"CNT"*;
Set COM *# Set of commodities #* **read elements from file** SETS **header** *"COM"*;

! A7.1.1 DECLARATION OF COEFFICIENTS FOR BasicARMINGTON   !
Coefficient
(All,c,COM)**(All**,s,CNT) C_L(c,s) *# Quantity of labor used in industry c, country s #*;
(All,c,COM)**(All**,s,CNT)**(All**,d,CNT) REVM(c,s,d) *# Tariff revenue derived by d on cif flows of c from s #*;
(All,c,COM)**(All**,s,CNT)**(All**,d,CNT) REVX(c,s,d) *# Revenue derived by s on on factory values of c to d #*;
(All,c,COM)**(All**,s,CNT)**(All**,d,CNT) VPUR(c,s,d) *# Purchasers value of flow c,s,d #*;
(All,c,COM)**(All**,d,CNT) VPUR_S(c,d) *# Purchasers value of c (from all sources) consumed in d #*;
(All,c,COM)**(All**,s,CNT)**(All**,d,CNT) C_SHA(c,s,d) *# Share of d's purchases of c that is sourced from s #*;
(Parameter) SIGMA *# Substitution elasticity #*;
(All,c,COM)**(All**,s,CNT)**(All**,d,CNT) VCIF(c,s,d) *# Cif value of c sent from s to d #*;
(All,d,CNT) C_LTOT(d) *# Aggregate employment in region d #* ;
(All,d,CNT) C_GDP(d) *# Nominal GDP in region d #*;
(All,c,COM)**(All**,s,CNT)**(All**,d,CNT) C_TX(c,s,d) *# Power factory-door tax imposed by s on flow of c to d #*;
(All,c,COM)**(All**,s,CNT)**(All**,d,CNT) C_TM(c,s,d) *# Power tariff imposed by d on cif flow of c from s #*;
(All,s,CNT) C_W(s) *# Wage rate in country s #*;
(All,c,COM)**(All**,s,CNT)**(All**,d,CNT) MARKETV(c,s,d) *# Market value of c flowing from s to d #*;
(All,c,COM)**(All**,s,CNT)**(All**,d,CNT) FACTORYV(c,s,d) *# Factory value of commodity c sent from s to d. #*;

! A7.1.2 SETTING INITIAL VALUES FOR THE COEFFICIENTS IN THE BasicARMINGTON MODEL AND DETERMINING INITIAL LEVELS SOLUTION !

Read
SIGMA **from file** OTHDATA **Header** *"SGMA"*;
MARKETV **from file** IODATA **header** *"DESV"*;
C_L **from file** IODATA **header** *"LAB"*;
REVM **from file** IODATA **header** *"REVM"*;

Formula
(Initial)(**All**,c,COM)(**All**,s,CNT)(**All**,d,CNT) C_TX(c,s,d)= 1;
(Initial) (**All**,c,COM)(**All**,s,CNT)(**All**,d,CNT) FACTORYV(c,s,d) =MARKETV(c,s,d)/C_TX(c,s,d);
(Initial) (**All**,c,COM)(**All**,s,CNT)(**All**,d,CNT) REVX(c,s,d) = MARKETV(c,s,d) -FACTORYV(c,s,d);
(initial) (**All**,s,CNT) C_W(s) = 1.0 ;
(**All**,c,COM)(**All**,s,CNT)(**All**,d,CNT) VCIF(c,s,d)
                 = FACTORYV(c,s,d)+REVX(c,s,d);*! No transport costs: fob= cif!*
(**All**,c,COM)(**All**,s,CNT)(**All**,d,CNT) VPUR(c,s,d) = FACTORYV(c,s,d)+REVM(c,s,d)+REVX(c,s,d);
(**All**,c,COM)(**All**,d,CNT) VPUR_S(c,d) = **Sum**(s,CNT, VPUR(c,s,d));
(**All**,c,COM)(**All**,s,CNT)(**All**,d,CNT) C_SHA(c,s,d) = VPUR(c,s,d)/VPUR_S(c,d);
(**All**,s,CNT) C_LTOT(s) = **Sum**(c,COM, C_L(c,s));
(**All**,d,CNT) C_GDP(d) = **sum**(c,COM, C_W(s)*C_L(c,d))
           + **sum**(c,COM, **sum**(s,CNT, REVM(c,s,d)))
           + **sum**(c,COM, **sum**(s,CNT, REVX(c,d,s)));
(**All**,c,COM)(**All**,s,CNT)(**All**,d,CNT) C_TM(c,s,d)= 1+REVM(c,s,d)/ VCIF(c,s,d);

! A7.1.3 DECLARATION OF VARIABLES FOR BasicARMINGTON MODEL !
Variable
(**All**,c,COM)(**All**,s,CNT) pfactory(c,s) *# Factory price of commodity c produced in s #;*
(**All**,c,COM)(**All**,s,CNT)(**All**,d,CNT) txMel(c,s,d) *# Dest-specific tax power by s on factory value c to d #;*
(**All**,c,COM)(**All**,s,CNT)(**All**,d,CNT) pmarket(c,s,d) *# Price just beyond the factory door of c,s to d #;*
(**All**,c,COM)(**All**,s,CNT)(**All**,d,CNT) pfob(c,s,d) *# Fob price of flow c,s to d #;*
(**All**,c,COM)(**All**,s,CNT)(**All**,d,CNT) pcif(c,s,d) *# Cif price of flow c,s to d #;*
(**All**,c,COM)(**All**,s,CNT)(**All**,d,CNT) p(c,s,d) *# Purchasers price of c,s,d #;*
(**All**,c,COM)(**All**,s,CNT)(**All**,d,CNT) tm(c,s,d) *# Power of tariff on flow c,s to d, applied to cif value #;*
(**All**,c,COM)(**All**,s,CNT)(**All**,d,CNT) qcount(c,s,d) *# Quantity of c (number of widgets) sent from s to d #;*
(**All**,c,COM)(**All**,s,CNT)(**All**,d,CNT) q_effect(c,s,d) *# Effective qty of c sent from s to d, see (7.1)-(7.3)#;*
(**All**,s,CNT) w(s) *# Wage rate in region s #;*
(**All**,c,COM)(**All**,s,CNT) aoMel(c,s) *# All input tech variable: output per unit of input in industry c,s #;*
(**All**,c,COM)(**All**,d,CNT) q_d(c,d) *# Qty of composite c consumed in d, not differentiated by source # ;*
(**All**,c,COM)(**All**,s,CNT)(**All**,d,CNT) aaMel(c,s,d) *# Pref variable for c,s to satisfy d's demands for c #;*
(**All**,d,CNT) f_mu(d) *# Country d's average propensity to consume out of GDP #;*
(**All**,d,CNT) gdp(d) *# GDP in d #;*
(**All**,c,COM)(**All**,d,CNT) p_d(c,d) *# Price of the c-composite in d #;*
(**All**,c,COM)(**All**,d,CNT) l(c,d) *# Quantity of labor used in industry c,d # ;*
(**All**,c,COM)(**All**,d,CNT) qotot(c,d) *# Total qty (no. of widgets) produced by industry c in region d # ;*
(**All**,s,CNT) ltot(s) *# Employment in country s #;*
(**Change**)(**All**,c,COM)(**All**,s,CNT)(**All**,d,CNT) d_revm(c,s,d) *# d's tariff revenue on flow c,s,d# ;*
(**Change**)(**All**,c,COM)(**All**,s,CNT)(**All**,d,CNT) d_revx(c,s,d) *# s's tax revenue on flow c,s,d # ;*
ave_wage *# World-wide average wage rate #;*

! A7.1.4 UPDATES FOR COEFFICIENTS IN BasicARMINGTON !

Update
(**All**,c,COM)(**All**,s,CNT)(**All**,d,CNT) MARKETV(c,s,d) = pmarket(c,s,d)*qcount(c,s,d) ;
(**All**,c,COM)(**All**,s,CNT)(**All**,d,CNT) FACTORYV(c,s,d) = pfactory(c,s)*qcount(c,s,d) ;
(**All**,c,COM)(**All**,s,CNT) C_L(c,s) = l(c,s);
(**All**,s,CNT) C_W(s) = w(s);
(**Change**) (**All**,c,COM)(**All**,s,CNT)(**All**,d,CNT) REVM(c,s,d)= d_revm(c,s,d) ;
(**Change**) (**All**,c,COM)(**All**,s,CNT)(**All**,d,CNT) REVX(c,s,d) = d_revx(c,s,d);
(**All**,c,COM)(**All**,s,CNT)(**All**,d,CNT) C_TX(c,s,d)=txMel(c,s,d);

! A7.1.5 EQUATIONS FOR BasicARMINGTON: PERCENTAGE CHANGE AND CHANGE VERSIONS !

Equation E_pfactory *# Equation (T7.1) Factory price , determined by input cost per widget #*
(**All**,c,COM)(**All**,s,CNT) pfactory(c,s) = w(s)-aoMel(c,s);
Equation E_pmarket *# (T7.2) Market price (just beyond factory), factory price & dest specific tax #*
(**All**,c,COM)(**All**,s,CNT)(**All**,d,CNT) pmarket(c,s,d) = pfactory(c,s) + txMel(c,s,d);
Equation E_pfob *# (T7.3) Fob prices. Same as pmarket in model without other taxes & margins #*

(All,c,COM)(All,s,CNT)(All,d,CNT) pfob(c,s,d) = pmarket(c,s,d);
Equation E_pcif # *(T7.4) Cif prices. Same as fob in absence of transport costs and other margins* #
(All,c,COM)(All,s,CNT)(All,d,CNT) pcif(c,s,d) = pfob(c,s,d);
Equation E_p # *(T7.5) Purchasers prices. Cif prices plus tariffs* #
(All,c,COM)(All,s,CNT)(All,d,CNT) p(c,s,d) = pcif(c,s,d) + tm(c,s,d) ;
Equation E_qcount # *(T7.6) Demands for comodities differentiated by source* #
(All,c,COM)(All,s,CNT)(All,d,CNT) qcount(c,s,d) + aaMel(c,s,d)
　　　　　　　　　　= q_d(c,d) - SIGMA*[(p(c,s,d)- aaMel(c,s,d)) -p_d(c,d)];
Equation E_p_d # *(T7.7) Purchasers prices for commodities undifferentiated by source* #
(All,c,COM)(All,d,CNT) p_d(c,d) = {sum(s,CNT, C_SHA(c,s,d)*[(p(c,s,d)- aaMel(c,s,d))])};
Equation E_q_effect # *(T7.8) Effective qty of c sent from s to d, see (7.1)-(7.3)* #
(All,c,COM)(All,s,CNT)(All,d,CNT) q_effect(c,s,d) = qcount(c,s,d) + aaMel(c,s,d) ;
Equation E_q_d # *(T7.9) Demand for composities: derived from Cobb-Douglas utility* #
(All,c,COM)(All,d,CNT) q_d(c,d) = - p_d(c,d) + f_mu(d) + gdp(d) ;
Equation E_l # *(T7.10) Industry's labor demand: output divided by productivity* #
(All,c,COM)(All,s,CNT) l(c,s)= qotot(c,s) - aoMel(c,s) ;
Equation E_w # *(T7.11) Demand equals supply of labor in each country*#
(All,s,CNT) C_LTOT(s)*ltot(s) = sum(c,COM, C_L(c,s)*l(c,s));
Equation E_qotot # *(T7.12) Total demand for commodity c produced in s* #
(All,c,COM)(All,s,CNT) **Sum**(d,CNT, FACTORYV(c,s,d))*qotot(c,s) =
Sum(d,CNT,FACTORYV(c,s,d)*qcount(c,s,d));
Equation E_gdp # *(T7.13) GDP, returns to primary factors plus indirect taxes* #
(All,d,CNT) C_GDP(d)*gdp(d) = [C_W(d)*C_LTOT(d)]*[w(d) + ltot(d)]
　　　　　　+ 100*sum(c,COM, sum(s,CNT, d_revm(c,s,d))) + 100*sum(c,COM, sum(s,CNT, d_revx(c,d,s)));
Equation E_d_revm # *(T7.14) Revenue derived from tariff levied by receiving country on cif values* #
(All,c,COM)(All,s,CNT)(All,d,CNT) 100*d_revm(c,s,d) =
　　　　C_TM(c,s,d)*VCIF(c,s,d)*[qcount(c,s,d) + pcif(c,s,d)+tm(c,s,d)]
　　　　　- VCIF(c,s,d)*[qcount(c,s,d) + pcif(c,s,d)] ;
Equation E_d_revx # *(T7.15) s's revenue from destination-specific tax on factory values* #
(All,c,COM)(All,s,CNT)(All,d,CNT) 100*d_revx(c,s,d)
　　　　= C_TX(c,s,d)*FACTORYV(c,s,d)*[qcount(c,s,d) + pfactory(c,s)+txMel(c,s,d)]
　　　　　- FACTORYV(c,s,d)*[qcount(c,s,d) + pfactory(c,s)] ;
Equation E_f_mu_cnt2 # *(T7.16) Average world-wide wage, convenient numeraire* #
Sum(tt,CNT, C_LTOT(tt))*ave_wage = sum(s,CNT, C_LTOT(s)*w(s));

! A7.1.6 ARMINGTON DECOMPOSITION OF WELFARE, see equation (7.29) and Appendix 7.2 !

Coefficient (All,d,CNT) WELFAREINDEX(d) # *Welfare index* #;

Formula (initial) (All,d,CNT) WELFAREINDEX(d) = 1.0 ;

Variable
(All,c,COM)(All,s,CNT)(All,d,CNT) peffob(c,s,d)#*fob price, effective unit of c sent from s to d*#;
(All,c,COM)(All,s,CNT) peffobave(c,s)# *Ave fob price, effective unit of c from s* #;
(All,d,CNT) welfare(d) # *Welfare, calculated as real consumption* #;
(change) (All,d,CNT) cont_prim(d) # *Welfare contribution, primary factors* #;
(change) (All,d,CNT) cont_tcf(d) # *Armington tax-carrying flow welfare contribution* #;
(change) (All,d,CNT) cont_toftA(d) # *Armington terms of trade welfare contribution* #;
(change) (All,d,CNT) cont_toftaddM(d) # *Melitz additional terms of trade welfare contribution* #;
(change) (All,d,CNT) cont_addTFP(d) # *Contributions of total factor productivity beyond tcf* #;
(change) (All,d,CNT) cont_total(d) # *Total of welfare contributions* #;

Update (All,d,CNT) WELFAREINDEX(d) = welfare(d) ;

Equation E_peffob # *fob price, effective unit of c sent from s to d*#
(All,c,COM)(All,s,CNT)(All,d,CNT) peffob(c,s,d) = pfob(c,s,d)- aaMel(c,s,d);
Equation E_peffobave # *Ave fob price, effective unit of c from s* #
(All,c,COM)(All,s,CNT) **Sum**(tt,CNT, C_TX(c,s,tt)*FACTORYV(c,s,tt))*peffobave(c,s)
　　= **Sum**(tt,CNT, C_TX(c,s,tt)*FACTORYV(c,s,tt)*peffob(c,s,tt));
Equation E_welfare # *Welfare, calculated in as real consumption* #

(**All**,d,CNT) welfare(d) =
    (1/**Sum**{cc,COM,VPUR_S(cc,d)})***Sum**{c,COM,VPUR_S(c,d)*q_d(c,d)};
Equation E_cont_prim *# Welfare contribution, primary factors #*
(**All**,d,CNT) cont_prim(d)= WELFAREINDEX(d)*(1/**Sum**{cc,COM, VPUR_S(cc,d)})
        *{**Sum**{c,COM, C_W(d)*C_L(c,d)*l(c,d)}};

Equation E_cont_tcf *# Armington tax-carrying flow welfare contribution, #*
(**All**,d,CNT) cont_tcf(d)= WELFAREINDEX(d)*(1/**Sum**{cc,COM, VPUR_S(cc,d)})
        ***Sum**(c,COM, **Sum**(s,CNT,[C_TM(c,s,d)-1]*VCIF(c,s,d)*q_effect(c,s,d)));
Equation E_cont_toftA *# Armington terms of trade welfare contribution #*
(**All**,d,CNT) cont_toftA(d) = WELFAREINDEX(d)*(1/**sum**{cc,COM, VPUR_S(cc,d)})
*{ **Sum**{c,COM, **Sum**(tt,CNT:tt **ne** d, C_TX(c,d,tt)*FACTORYV(c,d,tt))*peffobave(c,d) }
    - **Sum**{c,COM,**Sum**(s,CNT:s **ne** d, VCIF(c,s,d)*peffobave(c,s)) } };
Equation E_cont_toftaddM *# Melitz additional terms of trade welfare contribution #*
(**All**,d,CNT) cont_toftaddM(d) = WELFAREINDEX(d)*(1/**sum**{cc,COM, VPUR_S(cc,d)})
 * {**Sum**{c,COM, **Sum**(tt,CNT:tt **ne** d, C_TX(c,d,tt)*FACTORYV(c,d,tt)*[peffob(c,d,tt)-peffobave(c,d)])}
    - **Sum**{c,COM,**Sum**(s,CNT:s **ne** d, VCIF(c,s,d)*[peffob(c,s,d)-peffobave(c,s)])} };
Equation E_cont_addTFP *# Contributions of total factor productivity beyond tcf #*
(**All**,d,CNT) cont_addTFP(d) = WELFAREINDEX(d)*(1/**sum**{cc,COM, VPUR_S(cc,d)})
*{ **Sum**(c,COM, {**Sum**(tt,CNT,C_TX(c,d,tt)*FACTORYV(c,d,tt)*[q_effect(c,d,tt)-l(c,d)])})
  + **Sum**(c,COM, {**Sum**(tt,CNT,[C_TX(c,d,tt)-1]*FACTORYV(c,d,tt))}*l(c,d)) };

Equation E_cont_total *# Total of welfare contributions #*
(**All**,d,CNT) cont_total(d) = cont_prim(d) + cont_tcf(d) + cont_toftA(d) + cont_toftaddM(d) + cont_addTFP(d);

/***/
! Extra coefficients, evaluations, variables and equations required for   !
! converting the BasicArmington model into a Melitz model   !
/***/

! A7.1.7 DECLARATION OF ADDITIONAL COEFFICIENTS FOR MELITZ !

Coefficient (Parameter) ALPHA *# Parameter in Pareto distribution of firm productivities #*;
(**All**,c,COM)(**All**,s,CNT)(**All**,d,CNT) C_PHIT(c,s,d)*# Marginal productivity of typical c firm on sd-link #*;
(**Parameter**)(**All**,c,COM) DUM_MEL(c) *# One for Melitz commodity, else zero #*;

! A7.1.8 ADDITIONAL READ STATEMENT FOR MELITZ !

Read ALPHA **from file** OTHDATA **Header** "ALFA";
Read DUM_MEL **from file** OTHDATA **header** "DMEL";

! A7.1.9 ADDITIONAL FORMULAS FOR MELITZ !

Formula (Initial)(**All**,c,COM)(**All**,s,CNT)(**All**,d,CNT) *! see equation (6.1)!* C_PHIT(c,s,d)
            = DUM_MEL(c)*[2.0 + **if**(s=d,-0.9)] + [1-DUM_MEL(c)];
(**Initial**)(**All**,c,COM)(**All**,s,CNT)(**All**,d,CNT) *! see equation (7.26)!* C_TX(c,s,d) = [1/C_PHIT(c,s,d)]
            ***Sum**(j,CNT, MARKETV(c,s,j)*C_PHIT(c,s,j))/**Sum**(dd,CNT, MARKETV(c,s,dd));
(**Initial**)(**All**,c,COM)(**All**,s,CNT)(**All**,d,CNT) FACTORYV(c,s,d) = MARKETV(c,s,d)/C_TX(c,s,d);
(**Initial**) (**All**,c,COM)(**All**,s,CNT)(**All**,d,CNT) REVX(c,s,d) = MARKETV(c,s,d) -FACTORYV(c,s,d);

! A7.1.10 ADDITIONAL VARIABLES FOR MELITZ !
Variable
(**All**,c,COM)(**All**,s,CNT)(**All**,d,CNT) f_txmel(c,s,d) *# Exo to turn on Melitz factory-door tax rates #*;
(**All**,c,COM)(**All**,s,CNT)(**All**,d,CNT) f_aaMel(c,s,d) *# Exo to turn on Melitz love of variety #*;
(**Change**)(**All**,c,COM)(**All**,s,CNT) d_f_l(c,s) *# Exo to turn on Melitz total inputs to c-firms in s #*;
(**All**,c,COM)(**All**,s,CNT)(**All**,d,CNT) phi_tsd(c,s,d) *# Productivity of a typical c firm on sd-link #*;
(**All**,c,COM)(**All**,s,CNT)(**All**,d,CNT) n_sd(c,s,d) *# No. of c-producing firms (varieties) on the sd-link #*;
(**All**,c,COM)(**All**,s,CNT)(**All**,d,CNT) f_sd(c,s,d) *# Qty of inputs required to set up on the sd,c-link #*;

(All,c,COM)(All,s,CNT) n(c,s) # *Number of c-firms in country s #*;
(All,c,COM)(All,s,CNT) h(c,s) # *Qty of inputs for a c-firm to set up the opportunity to produce #*;
(All,c,COM)(All,s,CNT)(All,d,CNT) phi_min(c,s,d) # *Productivity of minimum prod'ty c-firm on sd-link #*;
(All,c,COM)(All,s,CNT)(All,d,CNT) q_min(c,s,d) # *sd sales of c-firm with min. prod. on sd-link d#*;
(All,c,COM)(All,s,CNT)(All,d,CNT) q_tsd(c,s,d) # *sd sales of c-firm with typical prod. on sd-link d #*;
(All,c,COM)(All,s,CNT) d_colrevx(c,s) # *Rev from dest-specific factory-door tax on c-firms in s #*;

! *A7.1.11 ADDITIONAL EQUATIONS FOR CONVERTING ARMINGTON TO MELITZ* !

Equation E_q_tsd # *(T7.17) Total quantity of sales (number of widgets) of c on the sd-link #*
(All,c,COM)(All,s,CNT)(All,d,CNT) qcount(c,s,d)= n_sd(c,s,d) +q_tsd(c,s,d);
Equation E_f_txMel # *(T7.18) Power of taxes to capture Melitz price effects from productivity differences #*
(All,c,COM)(All,s,CNT)(All,d,CNT) txMel(c,s,d) = aoMel(c,s) - phi_tsd(c,s,d) +f_txMel(c,s,d);
Equation E_f_aaMel # *(T7.19) Specification of preference variables to capture Melitz love-of-variety effects #*
(All,c,COM)(All,s,CNT)(All,d,CNT) aaMel(c,s,d) = (1/(SIGMA -1))*n_sd(c,s,d)+f_aaMel(c,s,d);
Equation E_d_f_l # *(T7.20) Melitz specification of total demand for inputs by c-firms in s #*
(All,c,COM)(All,s,CNT) C_W(s)*C_L(c,s)*(l(c,s) +w(s))=
((SIGMA-1)/SIGMA)*sum(d,CNT, MARKETV(c,s,d)*[n_sd(c,s,d)+q_tsd(c,s,d) -phi_tsd(c,s,d)+w(s)])
      + {(SIGMA-1)/(ALPHA*SIGMA)}*Sum(d,CNT, MARKETV(c,s,d)*[n(c,s) + h(c,s)+w(s)])
+ {(ALPHA-(SIGMA-1))/(ALPHA*SIGMA)}*sum(d,CNT,MARKETV(c,s,d)*[n_sd(c,s,d)+f_sd(c,s,d)+w(s)])
      + 100*d_f_l(c,s);
Equation E_n_sd # *(T7.21) Melitz specification of the number of c-firms on the sd-link #*
(All,c,COM)(All,s,CNT)(All,d,CNT) n_sd(c,s,d) = n(c,s) -ALPHA*phi_min(c,s,d);
Equation E_phi_min # *(T7.22) Melitz specification of the minimum productivity of c-firms on the sd-link #*
(All,c,COM)(All,s,CNT)(All,d,CNT) q_min(c,s,d) = phi_min(c,s,d)+f_sd(c,s,d) ;
Equation E_phi_tsd # *(T7.23) Melitz specification of the typical productivity of c-firms on the sd-link #*
(All,c,COM)(All,s,CNT)(All,d,CNT) phi_tsd(c,s,d) = phi_min(c,s,d);
Equation E_q_min # *(T7.24) Sales on the sd-link of a c-firm with pro'tivity level min of those on the sd-link #*
(All,c,COM)(All,s,CNT)(All,d,CNT) q_tsd(c,s,d) = q_min(c,s,d);
Equation E_nd # *(T7.25) Revenue from destination-specific factory-door taxes levied by s on c-firms #*
(All,c,COM)(All,s,CNT) sum(d,CNT, d_revx(c,s,d)) = d_colrevx(c,s);

!***!

WRITE (postsim) C_GDP **to** terminal ;   ! *allows GEMPACK to produce post-simulation values of coefficients* !

Closures

Table 7.9 lists in GEMPACK code two closures (exogenous variables) for the A2M system: one for generating solutions to the BasicArmington model and the other for generating solutions for MelitzGE. The relationship between the two closures is discussed in Sect. 7.2.

Appendix 7.2: Another Decomposition of Welfare for Armington and Melitz

In this appendix we derive the welfare decomposition set out in Eq. (7.29). The derivation uses the equations in Table 7.1 for the BasicArmington model. Notation is given in Table 7.2. The derivation is similar to that in Appendix 6.4. However, there are differences, e.g. new variables, aaMel and txMel, that were not in the earlier decomposition. Then we introduce Melitz equations to derive (7.35), (7.36) and (7.37).

Table 7.9 Closures for A2M system: solving the BasicArmington model or MelitzGE[a]

		Armington	Melitz
1	Dest-specific tax power by s on factory value c to d	txMel(c,s,d)	f_txMel(c,s,d)
2	Power of tariff on flow c,s to d, applied to cif value	tm(c,s,d)	tm(c,s,d)
3	All input tech variable: output per unit of input in industry c,s	aoMel(c,s)	d_f_l(c,s)
4	Pref variable for c,s to satisfy d's demands for c	aaMel(c,s,d)	f_aaMel(c,s,d)
5	Country 1's average propensity to consume out of GDP	f_mu ("CNT1")	f_mu ("CNT1")
6	Employment in country s	ℓtot(s)	ℓtot(s)
7	World-wide average wage rate	ave_wage	ave_wage
8	Qty of inputs required to set up on the sd,c-link	f_sd(c,s,d)	f_sd(c,s,d)
9	No. of c-firms in s for A, factory door tax collection for M	n(c,s)	d_colrevx(c,s)
10	Qty of inputs for a c-firm to set up the opportunity to produce	h(c,s)	h(c,s)

[a]Shaded rows indicate closure swaps

Derivation of (7.29)

We define the percentage change in welfare for country d as

$$\text{welfare}_d = \sum_c \text{MU}_{d,c} * q_{d,c} \tag{7.38}$$

where $\text{MU}_{d,c}$ is the share of d's household expenditure that is devoted to commodity c. We assume fmu_d in (T7.9) of Table 7.1 is zero. Then

$$\text{welfare}_d = \sum_c \text{MU}_{d,c} * \left(\text{gdp}_d - p_{d,c}\right) \tag{7.39}$$

Because the $\text{MU}_{d,c}$'s sum to one over c, (7.39) can be written as

$$\text{welfare}_d = \text{gdp}_d - \sum_c \text{MU}_{d,c} * p_{d,c} \tag{7.40}$$

Combining (7.40), (T7.13) and (T7.7) gives

$$
\begin{aligned}
\text{GDP}_d * \text{welfare}_d = {}& W_d * \text{LTOT}_d * [w_d + \ell\text{tot}_d] + 100 * \sum_c \sum_s \text{drevm}_{sd,c} \\
& + 100 * \sum_c \sum_s \text{drevx}_{ds,c} \\
& - \text{GDP}_d * \sum_c \text{MU}_{d,c} * \left[\sum_s \text{SHA}(s,d,c) * \left[p_{\bullet sd,c} - \text{aaMel}_{sd,c} \right] \right]
\end{aligned}
\tag{7.41}
$$

Substituting from (T7.14) and (T7.15) into (7.41) leads to

$$
\begin{aligned}
\text{GDP}_d * \text{welfare}_d = {}& W_d * \text{LTOT}_d * [w_d + \ell\text{tot}_d] \\
& + \sum_c \sum_s \left[\begin{array}{l} \text{TM}_{sd,c} * \text{VCIF}(s,d,c) * \left[\text{qcount}_{sd,c} + \text{pcif}_{\bullet sd,c} + \text{tm}_{sd,c} \right] \\ -\text{VCIF}(s,d,c) * \left[\text{qcount}_{sd,c} + \text{pcif}_{\bullet sd,c} \right] \end{array} \right] \\
& + \sum_c \sum_s \left[\begin{array}{l} \text{TX}_{ds,c} * \text{FACTORYV}(d,s,c) * \left[\text{qcount}_{ds,c} + \text{pfactory}_{\bullet d,c} + \text{txMel}_{ds,c} \right] \\ -\text{FACTORYV}(d,s,c) * \left[\text{qcount}_{ds,c} + \text{pfactory}_{\bullet d,c} \right] \end{array} \right] \\
& - \text{GDP}_d * \sum_c \text{MU}_{d,c} * \left[\sum_s \text{SHA}(s,d,c) * \left[p_{\bullet sd,c} - \text{aaMel}_{sd,c} \right] \right]
\end{aligned}
\tag{7.42}
$$

Rearranging we obtain

$$
\begin{aligned}
\text{GDP}_d * \text{welfare}_d = {}& W_d * \text{LTOT}_d * [w_d + \ell\text{tot}_d] \\
& + \sum_c \sum_s \left(\text{TM}_{sd,c} - 1 \right) * \text{VCIF}(s,d,c) * \text{qcount}_{sd,c} \\
& + \sum_c \sum_s \left(\text{TX}_{ds,c} - 1 \right) * \text{FACTORYV}(d,s,c) * \text{qcount}_{ds,c} \\
& + \sum_c \sum_s \text{TX}_{ds,c} * \text{FACTORYV}(d,s,c) * \left[\text{pfactory}_{\bullet d,c} + \text{txMel}_{ds,c} \right] \\
& - \sum_c \sum_s \text{FACTORYV}(d,s,c) * \text{pfactory}_{\bullet d,c} \\
& - \sum_c \sum_s \text{VCIF}(s,d,c) * \text{pcif}_{\bullet sd,c} + \sum_c \sum_s \text{TM}_{sd,c} * \text{VCIF}(s,d,c) * \text{pcif}_{\bullet sd,c} \\
& + \sum_c \sum_s \left[\text{TM}_{sd,c} * \text{VCIF}(s,d,c) * \text{tm}_{sd,c} \right] \\
& - \text{GDP}_d * \sum_c \text{MU}_{d,c} * \left[\sum_s \text{SHA}(s,d,c) * \left[p_{\bullet sd,c} - \text{aaMel}_{sd,c} \right] \right]
\end{aligned}
\tag{7.43}
$$

In BasicArmington there are no transport costs and no intermediate inputs. Consequently,

$$TX_{ds,c} * FACTORY(d, s, c) = MARKETV(d, s, c) = VCIF(d, s, c) \qquad (7.44)$$

and

$$W_d LTOT_d = \sum_c \sum_s FACTORYV(d, s, c) \qquad (7.45)$$

Working with these relationships and using (T7.1)–(T7.4) we reach:

$$
\begin{aligned}
GDP_d * welfare_d = {} & W_d * LTOT_d * \ell tot_d \\
& + \sum_c \sum_s \left(TM_{sd,c} - 1\right) * VCIF(s, d, c) * qcount_{sd,c} \\
& + \sum_c \sum_s \left(TX_{ds,c} - 1\right) * FACTORYV(d, s, c) * qcount_{ds,c} \\
& + \sum_c \sum_s TX_{ds,c} * FACTORYV(d, s, c) * pfob_{ds,c} \\
& - \sum_c \sum_s VCIF(s, d, c) * pcif_{\bullet sd,c} \\
& + \sum_c \sum_s FACTORYV(d, s, c) * aoMel_{d,c} \\
& + \sum_c \sum_s TM_{sd,c} * VCIF(s, d, c) * pcif_{\bullet sd,c} \\
& + \sum_c \sum_s TM_{sd,c} * VCIF(s, d, c) * tm_{sd,c} \\
& - GDP_d * \sum_c MU_{d,c} * \sum_s SHA(s, d, c) * \left[p_{\bullet sd,c} - aaMel_{sd,c}\right]
\end{aligned}
$$

$$(7.46)$$

Now we work on the last term of (7.46). We assume that country d consumes all of its GDP (zero trade deficit). Under this assumption $GDP_d * MU_{d,c} * SHA(s, d, c) = VPUR(s, d, c)$ where VPUR(s,d,c) is household expenditure in d on commodity c sent from s. Then using (T7.5) we obtain:

$$
\begin{aligned}
GDP_d * welfare_d = {} & W_d * LTOT_d * \ell tot_d \\
& + \sum_c \sum_s (TM_{sd,c} - 1) * VCIF(s, d, c) * qcount_{sd,c} \\
& + \sum_c \sum_s (TX_{ds,c} - 1) * FACTORYV(d, s, c) * qcount_{ds,c} \\
& + \sum_c \sum_s TX_{ds,c} * FACTORYV(d, s, c) * pfob_{ds,c} \\
& - \sum_c \sum_s VCIF(s, d, c) * pcif_{\bullet sd,c} \\
& + \sum_c \sum_s FACTORYV(d, s, c) * aoMel_{d,c} \\
& + \sum_c \sum_s VPUR(s, d, c) * aaMel_{sd,c} \\
& + \sum_c \sum_s TM_{sd,c} * VCIF(s, d, c) * pcif_{\bullet sd,c} \\
& + \sum_c \sum_s TM_{sd,c} * VCIF(s, d, c) * tm_{sd,c} \\
& - \sum_c \sum_s VPUR(s, d, c) * \left[pcif_{\bullet sd,c} + tm_{sd,c} \right]
\end{aligned}
$$

$$(7.47)$$

Because $TM_{sd,c} * VCIF(s, d, c) = VPUR(s, d, c)$, the last three terms in (7.47) contribute zero. Leaving these terms out and using (T7.8) and (T7.1)–(T7.4), we find that

$$
\begin{aligned}
GDP_d * welfare_d = {} & W_d * LTOT_d * \ell tot_d + \sum_c \sum_s (TM_{sd,c} - 1) * VCIF(s, d, c) * q_{sd,c} \\
& + \sum_c \sum_s TX_{ds,c} * FACTORYV(d, s, c) * [pfactory_{\bullet d,c} + txMel_{ds,c} - aaMel_{ds,c}] \\
& - \sum_c \sum_s VCIF(s, d, c) * [pfactory_{\bullet s,c} + txMel_{sd,c} - aaMel_{sd,c}] \\
& + \sum_c \sum_s FACTORYV(d, s, c) * aoMel_{d,c} \\
& + \sum_c \sum_s FACTORYV(d, s, c) * aaMel_{ds,c} \\
& + \sum_c \sum_s (TX_{ds,c} - 1) * FACTORYV(d, s, c) * q_{ds,c}
\end{aligned}
$$

$$(7.48)$$

Recognizing that the "diagonal" terms in the second and third lines on the RHS of (7.48) cancel and rearranging we obtain

$$
\begin{aligned}
\text{GDP}_d * \text{welfare}_d = {} & W_d * \text{LTOT}_d * \ell\text{tot}_d + \sum_c \sum_s \left(\text{TM}_{sd,c} - 1\right) * \text{VCIF}(s, d, c) * q_{sd,c} \\
& + \sum_c \sum_{s \neq d} \text{TX}_{ds,c} * \text{FACTORYV}(d, s, c) * [\text{pfactory}_{\bullet d,c} + \text{txMel}_{ds,c} - \text{aaMel}_{ds,c}] \\
& - \sum_c \sum_{s \neq d} \text{VCIF}(s, d, c) * [\text{pfactory}_{\bullet s,c} + \text{txMel}_{sd,c} - \text{aaMel}_{sd,c}] \\
& + \sum_c \sum_s \text{TX}_{ds,c} * \text{FACTORYV}(d, s, c) * q_{ds,c} \\
& - \sum_c \sum_s \text{FACTORYV}(d, s, c) * [q_{ds,c} - \text{aaMel}_{ds,c} - \text{aoMel}_{d,c}]
\end{aligned}
$$

$$(7.49)$$

Using (T7.8), (T7.12) and (T7.10) and rearranging gives:

$$
\begin{aligned}
\text{GDP}_d * \text{welfare}_d = {} & W_d * \text{LTOT}_d * \ell\text{tot}_d + \sum_c \sum_s \left(\text{TM}_{sd,c} - 1\right) * \text{VCIF}(s, d, c) * q_{sd,c} \\
& + \sum_c \sum_{s \neq d} \text{TX}_{ds,c} * \text{FACTORYV}(d, s, c) * [\text{pfactory}_{\bullet d,c} + \text{txMel}_{ds,c} - \text{aaMel}_{ds,c}] \\
& - \sum_c \sum_{s \neq d} \text{VCIF}(s, d, c) * [\text{pfactory}_{\bullet s,c} + \text{txMel}_{sd,c} - \text{aaMel}_{sd,c}] \\
& + \sum_c \sum_s \text{TX}_{ds,c} * \text{FACTORYV}(d, s, c) * [q_{ds,c} - \ell_{d,c}] \\
& + \sum_c \sum_s \left(\text{TX}_{ds,c} - 1\right)\text{FACTORYV}(d, s, c) * \ell_{d,c}
\end{aligned}
$$

$$(7.50)$$

Then using (7.30), (T7.2) and (T7.3) we quickly arrive at (7.29).

Derivation of (7.35)–(7.37)

If industry c is treated as Armington, then under standard assumptions $\text{aoMel}_{d,c}$ and $\text{aaMel}_{sd,c}$ are zero and $\text{TX}_{sd,c}$ equals one. Under these conditions, the c component of the combined last two terms in (7.49), and consequently in (7.50), is zero. Following the notation introduced in (7.35), these two terms can now be written as

$$
\begin{aligned}
\Delta\text{Efficiency}_d = {} & \sum_{c \in M} \sum_s \text{TX}_{ds,c} * \text{FACTORYV}(d, s, c) * [q_{ds,c} - \ell_{d,c}] \\
& + \sum_{c \in M} \sum_s \left(\text{TX}_{ds,c} - 1\right)\text{FACTORYV}(d, s, c) * \ell_{d,c}
\end{aligned}
$$

$$(7.51)$$

where M is the set of Melitz industries. Because for Melitz industries the collection of factory-door taxes is fixed on zero, the second term on the RHS of (7.51) is zero. Then using

$$W_d L_{d,c} = \sum_s FACTORYV(d, s, c) \tag{7.52}$$

we establish (7.35):

$$\Delta Efficiency_d = \sum_{c \in M} [\{\sum_s TX_{ds,c} * FACTORYV(d, s, c) * q_{ds,c}\} - W_d L_{d,c} * \ell_{d,c}] \tag{7.53}$$

In deriving (7.36) and (7.37) we restrict attention to Melitz industries, $c \in M$. Thus, we assume that the shift variables in (T7.19) and (T7.20) are zero. We start the derivation with (T7.20). Writing this equation from the point of view of country d, cancelling out the wage terms, and assuming that $h_{d,c}$ and $f_{ds,c}$ are zero, we obtain[18]

$$
\begin{aligned}
W_d * L_{d,c} * \ell_{d,c} \\
= [(\sigma - 1)/\sigma] * \sum_s MARKETV(d, s, c) * n_{ds,c} \\
+ [(\sigma - 1)/(\alpha\sigma)] * \sum_s MARKETV(d, s, c) * n_{d,c} \\
+ [(\alpha - (\sigma - 1))/(\alpha\sigma)] * \sum_s MARKETV(d, s, c) * n_{ds,c}
\end{aligned}
\tag{7.54}
$$

From here, (7.36) and (7.37) can be derived directly from Table 7.1 by a series of substitutions into (7.54). However, an alternative and instructive approach is to use a key result from Appendix 4.1: namely that costs in industry d,c are split in fixed proportions between production, set up of firms and setup on links. Noting that $\sum_s MARKETV(d, s, c) = \sum_s TX_{ds,c} * FACTORYV(d, s, c) = W_d L_{d,c}$, and using the fixed-split result we see from (7.54) that

$$\ell_{d,c} = \sum_s \frac{MARKETV(d, s, c)}{W_d L_{d,c}} * n_{ds,c} = n_{d,c} \tag{7.55}$$

Using (T7.21) in (7.55) together with (T7.22)–(T7.24) gives

$$0 = \sum_s MARKETV(d, s, c) * \phi_{\bullet ds,c} = \sum_s MARKETV(d, s, c) * q_{\bullet ds,c} \tag{7.56}$$

---

[18]With $f_{ds,c}$ equal to zero, (T7.22)–(T7.24) imply that $q_{\bullet ds,c} - \phi_{\bullet ds,c} = 0$.

Via (T7.17), (T7.8) and (7.56),

$$\sum_s \text{MARKETV}(d, s, c) * n_{ds,c} = \sum_s \text{MARKETV}(d, s, c) * q_{ds,c}$$
$$- \sum_s \text{MARKETV}(d, s, c) * aaMel_{ds,c} \qquad (7.57)$$

Substituting (T7.19) into (7.57) gives

$$\frac{\sigma}{\sigma - 1} \sum_s \text{MARKETV}(d, s, c) * n_{ds,c} = \sum_s \text{MARKETV}(d, s, c) * q_{ds,c} \qquad (7.58)$$

and then from (7.55)

$$W_d L_{d,c} * \ell_{d,c} = \frac{\sigma - 1}{\sigma} \sum_s \text{MARKETV}(d, s, c) * q_{ds,c} \qquad (7.59)$$

We obtain (7.36) and (7.37) by substituting from (7.59) into (7.35).

Appendix 7.3: The Theory of GTAP-HET

Akgul, Villoria and Hertel (2016), hereafter AVH, describe what they call GTAP-HET or GTAP with heterogeneous firms. Their aim is to incorporate the Melitz specification of trade with firm heterogeneity into a readily accessible version of the GTAP model. In our view, they fall a little short of the mark.

The most obvious problem is their version of market prices. In Melitz, the price of good c delivered from region s to region d by the typical firm on the sd-link reflects this firm's productivity. In terms of our BasicMelitz model (the Melitz model derived from the BasicArmington-A2M system) Melitz pricing requires

$$\text{pmarket}_{\bullet sd,c} = w_s - \phi_{sd,c} \quad \text{for all c, s, d,} \qquad (7.60)$$

where

$\text{pmarket}_{\bullet sd,c}$ is the percentage change in the market price (price just beyond the factory door) of good c from country s destined for country d;

w_s is the percentage change in the wage rate in country s (which, in our A2M system, is the cost of a unit of input to production of c in country s); and

$\phi_{sd,c}$ is the percentage change in the marginal productivity of the typical c-producing firm operating on the sd-link.

Instead of (7.60), AVH assume that[19]

$$\text{pmarket}_{\bullet sd,c} = w_s - \left(\frac{\sigma - 1}{\sigma}\right) * \phi ave_{s,c} \quad \text{for all } c, s, d \qquad (7.61)$$

where $\phi ave_{s,c}$ is the percentage change in the marginal productivity of the average c-producing firm in country s. This is defined more precisely in what follows. For now, the most important point is that the right hand side of (7.61) doesn't depend on the destination d. The coefficient $(\sigma - 1)/\sigma$ is the share of variable costs in the total costs of industry s,c.[20] It appears on the right hand side of (7.61) presumably because changes in $\phi ave_{s,c}$ operate on variable costs per unit of output, not total costs.

Equation (7.61) is inconsistent with Melitz theory. But does this matter? To investigate this issue we produced a version of BasicMelitz in which AVH's equation (7.61) replaces (7.60). To do this we started from the Melitz closure in Table 7.2. In this closure the percentage changes in the powers of export taxes [txMel$_{sd,c}$] are endogenously determined by equation (T7.18), while the shift variables [ftxMel$_{sd,c}$] in that equation are exogenous. Now, to move to the AVH version of the determination of market prices, we switched the closure so that txMel$_{sd,c}$ becomes exogenous and ftxMel$_{sd,c}$ becomes endogenous. With txMel$_{sd,}$ set on zero, equations (T7.1) and (T7.2) in the A2M system collapse to

$$\text{pmarket}_{\bullet sd,c} = w_s - \text{aoMel}_{s,c} \quad \text{for all } c, s, d, \qquad (7.62)$$

By setting aoMel$_{s,c}$ according to

$$\text{aoMel}_{s,c} = \left(\frac{\sigma - 1}{\sigma}\right) * \phi ave_{s,c} \quad \text{for all } c, s \qquad (7.63)$$

we can reproduce AVH pricing.

AVH specify equations to determine their $\phi ave_{s,c}$. In terms of the variables and equations in Table 7.1, their specification is[21]:

---

[19]By looking at AVH's equation (12) and the equation that follows immediately in their text, we deduced that (7.61) is a valid representation of the AVH treatment of prices translated into our simple model. We confirmed this by reproducing the simulations reported by AVH and observing that in these simulations the market prices for sd,c move in the same way for all d despite differences across d in $\phi_{sd,c}$.

[20]See the concluding paragraph of Appendix 4.1.

[21]Equations (7.64)–(7.66) correspond to AVH's equations (23) and (24).

$$\varphi ave_{s,c} = \sum_d SHRSMD(s, d, c) * \varphi_{sd,c}$$

$$+ \left(\frac{1}{\sigma - 1}\right) * \sum_d SHRSMD(s, d, c) * [n_{sd,c} - nt_{s,c}] \quad \text{for all c,s} \tag{7.64}$$

where

SHRSMD(c,s,d)   is the share of destination d in the market value of sales by industry s,c; and

$nt_{s,c}$ is the percentage change in the total number of links being operated by firms in industry s,c.

This is given by:

$$nt_{s,c} = \sum_d SHARE(c, s, d) * n_{sd,c} \quad \text{for all c, s} \tag{7.65}$$

where

SHARE(s,d,c)   is the number of c-producing firms on the sd-link [N(s,d,c)] divided by the total number of links being operated by firms in s,c.

That is,

$$SHARE(s, d, c) = \frac{N(s, d, c)}{\sum_{dd} N(s, dd, c)} \quad \text{for all c, s, d} \tag{7.66}$$

Substituting from (7.64) and (7.65) into (7.63) we see that AVH's model can be implemented in the A2M system by specifying $aoMel_{s,c}$ according to

$$aoMel_{s,c} = \frac{(\sigma - 1)}{\sigma} * \sum_d SHRSMD(s, d, c) * \varphi_{sd,c}$$

$$+ \frac{1}{\sigma} * \sum_d SHRSMD(s, d, c) \tag{7.67}$$

$$* [n_{sd,c} - \sum_k SHARE(c, s, k) * n_{sk,c}] \quad \text{for all c,s}$$

In the Melitz closure in Table 7.2, $aoMel_{s,c}$ was already endogenous. Adding another equation to determine it requires endogenization of a currently exogenous similarly dimensioned variable. This variable has to be $dcolrevx_{s,c}$: with all the rates, $txMel_{sd,c}$, exogenous as required for the AVH specification of market prices, collection of revenue from destination specific factory-door taxes on s,c firms must be endogenous.

We are now ready to answer the question we posed earlier: Does omitting destination-specific pricing from the Melitz model make much difference? In

Table 7.10 BasicArmington-A2M simulations: Melitz and AVH results for the effects of a 10% tariff imposed by country 2 on all imports from country 1 (percentage changes)

	Melitz		AVH	
	Country d = 1	Country d = 2	Country d = 1	Country d = 2
Real consumption (welfare)	*−1.321*	*1.044*	*−2.336*	*3.373*

Table 7.10 we compare Melitz welfare results from Table 7.4 with welfare results computed under AVH assumptions, that is with: $txMel_{sd,c}$ exogenous on zero; $ftxMel_{sd,c}$ endogenous; $aoMel_{s,c}$ specified according to (7.67); $dcolrevx_{sd,c}$ endogenous; and the rest of the closure the same as Melitz in Table 7.2. The comparison in Table 7.10 strongly suggests that the answer to our question is yes.

On further investigation we found, under AVH's treatment of market prices (no destination specificity), that variations in the specification of $aoMel_{s,c}$ (and hence $\phi ave_{s,c}$) have no effect on welfare or other variables of economic significance such as $q_{d,c}$, gdp_d, and w_s. In fact $aoMel_{s,c}$ can be treated as exogenous and given any value. Thus, AVH's use of the variable $\phi ave_{s,c}$ is not only inconsistent with Melitz but its specification via (7.64)–(7.66) has no relevance for AVH's results.

References

Akgul, Z., Villoria, N. B., & Hertel, T. W. (2016). GTAP-HET: Introducing firm heterogeneity into the GTAP model. *Journal of Global Economic Analysis, 1*(1), 111–180.

Balistreri, E., & Rutherford, T. (2013). Computing general equilibrium theories of monopolistic competition and heterogeneous firms (chapter 23). In P.B. Dixon, & D.W. Jorgenson (Eds), *Handbook of computable general equilibrium modeling* (pp. 1513–1570). Elsevier.

Hertel, T. W. (Ed.). (1997). *Global trade analysis: Modeling and applications*. Cambridge, UK: Cambridge University Press.

Melitz, Marc J. (2003). The impact of trade on intra-industry reallocations and aggregate industry productivity. *Econometrica, 71*(6), 1695–1725.

Chapter 8
Summary and Concluding Remarks

This chapter has two parts. The first is a check list of our principal findings with references to relevant parts of the book. The second contains conclusions about methodology and policy.

8.1 List of Principal Findings

(a) Armington is a special case of Krugman, which is a special case of Melitz, which is a special case of an encompassing model, AKME (Chap. 2).

(b) In a Melitz model for a sector, tariffs are the only distortion. This is despite monopolistic competition, economies of scale and prices that exceed marginal cost. In the absence of tariffs, the Melitz market satisfies given final demands in each country at minimum cost (Chap. 3).

(c) Optimality of Melitz solutions means that the envelope theorem can be useful in interpreting results (Sects. 3.3 and 6.2).

(d) Relative to Armington, a Melitz specification for a sector in a CGE model can be implemented with just one more parameter, the shape parameter for the Pareto distribution of firm productivities (Chap. 7).

(e) In moving from Armington to Melitz, we should not use the same value for the Melitz substitution elasticity between varieties produced by different firms and the Armington substitution elasticity between varieties produced by different countries. Instead, the Melitz elasticity should be calibrated so that the Melitz model gives similar trade responses to changes in tariffs as the Armington model (Sect. 6.5).

(f) Econometric estimation of the shape parameter for the productivity distributions in Melitz models can be undertaken using data on trade flows. However, it is not clear that current procedures are preferable to calibration based on views concerning shares in total costs accounted for by fixed costs associated with setting up firms and setting up on trade links (Chap. 4).

© Springer Nature Singapore Pte Ltd. 2018
P. B. Dixon et al., *Trade Theory in Computable General Equilibrium Models*,
Advances in Applied General Equilibrium Modeling,
https://doi.org/10.1007/978-981-10-8325-9_8

(g) Relatively small Melitz CGE models have been solved iteratively using GAMS software. The iterative method involves passing information backwards and forwards between Melitz sectoral models and an Armington global CGE model (the Auxiliary Armington model) (Sect. 5.3).

(h) The GAMS iterative method suggested to us that a Melitz solution for the effects of a tariff change can be interpreted as an Armington solution with additional productivity and preference shocks (Sect. 5.4).

(i) Iterative methods can be avoided by using GEMPACK software. With this software, even large-scale Melitz CGE models can be solved directly (Chap. 7).

(j) Using the insight from the GAMS iterative method, equations can be added to the GEMPACK code to decompose Melitz CGE welfare results into the parts attributable to standard Armington efficiency and terms-of-trade effects and the parts attributable to Melitz productivity and love-of-variety effects (Sects. 6.4 and 6.5).

(k) The envelope theorem suggests that productivity and love-of-variety effects of tariff changes in Melitz CGE models will approximately cancel out at the global level. This also applies at the country level in simulations in which there is little transfer of resources between Melitz and Armington sectors (Sect. 6.4).

(l) In interpreting Melitz results, it is helpful to work in effective units, that is, count quantities modified by changes in their ability to satisfy user requirements. Welfare decompositions based on effective units show that the main differences between Armington and Melitz results arise from industry-level economies of scale. Expansion of a Melitz industry reduces the cost per unit of effective output even if there is no change in the size of typical firms. Through variety effects, a bigger Melitz industry can more precisely satisfy user needs (Sects. 7.4 and 7.6).

(m) Working with effective units leads to Melitz results that are sometimes counterintuitive when viewed through an Armington lens. For example, in an Armington model, a country that imposes a tariff will normally receive a terms-of-trade benefit. In a Melitz model, output contraction in the exporting industries of supplying countries can cause increases in their costs per effective unit with resulting terms-of-trade loss for the country that imposes the tariff. Further experimentation with Melitz CGE models is required to determine the generality of results such as these (Sect. 7.6).

(n) Only minimal changes are required to the code for existing Armington models to give them Melitz sectors. Large-scale well-established Armington models such as GTAP can be given Melitz sectors by adding a small number of additional equations to the bottom of the computer code. Melitz and Armington solutions can then be computed with a few closure swaps (Sects. 7.2 and 7.5).

(o) Using GEMPACK software and the Armington to Melitz (A2M) conversion method described in this book, Melitz CGE models can now be created with almost no extra effort beyond that required for Armington models. This will facilitate the process of discovering empirical properties of the Melitz model (Chap. 7).

8.2 Concluding Remarks

Methodology

Over the last 50 years CGE modeling has made a major contribution to policy discussions in many countries over a wide range of topics. We hope that readers of this book will perceive another role for CGE modeling: as an investigative tool for establishing the properties of theoretical constructs. Throughout the book, CGE ideas and computations enhanced our understanding of Melitz theory and its relationship to Armington. For example, the CGE computations in Chap. 6 alerted us to the idea that Melitz productivity and love-of-variety effects sometimes cancel out. Having been alerted, we looked for the reason. The CGE computations in Chap. 7 alerted us to the idea that under Melitz assumptions a country that unilaterally imposes a tariff can suffer a terms-of-trade loss. Again, having been alerted, we looked for the reason.

The theory role of CGE modeling is facilitated by the use of linear percentage change equations [often referred to as hat algebra, Jones (1965)]. Writing the theory in this way allows us to derive interpretable and signable algebraic expressions for derivatives or elasticities of key endogenous variables with respect to key exogenous variables. These expressions become part of a two-way interaction between theory and computation: computations suggest results requiring explanation, hat algebra provides explanations, and these explanations can be checked by further computations. Linear percentage change forms were originally introduced to CGE modeling by Johansen (1960). This transparent way of representing outcomes of optimizing behaviour (e.g., consumer demand systems) was adopted in the ORANI model of Australia (Dixon et al. 1977, 1982) and later in GTAP (Hertel 1997). GEMPACK software uses linear percentage change representations of models and eliminates linearization errors via a multi-step procedure.

Policy

Trade policies are often controversial. Perhaps this is because these policies always involve transfers of resources between activities: between export-oriented production and import-competing; between manufacturing and services; and between one region and another. Consequently, trade policies always generate losers as well as winners. Economic models built along Armington lines have long implied that the overall welfare effects of proposed free-trade agreements and other changes in trade policies are small, often no more than a fraction of 1% of GDP. This is a disappointment to advocates of trade reforms. They are faced with explaining whether the benefits of their proposals are sufficient to outweigh the costs of disruption associated with implementation.

In response, reform advocates have often argued that Armington models underestimate the benefits of movements towards free trade by leaving out important sources of welfare gain. To them, the Melitz model, which builds in the possibility of trade-induced improvements in industry productivity, seemed immediately attractive. If for no other reason, Melitz has been a mandatory area for study by policy modelers such as ourselves.

What have we found out? The good news is that Melitz features can be included with relatively little difficulty in the detailed policy-oriented Armington-based models that have been developed by many researchers over past decades. Further good news is that interpretation of results from Melitz CGE models can be undertaken using methods familiar from Armington models. These methods include analysis of welfare decompositions and the undertaking of back-of-the-envelope (BOTE) calculations. A final piece of good news from Melitz is that CGE modelers now have a defence against critics who dismiss everything they have done on the unsupported but persuasive grounds that the welfare effects of trade are all about imperfect competition, economies of scale and the provision of variety.

The bad news is that the inclusion of Melitz in CGE models is not a knock-out blow. It does not lead to clear-cut new results. Zhai (2008) and Balistreri and Rutherford (2013) find that a CGE model with a Melitz specification can give considerably higher welfare gains from a tariff cut than a model built with a similar database but with an Armington specification. However, we doubt that this is a general result and was not our experience. In our illustrative Melitz model, we found in simulations of the effects of a tariff change that the extra welfare effects added to Armington by Melitz were offsetting. In our GTAP-A2M system, the region (NAmerica) that imposed the tariff (moved away from free trade) suffered a smaller welfare loss (in fact gained more) under Melitz assumptions than under Armington assumptions.

We do not see Melitz modeling as providing support for people who claim there are large gains from free trade. In a model such as Melitz in which agents are fully informed profit and utility maximizers, cuts in tariffs from their contemporary low levels will not generate large welfare effects. The most likely arguments to support large welfare numbers are still those associated with X-efficiency (Leibenstein 1966), rent seeking (Krueger 1974), technology transfer (Tarr 2013) and pro-competitive or cold-shower effects (Chand 1999).

As in Armington CGE models, in Melitz models terms-of-trade movements are important in the determination of welfare effects. Negative terms-of-trade effects are often dominant in simulations of unilateral tariff reductions. We do not see Melitz specifications as offering a panacea to those who would like to use general equilibrium modeling to support *unilateral* tariff reductions. In a Melitz world, as in an Armington world, tariff reductions make most economic sense when carried out on a multi-lateral or bi-lateral basis.

References

Balistreri, E., & Rutherford, T. (2013). Computing general equilibrium theories of monopolistic competition and heterogeneous firms (Chapter 23). In P. B. Dixon & D. W. Jorgenson (Eds.), *Handbook of computable general equilibrium modeling* (pp. 1513–1570). Amsterdam: Elsevier.

Chand, S. (1999). Trade liberalization and productivity growth: Time-series evidence from Australian manufacturing. *Economic Record, 75,* 28–36.

Dixon, P. B., Parmenter, B. R., Ryland, G. J., & Sutton, J. (1977). *ORANI, a general equilibrium model of the Australian economy: Current specification and illustrations of use for policy analysis* (pp. xii + 297). First Progress Report of the IMPACT Project, Vol. 2. Canberra: Australian Government Publishing Service.

Dixon, P. B., Parmenter, B. R., Sutton, J., & Vincent, D. P. (1982). *ORANI: A multisectoral model of the Australian economy* (pp. xviii + 372). Contributions to Economic Analysis, Vol. 142. Amsterdam: North-Holland Publishing Company.

Hertel, T. W. (Ed.). (1997). *Global trade analysis: Modeling and applications.* Cambridge, UK: Cambridge University Press.

Johansen, L. (1960). *A multisectoral study of economic growth.* Contributions to Economic Analysis, Vol. 21. Amsterdam: North-Holland.

Jones, R. W. (1965). The Structure of Simple General Equilibrium Models. *Journal of Political Economy, 73*(6), 557–572.

Krueger, A. O. (1974). The political economy of the rent-seeking society. *American Economic Review, 64,* 291–303.

Leibenstein, H. (1966). Allocative efficiency versus X-efficiency. *American Economic Review, 56,* 392–415.

Tarr, D. (2013). Putting services and foreign direct investment with endogenous productivity effects in computable general equilibrium models (Chapter 6). In P. B. Dixon & D. W. Jorgenson (Eds.), *Handbook of computable general equilibrium modeling* (pp. 303–378). Amsterdam: Elsevier.

Zhai, F. (2008). Armington meets Melitz: Introducing firm heterogeneity in a global CGE model of trade. *Journal of Economic Integration, 23*(3), 575–604.